Simon Winchester's

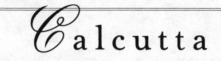

Simon Winchester's

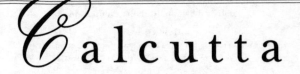

Calcutta

SIMON & RUPERT WINCHESTER

lonely planet

Lonely Planet Publications

MELBOURNE OAKLAND LONDON PARIS

SIMON WINCHESTER'S CALCUTTA

Published by Lonely Planet Publications

Head Office:
90 Maribyrnong Street, Footscray, Vic 3011, Australia
Locked Bag 1, Footscray, Vic 3011, Australia

Branches:
150 Linden Street, Oakland CA 94607, USA
72–82 Rosebery Avenue, Clerkenwell, London EC1R 4RW, UK
1 rue Dahomey, 75011, Paris, France

Published 2004
Printed through the Bookmaker International Ltd
Printed in China

Edited by Meaghan Amor
Designed by Gerilyn Attebery

National Library of Australia Cataloguing-in-Publication entry

Winchester, Simon.

Simon Winchester's Calcutta.

ISBN 1 74059 587 4.

1. Calcutta (India) - Description and travel. 2. Calcutta (India) - History.
I. Winchester, Rupert. II. Title.

915.414704

CONTENTS

Simon Winchester's

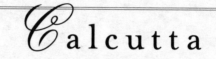

Calcutta

The Scent Behind the Smell

SIMON WINCHESTER

THE HOT STENCH OF THE SLOW-DECAYING POOR, the mobs flowing ceaselessly over the scalding bridge, the treacle of the Hooghly swamps below, the bent and broken limbs and the rotting rubbish piles and the screeching horns and the rickshaw bells and the infuriating calm of the cud-chewing cows — yes, such things as these I remember only too well about Calcutta, and my first long visit there, back in the early seventies in the time of war.

Everyone remembers such things. They are the familiar images, slivers of mosaic from the public nightmare that this city, above all others, has in the last century allowed herself to become. Before 1911, until which time she was capital of Imperial India, Calcutta was perhaps a little less of a hellish place. But these days, as when I first visited — I had been sent out from London by my newspaper, to write about the fighting that was then raging in Bengal — Calcutta has become a truly infernal city, as the writings that follow display all too clearly. And yet I find that for some initially inexpressible reason,

I cannot stop feeling an intense fondness for the place, and I still puzzle over exactly why that might be.

I think that what helps to sustain this affection, when I am assaulted from all sides by the customary memories of horror and dismay, seems to be a slide show of more curiously alluring images — images that manage, somewhat uncannily, to linger in my mind in much more vivid manner than any others. They are not sentimental memories, half-remembered moments of romance and beauty, mental pictures that could very obviously counter the customary awfulness; they are instead recollections that speak more of complexity and enigma, brief glimpses of this terrible city that offer up moments of unanticipated fascination. It is these, I think, that more properly reflect what Calcutta really signifies. They serve to remind us of what can occur in those rare moments of calm when, as Paul Scott once wrote, a visitor to anywhere in India — but to a dreadful place like Calcutta most especially — manages to capture what he called 'the scent behind the smell'.

Let me enumerate a few. First, I remember one evening, maybe only a couple of days after I had arrived by BOAC jet at what was then called Dum Dum Airport, and which I spent in the company of a very senior Indian soldier, a Bengali of great elegance, intelligence and courtesy. I had been interviewing him, in his own home, in a large and map-filled room cooled by a slowly turning *punkah*. I was there to ask him about the artillery and tank battles of the day that he had been directing against the East Pakistan army, and much of what he said was fairly unmemorable. What remains in my mind instead is a much more remarkable and surprising image — of watching the general later in the evening as he absently sipped on a pink gin and squinted through a magnifying glass at a fragile sheet of mulberry paper, a rare and precious antique that was tricked out with a four-hundred-year-old engraving that depicted, as he explained without batting an eyelid, Japanese court pornography.

It was not at all what I had supposed. He saw my surprise, and explained that he had wanted to turn aside from all this dull talk of military strategy, and share with me instead his real and abiding passion. It turned out that he was a keen collector of old Japanese erotica, was a student of the genre, and wrote learned essays about Oriental bedroom manners in a score of learned journals. Each night, this provided him with a form of relaxation. The following morning, however, he would go out, as he did every day during the short India—Pakistan war of the time, and do battle with his with Pakistani opposite number. To add further to the strangeness of the situation — and yet how could anything be much stranger? — he told me that the Pakistani was a man with whom he trained at Sandhurst twenty years before, and whom he counted still as a friend, although politics had temporarily rendered them into formal foes. That general, a Punjabi named Akbar Khan, did not, said my man with some asperity, have any untoward interests at all. 'Punjabi Mussulmen,' he said, 'are not like us. We Bengalis are a very different breed.'

I remember also going to see a gymkhana at the Tollygunge Club, an island of imperial memories hidden deep within the kind of neat and self-satisfied Calcutta suburbs that John Betjeman might easily recognise. Bob and Anne Wright were the managers of the club back then, and on the day I turned up their spottily adolescent daughter had pulled off some kind of minor triumph in the steeplechase, and was being feted for it by the club servants. The lawns were impeccable, the *malis* worked soundlessly trimming the shrubs, a small gang of men were employed to shoo away any crows that might try to steal the seeds. There was pink gin here as well, and I remember sitting long into the evening, nursing one, and talking about the fate of the Royal Bengal Tigers of the Sunderbans — a subject dear to Anne Wright's heart, and it seemed to me of far more moment than the fate of the millions of people who lived in the city that, invisible and all too easily forgotten, then surrounded us.

Without labouring the point, there were pink gins also up in the penthouse of a company called MacNeil & Magor, the famous and very ancient tea-broking firm that in those days had a magnificent office building on Chowringhee, right across from where farmers grazed their goats on the Maidan. I would go there from time to time to see a man who became a firm friend. He was called Pearson Surita, an Armenian who had become Calcutta's most celebrated boulevardier and was All-India Radio's legendary cricket commentator. He would sink one pink gin after another, while talking up the history of tea, and explaining his city's role as epicentre of the industry for which he worked. He couldn't stand drinking the stuff, mind you: gin was his tipple, from breakfast time to tiffin and well beyond. Fridays were his special favourite: he would begin drinking at ten in the morning, in celebration of what he called Poet's Day. Tagore? I once asked. 'Fool!' he bellowed. 'Piss Off Early, Tomorrow's Saturday.'

Contrast, conflict, contradiction – and of the kind found in these three encounters – always seemed to be underpinning my impressions of the city in those early days. Nor have they ever let up, in the dozens of times I have been back since. One brief story, bizarre and at this remove barely credible, serves perhaps to memorialise the strangeness of my times in Calcutta, the curious amalgam of the wholly delightful and the half insane that seems so firmly imprinted on the city's nature.

On this particular occasion I was in the city to photograph buildings for a book that I was writing on the relics of British imperial architecture. I had seen Lord Curzon's great mansion, I had wandered among the tombstones in Park Street Cemetery, I had gazed up at the Zoffany in St John's church baptistry. On the searing morning of this adventure I decided that I wanted to get myself to the great headquarters of the Indian Army's Eastern Command, a vast octagon that had been built a century before, behind a six-metre high castellated wall beside the Hooghly, and known to all passers-by as Fort William. Specifically, I wanted to see and photograph a nineteenth-century fortress deep inside it, the Dalhousie Barracks, said to be the largest military accommodation block in the world.

Inevitably, I couldn't get permission. I was turned away by legions of the Bengal babu-ocracy, men who suggested, fatuously, that in order to win approval I might write letters to high commissioners and foreign affairs ministers and high panjandrums in cities from London to Barrackpore and all places in-between. I was exasperated — though hardly surprised; I was by now living in India, and only too aware of how difficult life could be. I decided to circumvent the problem: I would simply contrive to weasel my way inside Fort William without permission, snap away some pictures with my quiet little Leica, and trust to the Fates that all would go well.

At first, it did. My driver of the time, a man named Ali whom I had known for fifteen years, had discovered on one remote corner of the fortress a ladder left by a construction crew, leaning up against the exterior wall. Making sure that no soldiers or police officers were watching us, Ali stood sentry as I shinned up the ladder onto the very top of the two-metre thick wall. I climbed hand over hand down a banyan tree I found on the inner side, and then was, astonishingly and not a little dangerously, now right inside the forbidden fortress.

There were soldiers everywhere, marching, shouting, drilling — doing what soldiers like to do. But no one challenged me. Indeed, no one noticed me. I walked around, managed to take pictures of the barrack block, the garrison church, the officers' mess. I was not particularly alarmed when eventually a sentry stopped me and asked if he could help me; nor was I especially unsettled when I was marched to the headquarters building and introduced to the garrison commander, a brigadier. We spoke for an hour about the history of Bengal and the threat of communism. (He particularly bemoaned the fact that one local Calcutta street had just had its name changed to Ho Chi Minh Sarani, an alteration he said he found preposterous.) He gave me tea, and afterwards, without ever asking to see my credentials or permission papers, offered me as escort for the remainder of my adventure a spruce young captain from the Education Corps.

It was only when it came time to leave, an hour or so later, when the captain asked which gate I had come in and whether he could see my entry pass to give back to the guardhouse, that I thought the game might well be up. I decided to fib. I had lost the pass, I mumbled, and then added for good measure that, so immense was the spread of Fort William, I could not exactly recall through which of the eight machicolated gates I had passed earlier that morning.

No problem, said the young officer. We'll take the brigadier's car — no one would dare challenge that. And so we piled into the khaki-coloured limousine, bright silver stars on the radiator and a red pennant flying from the roof, and we sped out through gates and across moats and under a portcullis, with sentries snapping to attention and saluting as we did so. And then, after a long and lazy circuit of the outside walls, we eventually found Ali, still waiting patiently with his car. The ladder was still standing innocently up against the wall. It was a symbol that the captain chose, discreetly, not to appear to notice.

And it was while the three of us — Ali, the officer and I — were talking to one another, offering up our thanks and farewells, that things took a final and unexpected turn.

From afar there was a sudden blare of a truck horn, a terrifying screech of brakes — and a huge petrol tanker appeared, sweeping down the road at full bore. It was on a collision course with where we had parked and, once its driver had jumped clear, it rammed itself — not into us, but into the brigadier's car, and promptly exploded, sending up a vast cannonade and an immense ball of fire that rose hundreds of feet into the air. The heat was intolerable, and we ran for cover. Chunks of car and truck and ladder and wall were hurled into the air and clattered back down onto the roadway. A huge crowd gathered: it was, at the very least, a splendid spectacle.

No one, it turned out, was hurt. The truck and the limousine were wrecked and were boiling in flames. The mild young captain, when last I saw him, was tearing his hair out at the thought of how he might explain all the ruin and disaster to his now car-less commander. Ali and I just grinned conspiratorially at one another, got into our car and drove stealthily away, leaving the fire and the wreckage to vanish into the mayhem of a customary Calcutta night. It struck me then, and it still strikes me today, that the entire event said something wonderfully symbolic about the city: it was an afternoon of broken rules, erudite conversation, disciplined courtesy, sudden disaster, spectacular mayhem. Calcutta, in other words, in a nutshell.

It is also perhaps worth noting that I fell for a girl in Calcutta around that time as well. Though she subsequently married sensibly and moved far away, we remain today the closest of friends. Her story, too, is something of a parable of the city.

Shukla was in her twenties when we found one another. She was a classic Bengali — the daughter of a Brahmin bureaucrat who worked as a babu in the Writers' Building, she was graceful, strong, clever, magnificent. She had been schooled at a Catholic convent in Darjeeling, had studied English and then comparative literature at university, had written a PhD thesis comparing the works of W. B. Yeats and Rabindranath Tagore, and then, finding no work suitable to her status, took a job as a receptionist at the Grand Hotel, where we met.

For several subsequent years she helped me with newspaper articles and books and essays, researching for me, opening doors, winning permissions to places more difficult to access than even Calcutta's army fort. Then she joined an American company, embarking on a career of managing hotels. She proved to be unusually adept at business, rose swiftly to become one of India's most powerful executives, serving on prime ministerial task forces and other exalted bodies before, in one dramatic plunge, the American company was sold, the senior executives were fired and Shukla lost her job.

Whereupon she decided that her goal for the remainder of her life would be the education of the indigent — a sector of the population with which Bengal in general, and the east's largest city in particular, is unusually well endowed. She cajoled and wheedled and pleaded for money from her old business friends, and with the immense fund that she raised, set up a number of small schools — places where children could be given eight hours each day of first-rate and entirely free education, could be equipped with uniforms and books and food and, essentially, the chance of a future. The only two qualifications which she asked of the applicants were that they have a burning desire to learn, and that they be unutterably and profoundly poor. The schools are now all oversubscribed; and Shukla, once a hotel receptionist, is now one of India's contemporary heroines. She is a woman destined, if there is any justice at all in India, for eventual honour and reward.

Shukla's story, like that of the soldier with his erotic engravings and the tea-broker who prefers gin, and the Wrights of Tollygunge with their obsessions with tigers, and, in a strange way, also just like the adventure that culminated in the exploding of the truck outside Fort William, is also a parable of the unexpected — a word that I keep tripping over whenever I look back and try to make out what, at this remove, I truly think of the city. Things unanticipated, unimagined and unimaginable always seem to keep happening in this dreadful, dreadful town.

You fly in to Dum Dum — now renamed Netaji Subhas Chandra Bose Airport, after one of the more curious villains of recent Bengal history — and you encounter a city that has, perhaps, a more grim reputation than any other major conurbation on the face of the planet. And you remain there — as I have done for weeks on end over decades past — and sure enough, day after day and night after night, it presents to the visitor a ceaseless surfeit of unanticipated events — some of the happenings great, some of them good, some delightful, some bizarre and some more dreadful than it is possible to suppose.

Calcutta is, in other words, a city in a state of permanent surprise, where amazement is around every crumbling corner, and astonishment lurks over every rickshaw-puller's shoulder. It is a city that never ceases to shock those who pass through; and it is also a city that on occasions so frequent as to warrant a guarantee, manages to delight and enthral those who are stalwart enough to stay and brave enough to make an effort to look and to see. To discern the scent, in other words, behind Calcutta's customarily terrible smell.

Quintessential Calcutta

RUPERT WINCHESTER

THE FIRST TIME I WENT TO CALCUTTA, I WAS ABOUT nineteen, on a generous university summer holiday. I was cheerfully at home in India, having lived there for a year or two as a child, and having spent many previous university holidays touring the country. But I had never been to Calcutta. It was certainly a place with a reputation, not all of it good, but it seemed as if you couldn't say you knew India until you'd tried Calcutta.

So, with the ready arrogance of youth, a friend and I boarded a train in Trivandrum, in the deep south of the country, bound for Calcutta. I can't remember the logic of this move, somewhat akin to spending half your holiday in Florida, and then suddenly deciding to take a train to Alaska. But perhaps that was the point: a certain erraticism was a useful marker in the perpetual traveller one-upmanship back home.

We boarded the train at Trivandrum Station in the late morning; there were baskets of plants and flowers, revivified by the recent arrival of the monsoon. The usual dramas of Indian station life were being played out along the steamy platform: sons off to the city, families going to a wedding, hawkers and beggars indolently working the throng. It would rain later in the day, but at that moment it was lovely.

Trivandrum to Calcutta is, or used to be, one of the very longest train journeys to be taken in India. There might have been a train to Amritsar that was further, but journeys east took longer. And so it was that fifty-six hours later, at the time our train was supposed to pull in to Howrah Station, we were sitting in southern West Bengal in a siding, because of a strike by a militant crypto-Marxist subset of some rail union – the wheeltappers or the boiler fitters perhaps.

Sitting in the carriage doorway, stifling in the huge heat, dirty, half-washed, hungry and overwhelmingly tired, I remember cursing the whole of West Bengal, and Calcutta in particular. What had made me want to come here? Why had I deserted the gentle mellowness of the south to put myself through this? My companion and I were hardly talking by that stage, but I managed to persuade her that we should try to get a room at the Fairlawn, an expensive hotel that the guidebook made sound like an oasis of clean, civilised respectability, and was just within our budget, considering how little we'd spent over the past three days.

Finally, nearly three days after we'd boarded so cheerfully, our train groaned over the Hooghly and dragged our sorry carcasses through the maelstrom of Howrah Railway Station. A bad-tempered taxi driver took us to the Fairlawn, where we were too exhausted to do anything but lie outrageously on the registration forms (Name: Mickey Mouse, Occupation: Dictator) and stumble towards a shower and clean, thin white sheets.

It was only the next morning, with the sun's determined streaming through the windows thwarted by the thick layer of net curtain, that we noticed what we'd stumbled in to. The Fairlawn Hotel was a piece of aspic, with an Anglo-Indian colonial hotel preserved cunningly inside. There were antimacassars, elephant's foot umbrella stands, coronation photographs, serviettes, tappable barometers, tiger-shoot pictures and copies of *Country Life* and the *Field* scattered about. Despite my delight at the crispness of the waiter's uniform as he brought me a *nimbu pani* in the jacaranda'd courtyard, the whole experience, as well as being horrible, wasn't what we had gone to India for.

Later the same day we found another place, a double room on a sixth-floor roof, with views out over other six-storey roofs, with the miasma of the city drifting continually as a cloud of dust and poverty and molecules and humanity, with the black kites soaring gracefully above the hubbub of the streets. We were glad of the overhead fan, as it was startlingly warm, even in the early hours. And I was smitten...

Calcutta rarely features on the Hippy Trail round India. Despite the existence of government-approved opium and ganja shops around most street corners, the city lacks the necessary indolence, the peaceful equanimity conducive to lying on a low-slung charpoy under a slowly turning overhead fan, thoroughly blissed-out on dirt-cheap *charas*. Instead, Calcutta seems to reek, to the would-be visitor, of frowsy desperation, of tangible need, of despair, of all-too-real, honest-to-god, life-or-death reality. Calcutta tends to attract people who want to help, who want to pit themselves against the worst the world has to offer, to measure themselves against a true benchmark of awfulness, to work in orphanages and leper homes and hospitals. Calcutta also attracts those lured by history — the history in its amazing selection of buildings, in its cemeteries, in its complex and fascinating past.

In Goa you know the beggars will always make a living. In Manali even the meanest can earn a crust duping newly arrived tourists with wildly overpriced dope. No one starves in Hampi, Trivandrum, Pondicherry or Mahabalipuram. But in Calcutta they do, and they seem to do so in front of your eyes. Calcutta seems a truer representation of life in India, the struggle and the hardship, than almost anywhere else. Indeed, the words 'struggle' and 'hardship' hardly seem appropriate to describe the scale of the injustice meted out on so many by an unforgiving fortune.

If this all seems a little depressing, it is not meant to be. Calcutta is a stirringly lovely city. It is hot and crowded and dirty and enchanting. On my last visit, I was on my way to the main post office one afternoon, with its vast cupolas and huge pillars, and I decided to cut across the centre of BBD Bagh, or Dalhousie Square as it was, or Tank Square as it was before that, when the city's drinking water came from the large tank in the middle of it. Cursing the noise and the traffic, I ducked into the tree-lined centre of the square, and was reminded of why I love Calcutta so much.

The tank itself is vast, several football pitches in size, and full of olive-green water. The late afternoon sun slanted through the trees on to its surface, which was pockmarked by insects and rising fish. To the north was the great bulk of the Writers' Building, that curious red-and-white gothic pile built to house the clerks of the East India Company, which resembles nothing so much as a large provincial French town hall. All around the edge of the tank, sitting on a low balustrade, were hundreds of people, doing not very much: holding *addas* (gossip sessions), playing cards, rolling cigarettes, reading the newspaper. A couple of wild-haired prostitutes were painting each other's toenails. Some people were bathing. A junkie was gently, reverently licking the flat of a piece of broken glass, and small boys were fishing, as adults looked on and offered advice. Suddenly the fumes and the honking of car horns seemed miles away, and I sat, transported, watching and being watched and enjoying the peace. Eventually I went on, subjecting myself to the dusty inefficiencies of the General Post Office, and the frantic maelstrom of the traffic, but with part of me still in the square, a place both Indian and British, so quintessentially Calcutta.

The same enchantment can be found on the huge expanse of the Maidan. Shepherds drive flocks of goats across it, between football matches and games of cricket, past political rallies and skinny horses cropping under trees. Mongooses can be found there, and jackals roam at night, their strange calls rising up eerily into the dark. At the south end, the Victoria Memorial stands bathed in light, sturdily magnificent.

There is a mythic quality to Calcutta, something close to indefinable, where its greatness comes from. It is no longer the city of palaces, neither is it the city of dreadful night. Rather, it is a much-maligned, sorely tried city that has taken the worst that history has thrown at it and survived, its humour and spirit not only intact but enhanced, its character moulded in adversity: passionate, thoughtful, intelligent, cultured and proud.

Calcutta:
A Brief History

SIMON & RUPERT WINCHESTER

THE CITY OF CALCUTTA WAS, TO ALL INTENTS AND PURPOSES, founded in 1690 by a British merchant named Job Charnock. It is perhaps appropriate that his name was Job, for, like his biblical namesake, the city he founded has had more than its share of iniquities heaped upon its head. Calcutta's afflictions, like Job's, are not of its own making, yet the suffering of the city has been all too real. Often a byword for squalor, filth, pestilence, famine, poverty and misery, Calcutta has absorbed all the vicissitudes that history and geography have thrown at her, and managed to retain her dignity, whilst forging a unique urban style and culture. There is no other city in the world like Calcutta, and nowhere it can adequately be compared to. The last three centuries have not been easy for Calcutta, but they have made it a truly remarkable place.

Job Charnock was an agent of the East India Company, the British trading company that became one of the most powerful commercial entities in the world. In 1686 he was appointed company agent in Bengal. A fascinating man, he appears to have been besotted by India, adopting local manners and, apparently, marrying an Indian widow whom he snatched from her husband's funeral pyre moments before she was immolated in the traditional practice of *sati*. It is this story that has helped to cement his reputation in India to this day; the concept of a widow remarrying still has a disturbing and profound potency for many Indians.

The Hooghly River, a large, muddy distributary of the Ganges, was a natural conduit for trade, and in the late seventeenth century the banks of the river were studded with European cotton, tea, rice and jute trading posts: the Dutch and Armenians at Chinsura, the French at Chandornagar, the Portuguese at Bandel, the Danish at Serampore, Prussians at Bhadeshwar and even the Greeks at Rishra. The British, through the East India Company, had their headquarters at Hooghly, some forty kilometres upstream from present-day Calcutta, but in the late 1680s hostilities between the locals and the British flared up, and Charnock was forced to look for a new base.

Over the next few years, Charnock moved up and down the river, from Sutanuti, near where Calcutta now stands, to Hijli at the mouth of the river on the Bay of Bengal. Finally, in 1690, the Company allowed him to make a permanent settlement, between the villages of Sutanuti and Govindpur, at the tiny hamlet of Kalikata. He landed on 24 August 1690, a date widely accepted as the founding of the city.

Charnock has often been attacked for choosing the spot he did: British residents complained about the unhealthiness of the site, built on a pan of alluvial mud and close to the malarial marshes of the Salt Lakes to the east. Rudyard Kipling, no admirer of Calcutta, called the spot fetid, unwholesome and impure, clammy and pestilential. In lines known and detested by every Calcuttan, Kipling went on to describe the city as:

Chance-directed, chance-erected, laid and built
On the silt —

Palace, byre, hovel — poverty and pride —
Side by side;

Calcutta may well have been chance-directed and chance-erected, but from a trading point of view, it was ideal. Sitting around an elbow of the Hooghly, it was protected to the west by the mighty sweep of the river, and to the east by the marshes, jungles and wetlands. The river was deep enough for easy navigation, even when steam replaced sail, and the curve of the river provided a spacious harbour. The east bank of the Hooghly was high enough to avoid flooding, and allowed enough space for the major building work that was to come.

In 1696 a fort, named after William III, was built in what is today known as BBD Bagh, now the commercial heart of the city, and in 1698 the East India Company won official permission from the local rulers to occupy the site of the three villages.

Charnock had died before this, in 1693, but is still to this day regarded by most as the sole father of the city. It was his insistence on the commercial and military advantages of the site, against the opposition of his superiors, that led to its founding, and his sympathies towards the local culture that helped to turn the trading post into a real community and, until early in the twentieth century, the capital city of India and the second city of the British Empire. In many ways Calcutta's history, its texture, its culture has always sprung from the mixture of Indian and Western influences, and Job Charnock's mulish insistence is that in microcosm.

Charnock's reputation became tarnished after his death: some of his successors accused him of theft, immorality, laziness, corruption and of having a violent temper, although these were traits exhibited by many who came after him to a much greater degree. His adoption of Indian culture meant that Calcutta was established in a much more cooperative manner than many of the British cities of the Empire.

On 1 January 2001, the first day of the new millennium, Job Charnock's city, sprawled across a bend in the Hooghly River, officially changed its name to Kolkata, in a stroke not quite managing to put its colonial past behind it. Unlike Bombay, which morphed into Mumbai, or Madras, which confusingly became Chennai, Calcutta chose a homophonic consonant, shifted vowels slightly and pleased its nationalists mightily, whilst irritating the rest of the world.

The Bengali has always been aware of the importance of the names of things. No guidebook to the city is complete without a table detailing the changes in appellation that its monuments and streets have gone through as influences and priorities have altered. From the obvious repudiations of colonial influences, like the towering Ochterlony Monument's mutation into the Shahid Minar (sadly ironic, because Sir David Ochterlony was a wise and enlightened man who loved India), to the gleeful mischievousness of changing the street that was home to the US Embassy, Harrington Street, into Ho Chi Minh Sarani, few streets have escaped a change in nomination.

With typical Bengali intellectual overcomplexity, there is no definitive answer as to the origins of the name Calcutta, and therefore no overwhelmingly obvious reason for the change of name to Kolkata. But theories are legion. One is the frankly risible suggestion that it is a corruption of Golgotha, the hill outside Jerusalem where Jesus was crucified, and so a good name for a place of great suffering.

Another unlikely but oft-heard theory has it that an early British arrival asked a local the name of the place, the local thought he had asked when the grass had last been cut, and replied, in Bengali, 'kal kata', or 'cut yesterday'. It is perhaps a measure of the Bengali's catholicity of intellect that such a story should even be repeated, such is its profound silliness. As perhaps is the suggestion that, in order to compete with the exports of the city of Calicut, which is where the word 'calico' comes from, the English stamped 'kalikat' on their own exports. Other suggestions for the origin of the name involve warehouses for unslaked lime, ancient tribes and excavations along the river banks.

More likely is the hypothesis that links the city's name to its most important deity, Kali. In the southern suburbs is an area called Kalighat – or Kali's landing – which is home to the main temple dedicated to Kali. As the focus for Hindus, it has always been important in the region, and it is more than likely that its name was taken to stand for the village which grew into the city. It doesn't explain why its name mentions a landing, when it is some distance from the river, but it seems to be the most plausible option. Ironically, the village of Kalighat was of far less importance than either Govindpur or Sutanuti, the other villages on either side of it. Its lack of importance meant that Charnock and those who came after him were afforded the space to settle as they liked, and to turn an undistinguished and obscure Bengali fishing village into one of the great cities of the world.

Of course, Calcutta being Calcutta (or Kolkata), Charnock's central role in the founding of the city has been disputed, and in the summer of 2003 the state government accepted a report submitted by a committee of historians, which had investigated and decided that the city had no founder and no foundation date. The committee had been set up after a Bengali cultural organisation had pushed for a judicial review of the evidence for Charnock's involvement in Calcutta's founding. The committee said in its report that Calcutta had no specific birthday and no individual should be referred to as its founder. The government said that henceforth Charnock would only be mentioned as 'an individual who had played a significant role in the development' of the city. Whilst providing reams of work for Calcutta's legions of bureaucrats, education officials and history teachers, the edict has been widely ignored in the city.

Charnock's mausoleum, a little striated plastered rotunda, sits in a quiet corner of the graveyard of St John's Church, the oldest in the city, dating back to 1787. Hard by the city centre, the churchyard is ridiculously tranquil for central Calcutta, with only the cawing of crows disturbing the sleepy peace. Tenement windows rise on all sides, and several buses are usually parked beside Charnock's tomb, the oldest piece of masonry in the city, their drivers asleep in its shade.

One of the mysteries of Charnock's story is the whereabouts of his wife's grave; there is no evidence to suggest that they are buried together, as custom would usually dictate. Indeed, she died before him, and he is supposed to have sacrificed a cockerel on her tomb every year, an act that would have been unthinkable in honour of a Hindu devout enough to have been prepared to commit *sati*. The sacrificing of a cockerel is more likely to have been a Muslim ritual, so it is possible that Charnock was even more multicultured than his reputation already suggests. His epitaph reads: 'He was a wanderer who after sojourning for a long time in a land not his own, returned to his Eternal Home.'

Over the next few years, Calcutta grew slowly but steadily. The three villages which Charnock had originally chosen as the site of his base were part of an estate owned by the Mughal emperor himself, but, in 1698, Charnock's successor, and son-in-law, managed to buy the *zamindari* rights, or revenue collection rights, for 1300 rupees. Within ten years, Calcutta had a population of around ten thousand, but the town needed more space, and the East India Company sent a gift-laden delegation to Delhi to negotiate further rights over the area. Eventually in 1717 the Mughal emperor Farrukhsiyar granted the Company freedom of trade over another thirty-eight villages, including Haora on the eastern bank of the Hooghly, in return for a yearly payment of three thousand rupees.

In many ways, this agreement was the making of Calcutta. The Mughal rulers were as venal and greedy as the Company and its officials, and Calcutta became the focus of a great deal of entrepreneurial activity, or 'shaking the pagoda tree' as it was euphemistically known, and both the Mughals and the Company began to make startlingly large amounts of money.

However, after the death of the Emperor Aurangzeb in 1707, the power and influence of the Mughals began to fade, as corruption became rife, and there was a corresponding rise in the power of the Marathas, the Hindu tribal confederacy from Maharashtra to the west. When the Marathas began sporadic incursions against the Mughals in the western districts of Bengal in the 1740s, Calcutta became alarmed, and the East India Company raised 25,000 rupees to build a ditch around the perimeter of the city. Known as the Maratha Ditch, it was never completed, because the threat from the Marathas began to recede, but it was later filled in and today's Circular Road follows its route. It also caused Calcuttans to be known across India as 'Ditchers'.

As the Mughals declined in power, so their relations with their representatives became more precarious, and in Bengal, the nawabs, or Mughal-appointed Muslim governors, became more and more independent. Coupled with the East India Company's thirst for more power, there were bound to be clashes. In 1740 Nawab Alivardi Khan managed to become almost wholly autonomous, but his death in 1756 led to a power struggle between his widow Ghasiti Begum and his grandson Siraj-ud-daula, a man variously described as haughty, fickle, arrogant, cowardly and 'a monster of vice, cruelty and depravity'. Eventually he succeeded to the nawabship, and, noting the wealth that the East India Company was generating for itself in Calcutta, decided to gate-crash the party.

Siraj-ud-daula demanded, as a way of showing off his power, that the fortifications of Fort William should be destroyed, so they could not be used against him. The Company ignored him, and in June 1756 he invaded the city and the fort with an army of fifty thousand and four hundred battle elephants. The woefully underprotected city fell swiftly, and most of the inhabitants fled. Siraj-ud-daula ordered that the prisoners be locked up for the night so they could be interrogated the next morning about the whereabouts of the Company's treasury. Unaware of Fort William's lack of detention facilities, his men locked the prisoners into a tiny room, on one of the hottest and most stifling nights of the year, in a city known for its oppressive heat.

It was with this decision that Calcutta first and most famously entered the world's lexicon as a byword for depravity, horror, native cruelty and injustice, with the creation of the story of the Black Hole of Calcutta.

Few incidents in India's history have been as analysed and debated as the Black Hole. The best-known account comes from John Zephaniah Holwell, who was there, in a letter he wrote to a friend shortly afterwards. Holwell's 'A Genuine Narrative of the Deplorable Deaths of the English Gentlemen and Others, who were Suffocated in the Black-Hole in Fort William, at Calcutta, in the Kingdom of Bengal; in the Night Succeeding the 20th Day of June, 1756' has been proved by scholars to be mostly incorrect, but the account has stood, partially because Holwell was a good storyteller, and partially because it helped to create a myth which British colonialism found it useful to foster.

According to Holwell, 146 Europeans were marched by Siraj-ud-daula's men into a room of only fourteen by eighteen feet, with just one small barred window. Late June in Calcutta, before the monsoon brings its cooling rains, is intolerably, suffocatingly hot and the prisoners, without water, soon began to keel over and die. Holwell claimed he managed to survive by drinking his own perspiration from his shirt, although he had to fight others from helping themselves to the same source. When the cell was opened in the morning, 123 of the prisoners were dead, many still standing up because of the crush, leaving only 23 alive.

As an example of the barbarism of India, the reaction to the Black Hole incident gave the East India Company carte blanche to subdue the natives, which they swiftly did. Karl Marx, writing on Indian history, talked of the incident as 'so much sham scandal'. Ever since, Indian scholars have tried to refute Holwell's account, calling him unreliable and suggesting that he merely wanted to make himself appear heroic (with some success: he eventually became acting governor of Bengal).

It is certainly true that it would be physically impossible to fit 146 well-fed Europeans into a room of four by five and a half metres. Indian scholars have shown that in all likelihood there were between sixty-four and sixty-nine prisoners, and that after the incident there were forty-three people unaccounted for. They note that the East India Company never claimed any compensation over the lives lost, despite presenting Siraj-ud-daula with a long and comprehensive list of damages during his occupation of Calcutta. The scholars claim that it wasn't Siraj-ud-daula who issued the order to incarcerate the prisoners, but that they were effectively forgotten due to confusion over the chain of command in his forces. Even so, locking some seventy people into a cell designed for perhaps half a dozen and then forgetting about them was never going to deliver a useful piece of propaganda, but the British made it into a more effective tool than Siraj-ud-daula could have foreseen.

The East India Company sent Robert Clive, later known as Clive of India, to retake Calcutta, which he did early in 1757, and on 23 June, at the Battle of Plassey, Clive defeated Siraj-ud-daula. The battle, which lasted only a few hours, is taken by some to mark the beginning of British rule in India, although the fact that Clive won because he had bribed the enemy commanders and soldiers is still a source of bitterness even today. Jawaharlal Nehru, in *The Discovery of India*, justly describes Clive as having won the battle 'by promoting treason and forgery', and pointedly notes that British rule in India had 'an unsavoury beginning and something of that bitter taste has clung to it ever since'.

John Holwell had an obelisk built at his own expense in 1760, in the northwestern corner of what is now BBD Bagh, marking the site of the Black Hole, although it was pulled down in 1821 because it had become 'an unsightly venue for local barbers'. In 1902 the viceroy, Lord Curzon, had another obelisk built, which stands, like Charnock's tomb, in a sleepy corner of St John's churchyard. The site of the Black Hole is now covered by Calcutta's vast main post office, and is not commemorated in any way.

Following Clive's retaking of Calcutta, the East India Company decided that the city needed to take a more serious approach to its defences, and, after clearing the inhabitants out of the southern village of Govindpur, built a new Fort William, next to the Hooghly. Costing the astonishing sum of two million pounds, the fort was gigantic and impregnable. It has never been used for the defence of Calcutta. It also had the unintended side effect, with the clearing of hundreds of hectares of jungle, of providing a clean line of fire should it come under attack, and of creating the Maidan, the amazingly huge swathe of green that bisects the city and acts as its lungs and its garden.

The next century or so were good times for Calcutta. Culturally, economically, architecturally, the city was thriving; indeed, life has never been as good since. The East India Company was parlaying its newly increased power after Plassey into greater abilities to make money. The port was busy with trade — jute, cotton and tea, and chests of the finest Patna opium, which the Company was selling to China, and eventually used to crack off a chunk of that country, in the form of Hong Kong. Because the Company's staff were allowed to trade on their own initiative, the plundering of Bengal's trade in favour of the white man meant that two very different Calcuttas came into being.

Physically, Calcutta was divided into what were known as the White and Black towns, in effect a European town and an Indian one, side by side, one servicing the other. The White Town developed around the nucleus of the old Fort William and grew to the south and east; the Black Town was centred round the Barabazaar, or great market, in the north of the city, and was haphazard and squalid. The feel of the city divide is still present in Calcutta today: the north of the city is crowded and frenetic, whilst to the south the impression is of wide, tree-lined streets and mansions, calmer and more European than the native north.

If there was a physical gulf between the two towns of old Calcutta, the day-to-day realities were astonishingly pronounced. Even thinking of the two halves as enclaves of masters and servants respectively, the scale almost beggars belief. Alexander Macrabie, the sheriff of Calcutta, who shared a house with three friends, wrote in 1775 of his household arrangements:

> *My own Establishment consists of a Sircar, a Broker and Interpreter, — a Jemmadar [steward, head servant] who stands at my Door, receives messages, announces Visitors and also rides by the side of my palanquin to clear the way. I am preceded in all my Peregrinations by two Peons or running Footmen and as many Hircarahs or Messengers... Eight bearers for my Palanquin complete my train... Mr F[rancis] keeps five horses and according to the cursed fashion of this idle country, has ten fellows to look after them, besides a coachman to keep the whole in order. He has moreover twelve Palanquin Bearers, for no reason that I can learn except his being a Councillor — four Peons, four Hircarahs, two Chubdars [staff-bearers] who carry silver staves,*

two Jemmadars. These are without Doors — Within, a Head Sircar, or Banyan, or Agent… A house-keeping comprador and his mate go to market, two cooleys bring home what he buys, and Consomar takes charge of it. Cook and two Mates dress it. Baker in the house. Butler and assistant take charge of Liquor, Abdar and his mate cool them. Two Side Board Men wait at Table. House — two Mertrannees [sweeper-women] to clean it, two watchmen to guard it, a Durwan to keep the door. Tailor, Washermen and Ironing Man for each Person. Mashalgees, torch bearers F[rancis] 4, M[acrabie] 2, L[ivins] 1, C[ollings] 1. Two Mallies or Gardeners, Cow and poultry feeder and Pork Man…

Let me see

Mr F	62
Mack	20
L & Coll	28
	110

One hundred and ten servants to wait upon a family of four People.

By any standards, having 110 servants for a household of four bachelors is excess on a grand scale. And while the servants existed to make life easier, other descriptions of the quotidian existences enjoyed by the British in Calcutta make it clear that life was less than onerous. James Mackintosh's *Travels in Europe, Asia and Africa* gives us an account of a day in the life of a typical Englishman in the 1780s:

About the hour of seven in the morning, his durvan opens the gate and the virandah is free to his circars [stewards], peons, harcarrahs, chubdars, huccabadars [hookah-bearers] and consumas, writers and solicitors. The head-bearer and jemmadar enter the hall, and his bedroom at eight o'clock. A lady quits his side, and is conducted by a private staircase, either to her own apartments or out of the yard. The moment the master throws his legs out of bed, the whole posse in waiting rush into his room each making three salaams, by bending the body and

head very low and touching the forehead with the inside of the fingers,
and the floor with the back part. He condescends, perhaps, to nod or
cast an eye towards the solicitor of his favour and protection. In about
half an hour after undoing and taking off his long drawers, a clean shirt,
breeches, stockings and slippers are put upon his body, thighs, legs and
feet, without any greater exertion upon his part than if he was a statue.
The barber enters, shaves him, cuts his nails, and cleans his ears. The
chillumjee [basin] and ewer are brought by a servant whose duty it is,
who pours water upon his hands and face, and presents a towel. The
superior then walks in state to his breakfasting parlour in his waistcoat;
is seated; the consuma makes and pours out his tea, and presents him
with a plate of bread or toast. The hairdresser comes behind, and begins
his operation while the huccaburdar softly slips the upper end of the
snake or tube of the hucca into his hand; while the hairdresser is doing
his duty, the gentleman is eating, sipping and smoking by turns. By and
by his banian presents him with humble salaams… If any of the solicitors
are of eminence, they are honoured with chairs. These ceremonies are
continued till perhaps ten o'clock, when, attended by his cavalcade, he is
conducted to his palanquin, and preceded by eight to twelve chubdars,
harcarrahs and peons… If he has visits to make, his peons lead and
direct the bearers; and if business renders his presence only necessary,
he shows himself, and pursues his other engagements until two o'clock,
when he and his company sit down, perfectly at ease in point of dress
and address, to a good dinner, each attended by his own servant. As it
is expected that they shall return to supper, at four o'clock they begin
to withdraw without ceremony, and step into their palanquins: so that
in a few minutes, the master is left to go into his bedroom, when he is
instantly undressed to his shirt, and his long drawers put on, and he
lies down on his bed, where he sleeps till about seven or eight o'clock.
Then the former ceremony is repeated, and clean linen of every kind,
as in the morning, is administered… After tea, he puts on a handsome
coat, and pays visits of ceremony to the ladies; returns a little before
ten o'clock; supper being served at ten. The company keep together till
between twelve and one in the morning, preserving great sobriety and
decency; and when they depart, our hero is conducted to his bed room,

> *where he finds a female companion to amuse him until the hour of seven*
> *or eight the next morning. With no greater exertions than these, do the*
> *Company's servants amass the most splendid fortunes.*

One of the interesting things to note about these two accounts is how the interaction between the races is so determinedly one-sided. The Indians, even in their vast profusion, are there merely to serve; the British are happy merely to be waited upon, and while they cherry-pick the best that the subcontinent has to offer, have very little real engagement with their adopted home. Smoking a hookah and sleeping with local women (often known as a 'sleeping dictionary' because they helped the sahibs to learn the local tongue) were no substitute for actively engaging with the local culture, which has perhaps tended to continue the sense of division between the two cultures, between the two towns.

However, although the Bengalis are seen only as servants, there was a small but growing wealthy mercantile class. Drawn from the *zamindari*, or absentee landlords of rural Bengal, as well as agents of the British, they were able to have their share of the wholesale plunder of Bengal led by the British. As Geoffrey Moorhouse puts it in his classic account of Calcutta, 'The way was almost open for a bright lad of the district to become as rich on his wits as any red-faced sprig from Kensington.' Although many Bengalis like to propound the suggestion that they are a race of lofty intellectuals who rarely deign to undertake commercial work, the fact is that the ranks of those made rich by Calcutta include large numbers of Bengalis. Acting as agents or *banyans* to Europeans was profitable, as was renting them properties. The Tagore family, for instance, probably Calcutta's most distinguished and certainly best known, had their fingers in a large number of highly profitable pies. The head of the family, Dwarkanath Tagore (1794–1846), was a well-educated *zamindar* whose willingness to take entrepreneurial risks paid off in spectacular fashion. Whilst working as a revenue collector for the East India Company, he founded a bank, with an Englishman as company secretary. He eventually moved into coal mining, tea growing in Assam, overseas shipping, life insurance, newspapers and railways.

Dwarkanath laid the extensive foundations of the Tagore family's wealth: he owned a number of gigantic mansions around the city, and when he made his first trip to Europe, he travelled in his own steamship, met Queen Victoria and Louis Philippe, the last king of France, dined with Dickens and Thackeray, and became the first Indian to receive the freedom of the city of Edinburgh.

Dwarkanath is also interesting because, unlike the majority of the money-grubbing British feasting off the riches of the city, he was concerned with the wellbeing of the people. He helped to found the Hindu College, to ensure access to education for Indians, and he played a major role in the founding of the Calcutta Medical College. He was also heavily involved with civil rights issues, the freedom of the press, the right to juries in civil courts, the suppression of *sati* and the organisation of the police force. Few Europeans in the history of Calcutta can boast as much. In many ways, Bengali figures such as Dwarkanath Tagore resemble the best elements of the city itself as it was in many ways: a blend of profit-driven magnificence coupled with high-minded spiritual and social care. As the best of Calcutta combines the best of both European and Indian cultures, so did Dwarkanath.

There was another group of Indians who prospered mightily as Calcutta grew: the Marwaris. Hailing from Rajasthan, the desert state in the west of India, the Marwaris were originally moneylenders to the princely courts. In Calcutta they prospered, first as moneylenders and traders, and then as property owners and developers and industrialists. They are often accused of sharp practices, such as the Great Ghee Scandal of 1917, where ghee, or clarified butter, on which the Marwaris had a city-wide monopoly, was found in many cases to be unrecognisably adulterated with substances unknown, but almost certainly abhorrent to Hindus, who use it in many religious ceremonies, as well as in cooking.

The Marwaris are also accused of having no attachment to the local community, being motivated solely by money and self-interest. This led, especially when the various communities in Calcutta were trying to unite in the name of independence, to them being deeply unpopular, although the British recognised that their self-interest made them highly useful as managers and senior executives. Unlike the wealthy Bengalis, who tended to live in the northern parts of the city and built their fabulous palaces above the Black Town, the Marwaris imported militia from Rajasthan to protect their businesses and warehouses in the centre of the city and moved themselves south of Park Street, well into the White Town of the sahibs.

The burgeoning wealth and importance of Calcutta during the nineteenth century meant that gradually it began to move beyond its colonial roots for the first time, and started to become a city that blended the influences of both East and West. The Bengal Renaissance, as it is known, is central to the pride Bengalis feel about their city, and a litany of names, most unfamiliar in the West, are known to everyone in Calcutta. Social reformers, educationalists, poets and nationalists became, and remain, household names in Calcutta, in a manner unknown in most other major cities of the world, but which seems entirely natural in Calcutta, high-minded as it is.

One of the drivers of the new attention to matters social and spiritual was the growth of printing. Bengalis have long been addicted to the *adda*, a group gossip and discussion session that can last for hours, and the printing press and periodicals allowed more Bengalis to participate in virtual *addas*. Around the bookshops that sprang up around Dwarkanath Tagore's Hindu College a culture began to grow that, not content with having *addas*, began to talk to greater numbers of people, through pamphlets and periodicals. All of the great names of the Bengal Renaissance used periodicals for both polemical and creative writing. Between 1818 and 1867 there were some 220 different periodicals published in Calcutta, mainly in Bengali, freely discussing politics, culture and spirituality.

Along with this, the young Bengalis of what was known as the *bhadralok*, or upper classes, began to form associations and societies to discuss and improve on many aspects of Calcuttan life. There were at least 120 societies formed in the middle years of the nineteenth century, covering subjects from libraries to science, drama to politics. So Calcutta was becoming wealthier and ideas were being widely disseminated: the perfect conditions for a rebirth of Bengali culture.

The most important figure in nineteenth-century Bengali culture, and one of the makers of modern India, was Rammohan Roy, a hugely important intellectual and social reformer. He first moved to Calcutta at the age of forty-two in 1814, after having made himself a considerable fortune as a financier working alongside agents of the East India Company. He also claimed to have travelled widely, 'in distant lands, over mountains and plains', and had certainly learned Sanskrit and Arabic, to which he later added Hebrew.

Living a conventionally wealthy life in Calcutta, he became friends with Dwarkanath Tagore, and began to explore spiritual and social matters more deeply. He ultimately came to reject orthodox Hindu teachings, which he felt held back too many people in the name of tradition: a more scientific and logical approach was needed for the betterment of the people of India. His religious views eventually became based on Vedanta, a branch of Hindu philosophy which focuses on reading and analytically interpreting the ancient Vedic writings. To this was added a belief in monotheism taken from both Islam and Christianity. In 1828, along with Dwarkanath Tagore, he founded the Brahmo Samaj, literally 'society of God', a religious movement of reformed Hinduism with Christian and Muslim overtones. The organisation was opposed to many of the traditional tenets of Hinduism, such as the caste system, animal sacrifice and idolatry. The organisation was hugely influential in its day, and is cited by many as one of the key influences in the modernisation of India and its rejection of many of the strictures of old Hinduism.

Roy's concern for social issues saw him agitate for the reform of Hindi law, protest against press restrictions and argue strenuously for Indians in government and the importance of an English system of education. He was almost certainly India's first feminist, writing in favour of the equality of women. He lobbied for and won from the governor general Lord Bentinck a ban on the practice of *sati*. He published periodicals in English, Bengali and Arabic, and stressed the importance of Western science and medicine.

In 1830 he was given the honorary title of raja, and went to England as a diplomat for the emperor to watch the passing of the Reform Act of 1832, which greatly affected the governance of India. His charisma and achievements made him many friends and admirers, but he caught a fever while staying with some of them in Bristol in 1833, and swiftly died. He is buried in Arnos Vale Cemetery in Bristol, in a Hindu-style canopied mausoleum paid for by Dwarkanath Tagore.

The next of the young Bengali reformers was the poet and dramatist Michael Madhusudan Dutt, a man often described as both a genius and 'erratic'. If the great Bengali reformers were the product of the synthesis of East and West, Dutt is seen as being on the more Western side of the equation, even going so far as converting to Christianity so as to gain acceptance of his writing in English (which is how he gained the forename 'Michael'). Some see him as a model of cross-cultural progressiveness, while others talk of his being 'besottedly anglicised'. What is not disputed is his importance as a Bengali poet and playwright, in terms of developing new diction and blank-verse forms and opening a new era of Bengali literature.

Dutt was a brilliant scholar and shone at Hindu College, especially at English, and he became convinced that his fame would come with works in English, along Miltonic lines (he even called his son Milton). His family supported him for a number of years as he tried to make a name for himself, despite his conversion and his refusal to marry a girl of their choice. Eventually, however, he was forced to earn a living and became a teacher in Madras, where he continued to churn out poetry in English to lukewarm reviews.

His best-known work in English, *The Captive Ladie*, found its way into the hands of Calcutta educationalist John Drinkwater Bethune, who sensibly suggested that Dutt should use his literary skills in his native language. As a friend pointed out, Bengalis did not need another Shelley or Byron in English, but rather an equivalent figure in Bengali literature, and this is what Dutt eventually became. He married the daughter of a Scottish indigo planter, moved back to Calcutta, got a job as a clerk and started writing in Bengali, quickly gaining recognition and finding himself at the centre of a literary salon. Most of his celebrated work used the psychology of Shakespeare and the structure of Greek tragedy while taking its themes from Hindu mythology.

In 1862 he moved to London to train as a barrister, and was joined by his second, French, wife. Family feuds meant his allowance was soon cut off, and he became reliant on friends for funds. He completed his studies and was called to the Bar before returning to Calcutta, although he remained deeply in debt until his death in 1873.

One of the friends who helped Dutt out when he was in a dire financial state was another of the great figures of nineteenth-century Calcutta, the Indian educator and social reformer Ishwar Chandra Vidyasagar. The name Vidyasagar was actually an academic title conferred by the Sanskrit

College in Calcutta, meaning 'ocean of knowledge', but all Calcuttans know who is meant by it. Indeed, the city's second bridge over the Hooghly, the magnificent Vidyasagar Setu, completed in 1994, is named after him, a testament to his enduring legacy in the city.

Born into a poor Brahmin family in a remote village in Midnapur, in the southwest of Bengal, Ishwar Chandra was recognised early as a bright boy, and sent to Calcutta to study. Travelling to the city on foot, aged seven or eight, he apparently taught himself Western numerals from the milestones along the way. He won a scholarship to Sanskrit College, and studied there for a decade, before taking up a variety of academic and administrative posts, including that of chief pandit, or learned man, of Fort William College. He then became head of Sanskrit College, and spent much time and energy reforming it along more Western lines.

Chandra wrote a number of Bengali textbooks, some of which are still in use today, as well as histories of Bengal. He also retold the English and Sanskrit classics and wrote about the lives of the great Western scientists such as Newton, Copernicus and Galileo, in order to encourage Bengalis to emulate their achievements. But not content with being the greatest educational reformer that Bengal had ever seen, he also embarked on a number of social reforms. He set up three dozen schools for girls, overcoming centuries of Hindu prejudice against the education of women.

He also campaigned, in the face of violent opposition, to allow the remarriage of widows. Once Rammohan Roy had — at least in the eyes of the law — ended the practice of *sati*, there were far more widows than previously, but they were prevented by Hindu law from remarrying, and faced terrible injustice, deprivation and prejudice. Polygamy also added to the problem, as elderly Brahmins could have any number of wives, often prepubescent, and when the husbands passed away the girls faced appalling discrimination. Vidyasagar

wrote several books on the subject and eventually succeeded
in having widow remarriage made legal, although it should be
noted that it is, even today, a highly contentious issue across
the country as a whole: widows are still highly marginalised
and there are still occasionally reports of *sati* being practised
in the remoter areas of Rajasthan. Vidyasagar also campaigned against polygamy, with less success.

In later life he left Calcutta and spent much time with
the tribal people of northern Bengal, away from his peers
and the British. He was known to many ordinary Bengalis as
dayer sagar, or 'ocean of kindness', because of his charitable and
philanthropic nature. The guru Sri Aurobindo once wrote,
'Vidyasagar, sage and intellectual dictator, laboured hugely
like the Titan he was, to create a new Bengali language and
a new Bengali society'.

Also from the district of Midnapur was Bankim Chandra
Chatterjee, widely considered to be the greatest and most
popular novelist of nineteenth-century Bengal. Educated at
Hooghly College, he became a deputy magistrate and collector
for the government, enjoying a thirty-three-year career.
His proximity to the British administration meant, perhaps
naturally, that his sympathies lay elsewhere, and though he
was familiar with English literature and thought, he could
be considered anti-British, although his feelings were coded
rather than overt in his work.

Alongside Chatterjee's government career, he wrote
fiction, and started a topical literary and cultural magazine.
His hugely popular novels, while mostly wide-ranging historical
romances, also brought up social and political issues facing
India, including education, the plight of widows and national
pride. His novel *Anandamath*, published in 1882, got him in
trouble with the British authorities for its portrayal of the
importance of patriotism and nationalist sentiment, and
he was forced to add a foreword to later editions distancing
himself from its message. Although he could probably have

survived on the money from his writings, he felt he had to continue his career to pay off debts he had inherited from his family. And while *Anandamath* is today considered an inferior piece of work, it gave Bengalis the anthem 'Bande Mataram' (Hail to the Mother), which became a patriotic hymn for Bengali and Indian nationalists, and is still popular across the country today.

The last important figure of the Bengal Renaissance is also probably the best known worldwide, the spiritual leader and reformer known as Swami Vivekananda. Vivekananda was a disciple of a Hindu priest called Ramakrishna, who officiated at a large temple in the north of Calcutta. Ramakrishna was a simple, pious and ascetic man, who preached tolerance and believed in the unity of all religions. Vivekananda, highly educated in a Western style, seemed an unlikely convert to Ramakrishna's homespun philosophies, but nonetheless was obviously drawn to them, and he joined the order and spent some years travelling India preaching.

In 1893 Vivekananda travelled to Chicago to speak at a congress of religions which was being held there, and gave a famous speech on Vedanta which made his name. He spent the next few years triumphantly travelling the West giving lectures explaining his philosophies and the meaning of true Indian spirituality, shorn of the excesses of Hinduism and tradition. In 1898 he returned to Calcutta and founded the Ramakrishna Mission. He built as its headquarters the Belur Math temple, which is still enormously popular with spiritual tourists.

Swami Vivekananda's message, propagated by the Belur Math and its dozens of missions around the world, is one of religious devotion, patriotism, social reform and good works. The Ramakrishna Mission also operates schools, orphanages and libraries and undertakes a wide variety of relief and charitable work. Vivekananda blended Eastern spirituality with Western material progress, and kick-started a fascination with Eastern spiritual philosophy and methods, such as transcendental meditation and yoga. The Ramakrishna Mission has remarkably few serious critics, as it provides enlightened spiritualism with a commitment to social service that is laudable. Swami Vivekananda died aged only thirty-nine, worn down by his efforts, but is recognised as a figure of undoubted importance, created from an enlightened Western education mixed with an Eastern spirituality – truly a child of Calcutta.

With the strengths of Hindu culture being more shrewdly appraised by Indians who were also the product of Western educations, it was perhaps inevitable that nationalism should become an issue in mid-nineteenth-century India, and most obviously in Calcutta, that most sustained synthesis of East and West. But while Calcutta's intellectual elite was struggling with how best to assert itself and its nascent nationalism, the rest of India caught fire, as the Great Mutiny swept the country.

In the years leading up to the mutiny there were a number of factors which created social and political unrest across the vast country. The political expansion of the East India Company at the expense of the native princes and of the Mughal court roused the ire of both Hindu and Muslim alike, and the increasingly swift introduction of European civilisation threatened traditional India in a vague but troubling manner.

Meanwhile, the regular Indian soldiers of the East India Company, the sepoys, were taking offence at a number of changes in their regulations, which they saw as part of a plot to force them to adopt Christianity. These beliefs were strengthened when the British introduced new rifle cartridges that had to be bitten before being fired. The cartridges were reputed to be coated with grease made from the fat of cows, which were sacred to Hindus, and of pigs, which was strictly taboo and highly insulting for Muslims.

The Company moved swiftly to dispel the rumours, claiming to have replaced the cartridges, but the sepoys' suspicions persisted, and in February 1857, a series of incidents began which saw the soldiers refuse to use the cartridges, and a swell of rebellion began to be felt in some of the army towns.

In late March of 1857, a sepoy named Mangal Pandey, based at Barrackpur close to Calcutta, attacked a senior officer, and although he was quickly tried and executed, the groundswell became a wave of rebellion breaking across the country. Pandey's name has, of course, joined the well-filled pantheon of brave Bengali freedom fighters, with more justification than many.

The mutiny had the most fierce impact in the towns of Meerut, Delhi, Lucknow, Kanpur and Jhansi, but the British, aided by Sikhs from the northwest frontier and Gurkhas from Nepal, were able to effectively put down the revolt by the middle of 1858. The rebellion was marked by the most ferocious savagery on both sides, to the honour of neither. The British, for instance, adopted the old Mughal punishment for mutiny, and rebels were often tied to the mouth of a cannon and blown to bits. Whole villages were wiped out for their pro-rebel sympathies, cities were sacked and hundreds of innocent women and children perished. It was barbaric and bloody, and was the crudest war India had seen in generations, but Calcutta came through it largely unscathed, due in large part to the loyalty of its people to the Company, the source of so much wealth and trade.

After the mutiny, the British government realised that it made no sense for a country the size of India to be governed by a private company, and instead introduced direct rule through the India Office, a British department of state, with a viceroy appointed to represent the crown. Almost exactly one hundred years after the Battle of Plassey, the East India Company was abolished.

The British also embarked on a much-needed program of reform. They tried to integrate the higher-caste Indians into the government, stopped land grabs, decreed religious tolerance and admitted Indians into the civil service. They also increased the number of British soldiers in relation to native ones and allowed only British soldiers to handle artillery. The viceroy — the first was Charles, second Viscount Canning — was quite naturally headquartered in Calcutta, and ran the entire country, aided by legislative and executive councils with an Indian-nominated element.

So Calcutta grew and prospered. It was around this period that it became known as the City of Palaces, as rich merchants vied to build themselves the most opulent homes. Calcutta University opened its doors, and the city got a telegraph line, a public sewerage system, a filtered water supply and horse-drawn trams within a few years of one another. And yet in Calcutta, perhaps more than any other Indian city, the embers of nationalism were still glowing. Resentment against the British was becoming stronger as educated Bengalis began to see more clearly how they were being exploited. 'How is he, who has appreciated the genius of Shakespeare and Bacon... who has read and discussed so much about the equality of man, to bear the influence of the civil servant or of the low-born English merchant whom he is obliged to call his master?' wrote a leading journalist in 1858, and this was a sentiment that was bound to spread.

The next opportunity for nationalist propagation in Bengal was the so-called Indigo Revolt (also known more prosaically as the Blue Mutiny) of 1861. For centuries Bengal had been exporting indigo, produced from a small shrub, around the world. However, during the nineteenth century supplies from other parts of the world began to dry up, and the British indigo planters in India stepped in to supply the world market. The planters also persuaded large numbers of Bengali peasant farmers to grow some indigo as well as their subsistence crops. This would have been acceptable had not the planters done the persuading through a system of small advance payments ahead of delivery.

Upon delivery of the indigo, it was claimed, the planters would offer rates that were far lower than agreed, and would often cheat in the measuring, effectively ensuring that the farmers ended up owing them money, rather than the other way round. Over the years, debts would increase amongst farming families, but it was impossible to escape the planters and their hired thugs, and complaining to the local magistrates was useless, as most of them were sympathetic to the planters, or even were planters themselves. One Englishman in the civil service is reported to have admitted that 'Not a chest of indigo reached England without being stained with human blood'.

The year after the Great Mutiny, the farmers slowly but surely began to rebel. In a village in what is now Bangladesh, two brothers walked out of a planter's indigo factory and succeeded in persuading the other villagers to stop planting the shrub, which was, to them anyway, valueless. The villagers' heroic resistance against the planters' hired goons meant that the resistance spread, albeit slowly. Within two years the mutiny had moved across Bengal and all farmers were refusing to grow the crop.

The mutiny gave the *bhadralok* of Calcutta an opportunity to organise and protest against the despotism of the indigo planters and, by association, Europeans in general. Intellectuals and journalists worked to rouse public opinion against the forced cultivation of the crop, and Bengal's first work of political drama, a play called *Nildarpan* (The Mirror of Indigo) was performed in 1860, containing lines like 'The indigo planters come like a needle, but go out like a ploughshare/And are devastating Bengal like swarms of locusts'. By the end of 1861, Bengal was producing negligible amounts of indigo. However, it is instructive to note that much of the production switched to the neighbouring state of Bihar, where the peasants were oppressed just as heavily.

It was not until 1917, when an ambitious lawyer called Mohandas K. Gandhi was persuaded to take on the Bihar farmers' case and won, using, among other things, the mantra of nonviolence, that this particular form of oppression came to an end in India. Gandhi of course learned some very valuable lessons from the Bihari indigo farmers, and the case had profound implications for the country as a whole.

In Calcutta, the Europeans of the city were divided about how to react to the new mood of nationalism. Some people were indignant that there should be any agitation at all. Geoffrey Moorhouse quotes from a letter to a Calcutta journal of 1884 complaining about Indians in government:

> With reference to the question of the Municipal Government of Calcutta, I beg to submit that the present system is perfectly preposterous. Calcutta is a purely English city. The city belongs and has always belonged to the English, and the native community in it is simply a foreign and parasitical community which would cease to exist if the English were to abandon it. Its site was selected and the land taken up for it was taken up by the English. They found it, built it, occupied it, maintained it, defended it, regulated it, and it is still from their commerce and enterprise that its revenues are now deployed. The English race, in its capacity for self-government, is admitted by all nations to have never been surpassed by any race that has ever been recorded in history... The end, however, is not far off. The nations of the world will refuse before long to be done to death by cholera and other loathsome diseases which are diffused from Calcutta over the surface of the globe, in order that Bengali babus may hold places of importance for which they are unfit and in which all they can do is exercise their talents for chatter, and enable Government to say 'See how liberal our administration is in India to the natives.'

Attitudes such as that must have done much to strengthen the resolve of Bengali nationalists in the years after the Great Mutiny.

On the other hand, there were far-sighted and humane Englishmen in India, and some of them were actively working to promote equality, if not a nationalist agenda. Viceroy Lord Ripon in 1882 wrote a memorandum intended to help Indians have an independent political life, and in 1883 he introduced what was known as the Ilbert Bill, which aimed to allow Indian judges sitting alone the power to try cases involving Europeans.

There was a huge uproar from the Europeans in Bengal, who thought the bill discriminatory: Indians had no right to judge them, as they were racially inferior. The British organised themselves and agitated against the bill, in a period known as the White Mutiny. When it was passed the next year, it had been heavily amended and specified that Europeans would have to be tried by a jury, at least half of whom would have to be their racial peers. Although this was a defeat for the Calcutta reformers, it showed them the lobbying power an educated minority could have, which they began to turn to their advantage. And despite the defeat, Lord Ripon is still remembered with great affection in India.

Another Briton who played a part in promoting political life among the people of Bengal was Allan Octavian Hume, a civil servant and ornithologist who, instead of retiring to England, moved north to Shimla and formed the Indian National Congress, with the aim of promoting liberal and secular ideals. In a circular letter of 1883 to the graduates of the Calcutta University, he asked them to 'make a resolute struggle to secure greater freedom for themselves and their country'. The Indian National Congress quickly became attractive to Bengalis as a forum for airing and directing their grievances, despite all its transactions being carried out in English. It concerned itself with matters such as the larger participation of Indians in the civil service, industrial and technical education, the separation of the executive from the judiciary and more representation of Indians in government.

A third Englishman, Viceroy Lord Curzon responded to these initiatives in a robustly British manner. A complex and fascinating man, Curzon had little time for organisations such as the Indian National Congress, which he thought prone to waffle: in a letter he complained about the Bengali's tendency towards 'rolling out yards and yards of frothy declamation about subjects he has imperfectly considered, or which he does not fully understand'. He set about reducing the elected portion of the Calcutta Corporation, a partially elected body of local councillors, to ensure British control, and he set up a commission of reform of Calcutta University — containing no Indian members — because he believed it had become too political. It has been argued that Curzon merely wanted to protect India from the Calcuttan *bhadralok*, whom he thought ineffectual and unrepresentative of the country's interests as a whole, but he merely managed to inflame Bengali and Indian nationalism still further.

Curzon's next step to counter the growth of Bengali nationalist sentiment was both bold and wildly counterproductive: the partition of Bengal. This was announced in 1903 and became a reality in 1905. Curzon called it an administrative measure, but in reality it was meant to divide and rule, creating as it did two separate Bengals: the east, which was overwhelmingly Muslim, and the west, which was predominantly Hindu. British officials were privately candid about their motives in the division of the state. The Home Secretary to the government of India, Herbert Risley is quoted as saying:

> Bengal united is a power; Bengal divided will pull in several different ways... one of our main objects is to split up and thereby weaken a solid body of opponents to our rule... A separate administration, a separate high court and a separate university at Dacca would give extra opportunities to the Muslim middle class to emerge from their backward state and weaken the economic base of the Hindu middle classes. The Hindu zamindari patrons to the Congress would find the Muslim peasantry ranged against them, secure in the support of the Dacca Secretariat. It would divide the nationalist ranks once and for all.

Curzon was equally frank in private:

> *Any measure in consequence that would divide the Bengali-speaking population; that would permit independent centres of activity and influence to grow up; that would dethrone Calcutta from its place as the centre of successful intrigue, or that would weaken the influence of the lawyer class, who have the entire organization in their hands, is intensely and hotly resented by them. The outcry will be loud and very fierce, but as a native gentleman said to me — 'my countrymen always howl until a thing is settled; then they accept it'.*

But this time, Curzon's confidence was misplaced. Partition was a horrible mistake from Britain's point of view, giving rise to the first mass movement in modern India, introducing purely nationalist forces and giving birth to a tradition of terrorism that survives to this day. And dividing Hindus and Muslims and exacerbating the differences between them has been disastrous for South Asia as a whole. And while Bengal, and Calcutta specifically, were most concerned with the partition, the whole of India turned its attention to the situation amid a rising tide of national consciousness. None of this was to concern Curzon overly: he quit his post two months before the change, and left Lord Minto to deal with the effects.

The effects of Partition were startling. The population became instantly more radicalised, and Calcutta became the centre of the agitation. Curzon had managed to divide the population, but British rule was losing its grip. Just before the division was made formal, it was announced at a mass meeting at Calcutta's Town Hall that all patriotic Bengalis would henceforth boycott all British-made goods from that point onwards. They swore that they would only purchase India-made goods, a movement which quickly spread and became known as *swadeshi*, from a Sanskrit word meaning 'of your own country'. The movement grew at an unexpectedly fast rate: Bengali newspapers recorded a quadrupling of their circulation figures within a few months, and the concept began to spread across the country as a whole. But along with the moves towards self-sufficiency like boycotts and passive resistance, came more extreme ways of achieving it: terrorism and extremism in general. Swiftly after *swadeshi* came calls for *swaraj*, or self-rule, which was really the last thing the British wanted to hear. More moderate political leaders began to be marginalised, and bombs were thrown, not just at the British, but between Hindus and Muslims.

Bengalis felt especially slighted by the partition because they felt the Muslims in the east of the state had been given an area in which Muslims were in a clear majority; and this struck at the Bengalis' nationalism. Muslims were, on the whole, perfectly happy with the new arrangement. But over the next few years, as sectarian violence became more common, the Muslims realised that Hindu nationalists were never going to allow them either peace or equality, and it convinced them of the need for a separate homeland. The Muslims were becoming politicised. In 1906 they formed the political organisation that was to become the Muslim League, to safeguard the political rights of Muslims in India, and within a few years its leaders were proposing, then demanding, the creation of a separate Muslim India.

So the violence in Bengal mounted, as did the repression by the British authorities that came in its wake. And as the cycle worsened, the British realised that something needed to be done. Lord Minto tinkered with various pieces of legislation, with the aim of gently encouraging parliamentary democracy in India, and an Indian was appointed to the viceroy's executive council in 1909. But these changes were too little, too late, to staunch the resentment over Partition. In 1910 Minto left for England, to be replaced by Lord Hardinge. One of Hardinge's influential advisors was King George V, who had visited India in 1905, and had thought Partition a mistake. Wanting to venture east to India again, and believing the ending of Partition would ensure him a great welcome, he and Hardinge decided to end the division of the state in 1911.

In the same year, in a move that was the first of the major body blows that Calcutta suffered, it was decided to move the capital of India from Calcutta to the ancient city of Delhi. It was thought that the cooler climes of the northern city, along with its history as the seat of power of both Muslim and Hindu rulers, would assert a calming effect. Also, by removing power from a by now highly volatile and politicised Calcutta, the British would be able to rule once again with the effortless serenity they expected. And Delhi was geographically central; important in such a vast country.

Whilst nowadays both cities present similarly crowded, hectic and polluted faces, in 1911 they were very different. Calcutta boasted around 14,000 nonmilitary British residents, while Delhi had less than ninety. Curzon, amongst others, argued against the move, calling Delhi a 'cemetery of dead monuments and forgotten dynasties', but it went ahead anyway.

For Bengalis, the end of Partition was a victory, and the shifting of power to the northwest was of surprisingly little importance. For the British of Calcutta, the move was a disaster. The proximity of legislative power to their trading interests was of paramount importance, and the letters pages of the Calcutta newspapers were full of their hair-tearing and lamentations. For them the move was akin to moving the capital of England to a more ancient but infinitely less important city, like Bath or York. But beyond their sulking, there was perhaps the realisation that this was the first time that the British Raj had ever actively retreated before its subjects. There was a terrific symbolism about the ending of Partition and the shift of capitals; if the British weren't exactly on the run, they were picking up speed, away from the city they had created, and the country they had done so well out of.

But if a momentum was building that would inevitably see the British relinquish India, news of it hadn't reached the British in Calcutta. When Queen Victoria died in 1901, Lord Curzon proposed a 'great imperial duty': the erecting of a memorial to her memory. It is ironic that what Curzon saw as a memorial to a woman who had never visited India became a memorial to the entire Raj itself. Undoubtedly the greatest physical monument left behind by the British in India, the Victoria Memorial is an astonishing confection of white marble and hubris, occupying a vast site at the southern end of the Maidan. Blindingly white in the fierce Bengali sun, classically ordered yet somehow busy, it looks best at night, sumptuously lit and reflected in the great ornamental pools that surround it, serene and magnificent.

Curzon in many ways saw the memorial as a British Taj Mahal — if not as a tomb, at least as a fabulous token of love and devotion. The building is faced with marble from Makhrana in Rajasthan, where the Taj Mahal's came from. W. H. Auden claimed that when he visited it in the 1930s he was assured by a local that both buildings were built by the same architect. And while the Taj is essentially a sad building, commemorating a woman who died young, the Victoria Memorial celebrated a long and important life, and the building itself was to be stuffed to the brim with the relics and proofs of imperial success. Lord Curzon saw the memorial as 'a building stately, spacious, monumental and grand... where all classes will learn the lessons of history and see revived before their eyes the marvels of the past'. Curzon also thought, overoptimistically, that the building might stop the rising tide of Indian nationalism, by providing a focus on what he saw as the shared triumphs of Empire. And indeed, the *bhadralok* and the Indian aristocracy were happy to fund the entire cost of the building, which came to more than ten million rupees and took sixteen years to complete. The site covers some sixty-four acres, and a prison had to be demolished to make way for it.

It is designed in a style that could be broadly described as Italian Renaissance, with a suggestion of orientalism, although some architectural critics see it as owing much to British civic classicism, and to Belfast Town Hall in particular. The great central dome reaches to fifty-six metres, and is topped by a five-metre, three-tonne figure of victory. The foundation stone was laid by George V, and the monument was opened in 1921 by the Prince of Wales, later Edward VIII. Curzon himself never saw it; he left India before the foundation was even laid.

The inside is less awe-inspiring than the exterior. The collections, whilst certainly eclectic, have a somewhat random and uncared-for air about them. Queen Victoria is the main focus, naturally, and there are a large number of copies of paintings from the Royal Collection in Britain showing scenes from her life. There is the piano she practised on as a girl, and an armchair and writing desk she used from Windsor Castle, and the last letter she wrote to her Indian subjects. There are photographs of her, and stained glass depicting scenes from her life, with heavy allegorical overtones.

Elsewhere in the museum there are more portraits of prominent Calcuttan worthies: Holwell of Black Hole fame, Clive of India, Sir David Ochterlony, Bishop Heber, Dwarkanath Tagore and Michael Madhusudan Dutt. There are lithographs and aquatints, weapons and armour, treaties and manuscripts, coins, stamps and other artefacts of the Raj, although their arrangement can tend towards the haphazard. Some later galleries have been added that deal with Indian leaders and with the growth of Calcutta, and these are better arranged and thought out.

The memorial is hugely popular with the people of Calcutta; coachloads of tourists and pilgrims visit, crocodile lines of schoolchildren troop open-mouthed through its echoing halls, lovers meet in the precious space of its gardens, and groups of walkers meet in the early mornings to stroll and hold their *addas* in the cool of the day. But perhaps the greatest testament to the pride that Calcuttans feel towards the memorial is the fact that it has never been molested by the frenzied mobs whipped into passionate anti-British fervour close by on the Maidan, and that despite Calcuttans' fondness for renaming things, it is still, resolutely, the Victoria Memorial.

The years following the end of the partition of Bengal were uneasy ones in Calcutta. The Muslims were the people who had gained the most from the partition, and consequently felt that they had lost the most when the scheme came to an end – an end that had been engineered mainly by the Hindus with whom they lived in the city. Coupled with this, the First World War brought with it a hefty increase in the price of staple goods such as rice, salt and cooking oil, which hit poor Muslims, and increased their general resentment. And the imams were starting to preach jihad and were encouraging Muslims to put Islam before India. To add to the mix, the British were still playing off one faith against the other in order to divide and rule. The stage was set for the antagonism between the two faiths to lead to a number of terrible riots in the next three decades.

The first of these happened in 1918, although the Muslims' target was the Marwari community, whom they suspected of hoarding foodstuffs and driving up prices (which was almost certainly true). Shops were burned, dozens were killed (although no Hindus) and the city began to live with a communal tension that lasted for decades.

In 1926 a Hindu organisation held a march through north Calcutta. Passing a mosque during its call to prayer, they were asked if their band could cease playing while they passed by. It appears they could not. Muslims from the mosque attacked the procession and almost instantly battle was joined, lasting for two weeks. Mosques and Hindu temples were desecrated and torched, hundreds were injured and dozens killed. The army eventually stopped the fighting, only for it to break out again a couple of weeks later, with seventy dead and four hundred injured. This was a pattern that was to continue for many years.

While the Hindus and Muslims were learning how to hate each other as a way of life, the opposition to the British was a steady undertone from the Hindu community. There was a general strike called by Gandhi in 1921 to mark the Prince of Wales' visit to India. The people of India were becoming increasingly politicised, and the people of Calcutta were becoming addicted to politics, as they still are today. There were sporadic acts of terrorism against the British, which cumulatively began to weary the colonisers, who had only really wanted Calcutta for what it could provide.

In 1930 three young anti-British revolutionaries managed to meet with a Colonel Simpson, a prisons inspector, in the Writers' Building, the administrative building on Dalhousie Square. They shot him, rather messily, and then two of them ate cyanide and died on the spot. The third was hanged not long after. Despite the high cost in terms of lives lost, and the spectacular pointlessness of the act, the square was later renamed BBD Bagh – after the assassins Benoy, Badal and Dinesh – and nowadays taxi drivers occasionally point out the significance of the name with a certain pride as you drive through the square.

But the pride in the largely irrelevant Benoy, Badal and Dinesh is as nothing compared to the deification of another Bengali revolutionary, Subhas Chandra Bose, known to every-one in Calcutta as Netaji, or 'revered leader'. Calcutta's airport was known for many years as Dum Dum, made famous because of the hollow-point bullets invented there – but now travellers are greeted by signs welcoming them, not entirely clearly, to NSCBI Airport, or Netaji Subhas Chandra Bose International. Some speak of Bose as a figure to rival Gandhi, although outside Bengal his status is much lower.

A firebrand in his youth, Bose was expelled from Presidency College for leading an assault on an English teacher, but went on to Cambridge, from where he was to write in a letter home that 'what gives me the greatest joy is to watch the whiteskins serving me and cleaning my shoes'. He passed the exams to join the Indian civil service but quickly resigned and joined Gandhi's nascent independence movement. However, he disagreed with Gandhi's insistence on nonviolence, and joined a more extreme faction struggling for independence.

He was jailed by the British on a number of occasions on terrorism charges during the 1930s, and yet in the same period managed to become chief executive of the Calcutta Corporation, and mayor of the city.

When the Second World War broke out, Bose argued that Britain should immediately hand over power, but he was quickly arrested on charges of sedition, and fled Calcutta disguised as a Muslim. He got as far as Kabul, where the Italian embassy gave him papers, and he eventually made it to Berlin in March 1941. For the next couple of years he was involved in anti-British propaganda, and trying to persuade Hitler to let him parachute brainwashed Indian troops captured in North Africa into India to defeat the British.

In 1943 he went by submarine to Japan, where he was something of a hero, and became head of what was known as the Indian National Army, composed of captured Indian troops sympathetic to the cause. He soon declared war on the Allies, and his 25,000 troops actually managed to cross the Indian border after fighting their way through Burma. However, they advanced no further, and were routed by General Slim's Fourteenth Army. Making his way to Russia, Bose's plane crashed mysteriously on the island of Taiwan, and he died.

Despite this fairly dishonourable history, certainly during the war years, Bose is revered across Bengal. Many people think he didn't in fact die in the plane crash, but rather that the British somehow managed to kidnap and imprison him. As well as the airport, there is a major road named after him, and a number of statues around the city, where huge crowds gather on his birthday to sing patriotic songs. They refuse to believe the well-documented facts that this aesthetic Hindu figurehead smoked, drank alcohol, ate beef and fathered a daughter by a non-Hindu. They refuse to concede that trying to involve Hitler and Mussolini in India's struggle for independence was colossally irresponsible. His moon-face gazes out serenely from any number of posters and portraits around the city, a source of delight for most Calcuttans. The fascism and the glorifying of violence are conveniently ignored; the fact that Calcutta once had an undoubtedly brave figure fighting to free them from the British has set his reputation in stone.

During the Second World War, Calcutta suffered another of the body blows that have come to characterise its recent history: the Great Famine of 1943. Although Bengal did not suffer the worst food shortages in India, it had seen famine before. But 1943 saw famine on a new and terrible scale, and one which was caused not by a failure of crops or the monsoon, but by greed. No one knows exactly how many people died, but the best estimates now put the figure at between three and four million.

There had been a few poor rice harvests in the years leading up to 1943, and Bengal had been importing large quantities from abroad almost every year since 1934. However, by 1943 one of the major sources of imports, Burma, had been invaded by Japan, so ending the supply. Over the winter of 1942–43, the winter rice crop failed because of a cyclone and huge flooding, and the peasant farmers across Bengal began to stockpile what they had. The British administration, in some disarray because of the war, had little idea how much rice Bengal needed, and allowed much of the winter crop to be exported. Soon, poor landless peasants began to flood in to Calcutta looking for food. Already battered by the flooding over the winter, tens of thousands of the destitute and starving began filling the streets, sleeping on the pavements and at the train stations. They had sold all of their belongings in an attempt to buy food, and now they had nothing. The stories of poverty and desperation are as awful as of any famine, but this one was worse because the middle classes of the city were not starving: they could afford to keep on buying the stockpiled grain and pay the prices charged by the profiteers.

The *Manchester Guardian* caught some of the flavour of the time: 'Thousands of emaciated destitutes still roam the streets in a ceaseless quest for food, scouring dustbins and devouring rotten remains of castaway food and fruit. Rickety children clutching imploringly the tattered garments barely covering the bones of their mothers are seen in all quarters of the city.' People were eating snails, refuse from hospital waste, dogs and grass. Mothers were abandoning their children to their fate, and Hindus and Muslims were eating scraps of food that the other had touched, normally the greatest taboo.

While many people blame the British for the famine, the Indian Provincial Government in Calcutta was doing equally little to stem the tide of starving refugees or to feed them. The Food Minister, H. S. Suhrawardy — later to become president of Pakistan — declared that there were no major problems with food production: this at a time when food prices had risen by 600 per cent in a state where there were 46 million landless peasants. In July of 1943 Suhrawardy denied a request that Bengal be declared a famine area, because he could see plenty of food in the shops. And the need couldn't be too bad, he reasoned, if the starving weren't looting it. But the truth was that the people dying were mainly village folk, who didn't understand what was happening to them, or how to fix the situation. And the better-off Calcuttans simply didn't help their compatriots enough or understand the situation. It wasn't until October that Suhrawardy finally relented and asked for outside help. By then 11,000 people a week were dying in Calcutta. And in the wake of the famine came cholera, which wiped out many more poor Bengalis.

While few Calcuttans covered themselves with glory during the famine, the British were perceived as deserving far more of the blame, and the famine served to drive the wedge even further between the Raj and India. And it is surely only right that this should be the case. Despite the war, the idea that tens of thousands of people should be dying every month, hideously and piteously, and begging for rice and water, in the second city of the British Empire, is a revolting one, when we know it could have been prevented by better administration. If that was the best the British could do, then it must be nearly time for the Indians to try for themselves.

Part of the blame for the famine was also put upon the Muslims, and the Muslim League, who were of the majority in the Indian Provincial Government. In 1946 H. S. Suhrawardy formed a new Muslim League administration. By now, it was clear that British rule wasn't going to be lasting for a great deal longer, and Mohammed Ali Jinnah and his Muslim League, and Jawaharlal Nehru's Congress Party were beginning to have the argument about how to divide the country between Muslim and Hindu. Suhrawardy, of course, supported Jinnah, and agreed with him on the need for a 'Direct Action Day', on 16 August 1946, where Muslims would cease all business. The commerce ceased, but the business they had with the Hindus of Calcutta took centre stage, and the city descended into violence and madness.

A mass meeting of Muslims was called at the foot of the Ochterlony Monument, and the crowd grew increasingly fractious. At the end of the meeting they took off across the city in an orgy of looting, stabbing and burning. Hindus huddled in their houses as rampaging mobs set fire to buildings, hurled Hindus into sewers and hacked at them with axes. A curfew was ordered, but made little difference. Piles of bodies were appearing on street corners and the stench of death began to waft through the streets again, as it had in 1943. Hindu and Muslim leaders organised peace talks, but the fighting continued. It took a week for the police and troops to restore order to the city, and it took 45,000 troops to do it. An estimated 100,000 people fled the city, and about the same number were made homeless. Figures for the dead are unknown, but they probably numbered about seven thousand, with twice that number injured.

And still the fighting continued, sporadically, across the city, a 'small butchery' which saw a few die every day. In an effort to calm tensions, Gandhi himself came to Calcutta for Independence, which it had been decided would be declared on 14 August 1947. He moved into a house together with Suhrawardy to show amity and mend fences. On 15 August 1947, the mood in the city changed, and fraternity swept across it; Hindu and Muslim briefly united to celebrate India's independence from the British, ten days short of 257 years since Charnock had established his trading post on the Hooghly.

As if enough indignities had not already been heaped upon Calcutta's head, the period after Independence saw a repeat of the Partition of Bengal, with the creation of Muslim East Pakistan. Some four million Hindu refugees left the country and made for Calcutta, which is only sixty-five kilometres from the border. The torrent of refugees seemed unstoppable, and there was nowhere for them to live. Vast relief camps were set up, ironically called 'colonies', but these were woefully inadequate for the task of housing the numbers arriving. By the time of the Kashmir Crisis of 1951, Calcutta had virtually become one vast relief centre. Families squatted on every street corner, the gorgeous palaces of the British were filled to bursting with the indigent, and railway platforms and warehouses held countless numbers of the unfortunate. For those who didn't succumb to starvation or disease, a life of beggary on the streets was all they had to look forward to.

In many ways this is the vision of Calcutta that many in the West carry around with them: a vision of a destitute and filthy population eking out an existence in the gutters of a city built on the proceeds of the looting of a country; a vision of death, disease and despair. And in many ways it was an accurate picture for many years, although it ignored the astonishing wealth of the rich *bhadralok* and Marwari families, and the British traders who remained. And these inequalities did not go unnoticed in Bengal, which was busy embracing Marxist political policies with great enthusiasm.

In 1967 there was another famine in India, due to drought, and the higher prices of staple foodstuffs meant a reduction in the purchase of consumer goods. Consequently thousands of manufacturing jobs were lost in Bengal. This had a knock-on effect which saw the Congress Party lose power to a loose grouping of political parties allied to two different Communist factions. Determined more than anything else to stay in power, they utilised a time-honoured method for rallying peasant support – they agitated for the redistribution of land.

There is no doubt that the system of land ownership in Bengal was in need of being distributed more equitably. The average size of land-holding was, at about one and a half hectares, tiny, and the majority of peasants had no tenure, and therefore no security. The administration began to encourage heavily armed gangs of landless peasants to march on the property of the larger landowners and claim it as their own. At first the police tried to enforce law and order but were instructed that the land grab was part of a legitimate and democratic struggle, and told not to interfere. Within six months the Communist Party of India (Marxist) had increased its membership by 450,000 in the rural areas of Bengal.

A more politically astute, or politically mature, party might have seen that it was creating a monster in encouraging violent land redistribution, but not the CPI(M). The situation quickly began to spiral out of control, particularly in a district up in the hills of Darjeeling known as Naxalbari. The area had long been a hotbed of political radicalism, and there had been two uprisings there earlier in the century. Peasants in the area were more enthusiastic than most about redistributing land, and eventually the government began to realise that things were getting out of control. After a number of violent clashes between police and activists in the area, the CPI(M) decided to start expelling troublemakers from the party. China's government took note of this, and an editorial in the Beijing *People's Daily* newspaper forecast the 'approach of a great people's revolution in India with armed struggle as its major force'. The expelled Communists began to rally under the banner of the Naxalites, and a new revolutionary political force was born.

Although essentially a peasant force, the Naxalites attracted the educated youth of Calcutta from the start, inflamed by what they saw as oppression of the peasants. These idealistic young people became the driving force of the Naxalites, living with the peasants and in the slums, preaching Maoist propaganda and grass-roots armed revolution. They were responsible for innumerable killings (Red Guard Actions) in the countryside, but by 1970 these reached Calcutta, and violence started to engulf the city once more. Bombings, arson, robbery, assault — all began to soar, and eventually Bengal's governor suspended the regional government and handed power back to the central government, who sent in the troops.

Towards the end of 1971, the brutality and oppression of the army began to calm the city, and the Naxalites' revolution was essentially, but not entirely, over. In 1999 the Naxalites claimed 144 lives, 35 of those police officers, and 211 Naxalites were killed by the police. In 2003 the chief minister of Andhra Pradesh narrowly escaped death in the form of a Naxalite mine.

'Perhaps there will be another kind of disaster before Calcutta is left to its plague,' wrote a gloomy Geoffrey Moorhouse in 1970. And indeed there was yet another great indignity in store for the City of Palaces: the 1971 India–Pakistan War, which led to the birth of Bangladesh.

Since Partition at Independence, East Pakistan had been dominated and often neglected by West Pakistan, and these tensions turned into a struggle for independence for the east. The great cyclone of 1970, which killed some 200,000 in East Pakistan crystallised for many there the need for independence from West Pakistan, which, in turn, plunged the country into more chaos and violence. And, as usual, Calcutta got the refugees fleeing the bloodshed, the hundreds of thousands of poor, hungry, desperate, sick and bewildered who made their homes on the city's groaning streets. The refugee problem led to India's intervention, the 1971 India–Pakistan War and the eventual declaration of the new, independent state of Bangladesh.

These constant running problems on the streets of Calcutta produced another of the city's enduring icons, in the shape of a tiny Albanian nun called Agnes Gonxha Bojaxhiu, better known to the world as Mother Teresa (the name she took after St Teresa of Lisieux when she undertook her religious vows). Close to her main home for the destitute near Kalighat in the south of the city is a fifteen-metre high mosaic of the smiling old lady. Next to it is an advertising hoarding, which declares that it is a space 'Reserved for Kolkata's Best Brands', which seems ironically accurate: Mother Teresa is a brand which has helped to make Calcutta famous, but not one that has helped the city overmuch. In many ways Mother Teresa helped to propagate the idea of Calcutta as a squalid sump-hole of filth and poverty, and many in the city are at best ambivalent about her becoming the best-known face of the city.

Born in 1910, Bojaxhiu joined the Irish order of Loreto nuns, and was sent to teach in Darjeeling. By 1931 she was in Calcutta, and became horrified by what she saw on its streets: the death and poverty. In 1943 there was the Great Famine and in 1947 there was the post-Partition refugee influx, and she was constantly tormented by the scenes she saw. In 1950, with permission from Rome, she founded a new order, the Missionaries of Charity, recognisable by the simple blue-bordered white cotton saris the nuns all wore. She worked tirelessly and quietly, setting up homes for the dying, for lepers and for children, nursing tens of thousands of the poorest and most destitute as they died, easing their final pains with basic medical attention.

In 1968 a British journalist and Catholic convert, Malcolm Muggeridge, broadcast an enthusiastic television program about Teresa's work in Calcutta, and she started to become an icon of charitable compassion, selfless dedication and goodliness. She was awarded the Nobel Peace Prize in 1979, and before her death was often cited as the most respected woman in the world. The Catholic Church is moving swiftly to have her canonised, and in late 2003 she was beatified, more quickly than any other saint in Catholic history.

Despite all this, Calcutta is not entirely comfortable with the legacy of the old lady (she died in 1997, on the day Princess Diana was buried, so shunting her down the news agendas around the world). There is no statue of her, in a city that loves its statues. There has been no road named after her, in a city with a positive mania for renaming roads after its heroes, no matter how obscure. The reasons for this are complex, but instructive.

The criticisms levelled at Teresa are many. Her medical facilities are routinely described as atrocious; there is little pain medication, although it is cheap and widely available nowadays, and her mission's approach to treating leprosy is regarded as primitive. In a city with as many needs as Calcutta, it would probably be sensible to plough money into prophy-lactic medication and education, but the sisters only want you when you're dying, so you can die a Catholic death. The point isn't treatment.

The Missionaries of Charity are also accused of having an awful lot of money, hundreds of millions of dollars, which is kept outside India, because of its laws on charities keeping their records open for scrutiny. The order now has convents and nunneries in 120 countries, and many see its vast wealth being used only to open dogmatic religious institutions, rather than solving the world's problems. Teresa herself is accused of being a highly savvy media operator, hugely ambitious to promote a highly orthodox and conservative Catholicism, and a right-wing ideologue.

But in Calcutta itself, many think Teresa and her myth is a counterweight to progress. Not only is she the most famous figure of recent years to hail from the city, but she was Christian, in a proudly Hindu city. The myth also requires the people of the city to play the part of hapless victims, to be lifted up by Teresa. As British journalist Christopher Hitchens put it:

> From Mother Theresa and from her fans you would receive the impression that in Calcutta there is nothing but torpor, squalor and misery, and people barely have the energy to brush the flies from their eyes while extending a begging bowl. Really and truly that is a slander on a fantastically interesting, brave, highly evolved and cultured city, which has universities, film schools, theatres, book shops, literary cafes, and very vibrant politics. There is indeed a terrible problem of poverty and overcrowding, but despite all that there isn't much mendicancy. People do not tug at your sleeve and beg. They are proud of the fact that they don't. The source of Calcutta's woes and miseries is the very overpopulation that the church says is no problem, and the mass influx of refugees from neighbouring regions that have been devastated by religious and secular warfare in the name of God.

There is no doubt, however, that Mother Teresa has had an effect on many lives (or deaths) in Calcutta. She threw up a challenge to the city's administrators, which they have yet to answer properly. But she is not one of Calcutta's best brands, merely one of its most famous. The Calcuttan author Aroup

Chatterjee, in a painstaking analysis of Mother Teresa's deleterious effects on the city, calculates that since 'the Teresa bandwagon really took off in the mid-1970s' she has cost Calcutta $4.5 billion in terms of lost tourist revenue; Western tourists are frightened off by the images that the Missionaries of Charity rely on propagating.

For many people, Teresa's fame was sealed with the award of the Nobel Prize in 1979, but she wasn't the first resident of the city to win a Nobel Prize; far from it. The city got its first in 1902, when Surgeon-Major Ronald Ross was awarded the prize for medicine, for his discovery of the mechanism for the transmission of malaria. He had discovered the role played by mosquitoes by sending his servant Mahomed Bux into the steamy Calcutta streets to capture them, and then be bitten by them, while Ross closely observed the results.

But more famous than Ross, far more beloved than Mother Teresa or any member of the Bengal Renaissance, and more celebrated in Calcutta than even the buffoonish Subhas Chandra Bose, was the winner of 1913's Nobel Prize for literature, Rabindranath Tagore.

Tagore, born in 1861, was the grandson of the great businessman and philanthropist Dwarkanath Tagore. The youngest of fourteen children, he was educated at home, and was precocious; he wrote his first poem at the age of seven, and was apparently translating Shakespeare into Bengali by the age of twelve. He was sent to England at seventeen and studied in London, but returned to Calcutta after a year and a half without a degree.

Because of the wealth of the Tagore family, he spent the next few years writing poems, plays, short stories and novels, without the necessity of earning a living. However, when he was thirty he was sent to manage some of the family's estates, where he spent much time with the rural poor, who influenced him deeply. In 1901 he founded a school at Shantiniketan, north of Calcutta, with the intention of blending Indian and Western methods of education, which eventually became Bengal's Vishva Bharati University. And he continued to write, turning out poems, novels, textbooks, a history of India and treatises on education. He travelled the world giving lectures and meeting the great and the good. W. B. Yeats is said to have been overcome with emotion upon meeting him.

During this time, Tagore's wife, son and daughter all separately died, which affected him deeply, but he translated his emotions into his poetry, and in 1910 he published *Gitanjali*, which won him the Nobel Prize (the first non-European to win). Described by the Nobel committee as 'profoundly sensitive, fresh and beautiful verse, by which, with consummate skill, he has made his poetic thought, expressed in his own English words, a part of the literature of the West', and by others as 'windy mysticism', it certainly cemented his reputation in the West as a messiah from the East, and perhaps meant that he is seen there as more of a mystic than as the towering poet and national figure he is in Bengal.

In 1915 he was knighted, but he returned the honour in 1919 in protest over the Amritsar Massacre, which saw four hundred peaceful Indians gunned down by British troops, one of the most shameful episodes in all of Britain's colonial history. Tagore continued to write and compose music, and wrote the Indian national anthem, 'Jana Gana Mana'. In his sixties he decided to teach himself the principles of painting, and over the last twenty years of his life produced a large number of impressive paintings in a modernist and expressionist mode.

Although he didn't often write specifically about Calcutta, when he did it was with a certain unmistakable *tendresse*:

> *When I was a little boy Calcutta city was not as wakeful at night as it is now... In those old times which we knew, when the day was over, whatever business remained undone wrapped itself up in the black blanket*

of the night and went to sleep in the darkened groundfloor premises of
the city… In the hot season… the hawkers would go about the streets
shouting 'I-i-i-ce'… No one but myself knows how my mind thrilled
to that cry as I stood on the verandah facing the street… The air was
full of the scent of the thickly strung bel flowers which the women and
girls wore in their hairknots.

Tagore died in Calcutta in 1941, his gentle humanism untested
by the horrors that famine and Partition brought to his home.
He is Calcutta's most important icon, and deservedly so.

Calcutta has been home to a surprising number of other
Nobel laureates. Sir Chandrasekhara Venkata Raman got
one for physics for his work on the scattering of light and
for the discovery of the effect named after him. Economist
Amartya Sen won in 1998 for his work in the field of welfare
economics, prompted to an extent by his upbringing in famine-
struck Calcutta. The city also has partial claim to the Nobel of
Pakistani nuclear physicist Abdus Salam, who did his Masters
in science at Calcutta University.

Calcutta has had other residents who have trod the world
stage: William Makepeace Thackeray the novelist was born
here, as was the luminously beautiful Hollywood actress Merle
Oberon. But in the world of films, one Calcuttan stands
far above Oberon, and indeed above the achievements of
Bollywood, on India's western coast: Satyajit Ray. Often
referred to as a Bengali Bergman, he is another figure revered
in Calcutta. Cinema has always been popular in the city (there
were showings as far back as 1898), and the first film in Bengali
came out in 1919. This being Bengal, the city's films tended to
be more theatrical and cerebral than those of Bombay's.

Born in 1921, Ray studied art at Tagore's university at
Shantiniketan, and then joined an advertising agency, where
he became adept at visual design. In 1950 he was asked to do
some illustrations for a children's book version of *Pather Panchali,*

a well-known Bengali novel, and his visualisation of the book became the kernel of the film he would make in 1955, which would bring him to the attention of the world. Between then and his death in 1992, he made some forty films and documentaries, and he was awarded a lifetime achievement Oscar in 1991.

Ray's films are all sodden with Calcutta and Bengal; they ooze it from every pore. Few of the world's great film directors can be identified so closely with a specific city — Woody Allen with New York, perhaps. Ray's films, while unflinching, never sentimentalise, and they are deeply thought-provoking. Ray always seemed to push realism beyond simple observation, so scenes are pregnant with hidden meanings. Whether set in modern-day Calcutta or during the Bengal Renaissance, his films pulse with a purely Bengali heartbeat. Certainly, no other Calcuttan has pushed Bengali language and culture so firmly into the consciousness of the West as Ray; his value to the city and to the world is incalculable.

What is interesting about Calcutta's Nobel Prizes, and Oscars, is that all of them represent a synthesis of Western, or scientific, thinking and the city itself. Mother Teresa, Rabindranath Tagore, C. V. Raman, Amartya Sen, Ronald Ross and Satyajit Ray all used the city itself to produce the work for which they were honoured. As Calcutta itself is the product of the mixing of cultures, so is its most distinguished work.

Politically, too, Calcutta remains a synthesis, a mixture of progressive social thinking and obscure Marxist-Leninist dogma. The Left Front has been almost continually in power in West Bengal since 1977, and has presided over a great deal of decline, as its ideological partners, such as the Soviet Union, gave up on Marxism. Calcutta is plagued by poor labour relations: strikes are common and mass rallies are a daily feature of life in the city. Many residents despair that the government spends more time debating whether to change the state's name to Bangla than they do to providing halfway decent services to the people who live there. A recent article in the *Statesman* captures what a long way Calcutta has come since being able to describe itself as the second city of the Empire:

> *Wards 19 and 20 of Howrah have been declared 'Cholera Endemic'…*
> *an investigation revealed that the numerous indigenous units working*
> *with aluminium nuggets or bars to produce parts and spares use toxic*
> *chemicals and acids, but there is no system for the disposal or treatment of*
> *the industrial waste. Perhaps that is the reason why the stench emanating*
> *from these open drains is different from the foul smell characteristic*
> *to Howrah. The dark fluids coagulating with the gutter juice and the*
> *noxious fumes from the dwarf chimneys of the galvanising furnaces*
> *are what the residents of the area claim to be the causal factor of all*
> *the illness prone to the locality… The water used by people in Wards*
> *19 and 20 is unfit for drinking. A couple of hours after being drawn*
> *it turns an ugly shade of brick red.*

In relation to Howrah's sewerage problems, it emerged during the cholera scare that the authorities had no maps of the sewerage system dating more recently than the 1930s, and they were also still using maps from 1841, 1793 and 1784. But lack of infrastructure aside, as the piece made clear, the cholera was, astonishingly, the fault of the Muslim residents of the area:

> *Mr Mukerjee [The mayor] vehemently put the blame on the shoulders*
> *of the residents themselves. 'They are dirty, they don't clean their hands*
> *before eating, the ladies don't breastfeed their children properly, that's*
> *why they keep getting diarrhoea. It is a normal occurrence in that*
> *area. There is no cholera problem, they probably ate too much during*
> *sabebarat [a Muslim holiday].'*

One of the features of Calcuttan life that the visitor notices immediately is its transport system, which is confused and contradictory, and entirely its own. The traffic in Calcutta is, in my experience, the worst in the world. Bangkok, Los Angeles, Beijing, Lagos, Caracas — all pale in comparison to the choking, terrifying melee that is Calcutta's road traffic. When moving, the traffic goes at a furious velocity, with drivers hurtling through the tiniest of gaps. At the often interminable junctions or traffic lights, all the drivers switch off their engines and an eerie quiet descends over the sea of rooftops baking gently in the sun. At some mysterious signal (not usually the lights, which are mostly broken) all the engines are started and the vehicles rumble into life, shaking their roofs and seeming like some vast scaly animal rousing itself from sleep. The air fills anew with thick, choking brown clouds of exhaust smoke, often cutting visibility down to a matter of metres.

The use of the horn while in motion is practically constant, although apparently illegal. Some drivers lean constantly on the button, while others tap out delicate fusillades of rhythm. At major intersections the noise can become almost unbearable until, after a few days, you find yourself becoming used to it.

There are thousands upon thousands of buses with people leaping gracefully on and off. There are trams of the most advanced dilapidation. There are holes in the roads deep enough to hide a coffin in, gouts and welts and ridges of asphalt like frozen waves upon a beach. Short journeys can take hours, but there is never a shortage of things to watch on the streets.

One often sees traffic accidents, fender benders, or pedestrians upended with a shocking suddenness as they try to weave through the cars and buses; as the blood begins to pool you reflect that that is undoubtedly the start of another of Calcutta's bad luck stories.

Despite the prehistoric nature of Calcutta's road traffic, the city can boast that most unlikely and modern of transport systems, the underground metro. What makes this particu-

larly unlikely is that Calcutta is perhaps the last city in which
you would want to build an underground system, due to the
fact that it is largely built on a swamp. It was the first one in
India and only the fifth in Asia, a fact of which Calcuttans
are inordinately proud.

The metro system was first optimistically proposed in 1949,
but it wasn't until 1972 that ground was actually broken. A dozen
years later, after 'overcoming innumerable hurdles and crossing
all barriers of disbelief', as the metro's own history admits, the
first three-kilometre stretch of line opened, between Esplanade
and Bhowanipore. Nowadays it has seventeen stations, running
north–south, covering some dozen miles.

The years of construction were notable in the city for
the chaos they caused. The only way of feasibly building a
metro was to use a method known as 'cut and cover', which
is extremely disruptive, involving as it does digging a huge
trench, building a tunnel inside the pit, and covering it back
over with earth. The fact that they followed the roads (to
maximise the possible interfaces between surface traffic and
the new system) meant years of terrible congestion for the
city, with sewers, water pipes, telephone and power cables,
and gas mains all having to be diverted as well. But built it
was, and sensibly, and it has given Calcutta much to be proud
of. It is fast, clean, cool and efficient, and by far the best way
to travel along the spine of the city.

It was designed pragmatically in other ways too: the
tunnels and walkways have channels set into the floors along
the edges of the walls for commuters to spit their *paan* into.
The designers knew, apparently, that people would carry on
spitting despite their civic pride, so decided to work with it
rather than trying to discourage it.

Another curious addition to the rail system are the
televisions mounted on every platform. We've watched groups
of Bengali commuters watching the Californian hard-rock
group Audioslave in a video that involved them driving across

the desert and crashing their car into a bulldozer. Several of the band resemble Shivaite sadhus with their long hair, bare chests and ragged clothes. There, just below the city of Swami Vivekananda and Rabindranath Tagore, the inanities of MTV were being played out to a rapt audience. It was hard to know who was the more bemused by this cross-cultural melange, but Calcutta has always shown a great aptitude for learning what it needed to from the West and rejecting the rest; we suspect it is safe from the baleful influence of Audioslave for some time yet.

An area of public transport that could do with improvement is Calcutta's bridges. No major city in the world is as badly off for bridges as Calcutta, for it has only two. London, for instance, with half Calcutta's population of fourteen million, has sixteen. Consequently, Calcutta's bridges are busy, to say the least. The Howrah Bridge, built in 1943 (to replace a much older pontoon bridge on the same spot) is the world's busiest bridge. Reliable estimates vary, but it is thought that 100,000 vehicles cross it every day; the numbers of pedestrians is probably incalculable. The great grey bulk of the bridge is one of the city's most recognisable landmarks, which is ironic, as taking photographs of it is strictly forbidden.

Because of the huge volume of traffic, it can take anything up to an hour to cross the seven hundred metres of the single span, mainly because of the chaos at either end. Crossing to the western side you debouch into the area around Howrah Railway Station, already teeming with more people, cars and animals than one would imagine possible; going eastwards the bridge dumps its travellers into Barabazaar, one of the most densely populated places on earth.

Calcutta's second bridge, the Vidyasagar Setu, was opened in 1992, after an astonishing twenty-two years of construction. A magnificent-looking bridge only a kilometre and a half south of the Howrah Bridge, it is also permanently jammed, mainly because of the lack of suitable approach roads. The length of construction, astronomical cost and relative inefficiency has meant that Calcutta's Municipal Corporation have shied away from building any more bridges, despite the evident need for them.

No discussion of Calcutta's transport system would be complete without considering one of the features about which the city is most ambivalent: the hand-pulled rickshaw. Originally invented in the Himalayan hill station of Shimla in the 1880s, the human-pulled rickshaw appeared in Calcutta around the turn of the century, when the Chinese community introduced them for moving cargo around the city. In 1914 they became licensed to carry passengers, and their numbers exploded. Although the authorities decided in 1939 that it would issue only six thousand licences, there are estimated to be some thirty thousand rickshaw pullers in the city.

Calcutta is the only city on earth to still allow hand-pulled rickshaws (Hong Kong has half-a-dozen, but only for tourists to photograph themselves in front of), and the city is deeply embarrassed by their very existence. How can it project itself to the world as a successful and cosmopolitan city when it still exploits people quite so blatantly and inhumanely as to use them as human mules?

There is no doubt that pulling a rickshaw is incredibly hard work. None of the pullers seem to possess shoes. Heat in the summer can rise to forty-five degrees. The police apparently can make life very difficult for pullers, exploiting the fact that many are unlicensed. Many of them rent their rickshaws from criminal syndicates. And the impact on the pullers' health is extremely serious: in a city where 47 per cent of the population have respiratory problems due to the air pollution, the rickshaw pullers suffer more directly than any other group. So human-rights groups and the Calcutta government are engaged in a long-running battle with the pullers to ban them, which the authorities seem to think they will win through a process of attrition, simply waiting for the pullers to die out.

But the rickshaws have many supporters, despite the seeming inhumanity. They are very flexible, and can travel through Calcutta's frequently flooded streets when no other mode of transport can. They are nonpolluting, and provide cheap, reliable and consumer-friendly transport options in a city where the buses are incredibly dirty, crowded and dangerous, and the car and taxi unaffordable for many. Every rickshaw journey is a journey that is not being made by another form of transport that would be more polluting. They are particularly useful for women, the elderly, the frail and the disabled. The rickshaw pullers will take customers at any hour of the day or night, and are often used to take children to and from school in a city where personal care and reliability are highly valued. And they fit models of sustainable development perhaps better than any other mode of transport.

Most importantly, they allow the pullers to labour, with self-respect, rather than be unemployed on the streets. Most of the pullers are migrant labourers from poor states neighbouring West Bengal – Bihar, Jharkhand and Orissa – and they send much of their wages home to provide support in impoverished rural communities.

For Western visitors to Calcutta, it is uncomfortable to see man pulling man, usually a poor unskilled man pulling a more skilled man. Geoffrey Moorhouse predicted that the revolution would come to Calcutta heralded by the sound, familiar in the city, of the rickshaw pullers' bells being tapped against the shafts of their vehicle, and an uprising against the social injustice led by 'the rickshaw men who have pulled so many rich people around Calcutta like animals all their lives'. It hasn't happened yet, and the pullers' place in Calcutta seems assured for some time yet.

About Calcutta

from

Days and Nights in Calcutta

CLARK BLAISE & BHARATI MUKHERJEE

I HAD BEEN AWAY FROM CALCUTTA FOR FOURTEEN YEARS. My parents no longer lived there and I had never written letters, nor even sent birthday cards, to friends and relatives during this period. Yet after all these years, their first question invariably was: 'Has Calcutta changed very much?' And my response was what I knew they wanted to hear: 'No, it's just the way I remember it.' Then it was their turn to smile benevolently at me and whisper: 'You know, you might have a Canadian husband and kids, but you haven't changed much either.' I was not lying, merely simplifying, when I agreed with friends I had not seen since our missionary school days that nothing had changed. Because in Calcutta, 'change' implies decline and catastrophe; friendship is rooted in the retention of simplicity. The fact that after fourteen years away I was still judged 'simple' was the greatest compliment my friends and relatives could bestow.

I was born in Ballygunge, a very middle-class neighborhood of Calcutta, and lived the first eight years of my life in a ground-floor flat on a wide street sliced in half by shiny tram tracks. The

flat is still rented by my *jethoo*; the tram tracks still shine through
the mangy blades of grass in the center of the street; and the
trams are still owned by British shareholders most of whom have
never seen Calcutta. Ballygunge remains, in these small, personal
terms, a stable society. Wars with China and Pakistan, refugee
influxes from Assam, Tibet, Bangla Desh, and Biliar, Naxalite
political agitations: Nothing has wrenched out of recognizable
shape the contours of the block where I grew up.

In those first eight years, though I rarely left Ballygunge, I
could not escape the intimations of a complex world just beyond
our neighborhood. I saw the sleek white trams (perhaps never sleek
nor white) and I associated them with glamour and incredible
mobility. My own traveling was limited to trips to the *mamabari*
a few blocks away, and to school which was in the no man's land
between Ballygunge and the European quarters. These trips were
accomplished by rickshaw. My mother had a tacit agreement with
one of the pullers at the nearby rickshaw stand, and whenever
he saw her approaching with her three little daughters, he would
drag his vehicle over at a trot. Rickshaws were familiar — the same
puller and the same route over back streets with light traffic. Only
trams promised journeys without destination. And sometimes
trams promised drama. While swinging on the rusty iron gate
that marked the insides and outsides of properties but was not
intended to keep trespassers out, I had seen a man (a pickpocket,
I was later told by an older cousin) flung bodily out of a moving
tram by an excited crowd. And once I had seen the heaving body
of a run-over cow on the tracks just in front of our house. The
cow had drawn a larger crowd than the pickpocket. The head
had not been completely severed from the body; I think now
that a fully severed head might have been less horrible. I saw
it as an accident, cruel, thrilling, unnecessary, in a city where
accidents were common.

I saw processions of beggars at our front door, even
Muslim ones, and it was often the job of us small children to
scoop out a measure of rice from a huge drum in my widowed

grandmother's vegetarian kitchen and pour it into the beggars' pots. I was too little to lean over the edge of the drum and fill the scoop, and for that I was grateful. The beggars terrified me. I would wait for them to cluster at our front door, but when they were actually there, I would hide behind my older cousin Tulu (now a geneticist in Hamburg), who would issue efficient commands to the beggars to stop fighting among themselves and to hold out their sacks and pots. It is merely a smell that I now recall, not the hungry faces but the smell of starvation and of dying. Later, my mother, a powerful storyteller, told me how millions had died in the 1943 Bengal famine — she did not care about precise statistics, only about passion — and how my father had personally organized a rice-gruel kitchen in our flat. I had no concept of famine; I only knew that beggars were ugly and that my father was a hero.

As a child in Ballygunge, I did not completely escape World War II. My mother told me later, especially after we had been to war movies at the Metro Cinema, that there had been periodic air-raid sirens in the fields just beyond the landlord's palm trees, and that my father had set aside a small room as air-raid shelter for the forty-odd people who were living at the flat at the time. She remembered the tins of imported crackers, the earthenware pitchers of water, the bedrolls, and the complaints of the younger uncles who felt that tea made on a hot plate in the shelter did not taste as good as tea made on the regular open stove. She said she had not been frightened at all during the raids, not even after the bombing of the Kidderpore docks, and that sometimes instead of rushing to the shelter at the first wail of the siren, she had settled us in, then raced to the street to admire beautiful formations of the Japanese planes. The Japanese, she insisted, meant us Indians no harm. She talked of prewar Japanese hawkers who had come to the front gate with their toys and silks. I did not see the Japanese planes. I do not remember the sirens. But in the last year of the war, as I was sitting in the first-floor balcony of the *mamabari* on Southern Avenue, I saw a helmeted soldier on a motorcycle swerve around a car, then crash into a stalled truck. His body was flung high (all the way up to the level of the second-floor windows, my aunts said), before it splattered against the sidewalk. That is my only memory of the war: street children scurrying after the dead soldier's helmet. My aunts said that the soldier must have been drunk, that all soldiers were drunk and crude. I was shocked that a soldier who was drunk could also be Indian. I had never seen a drunk person.

And immediately after the war, when many British-owned Wolseleys, Rovers, and Austins bore gigantic white V's on their hoods, I became aware of signs of violence of another sort. Funeral processions for teenage freedom fighters passed our house. At the head of these processions were bullet-ridden bodies laid out on string beds and covered over with flowers. In those days, we thought of them as freedom fighters and martyrs but called them 'anarchists' and 'terrorists,' for we had accepted the terminology of the British without ever understanding or sharing their emotions. Later still, during the communal riots between Hindus and Muslims at the time of Partition, I saw from the roof (where we always rushed at the first signal of a possible invasion of our block) giggling young men loot a store and carry off radios and table fans. This was comic, but I knew that in other parts of the city, looters were vandalizing households and murdering everyone in sight. A week later, my father and the workers in his pharmaceutical plant were besieged by a Muslim group and had to be rescued by troops. The event might have been tragic for our family — and in fact, three workers were killed by the rioters before the troops arrived — but my father delivered the account with so much elegance and wit that I have never been able to picture it as a riot.

It is that Ballygunge which has not changed. It is still possible for my parents' separate families to continue renting the flats they have lived in since I was born, to conduct discreet and fairly stable middle-class lives, although each year the periphery of violence draws a little closer to the center.

THERE WAS A BAGGAGE HANDLERS' STRIKE ON THE NIGHT *chhoto-mamu* and I arrived. Several wagons of suitcases stood uncovered for forty minutes next to the delivery chute, pelted by monsoon rains, while three planeloads of passengers milled around inside waiting for porters. Finally one businessman crawled the length of the chute, then out the narrow opening to the wagons and started unpiling the bags in order to get to his own. A second man, seeing his bags being roughly handled and dumped in a puddle, squeezed through the opening in order to teach the first one a lesson. Pushing and name-calling broke out. 'Who you are calling a bastard? You have insulted my mother, you bastard.' They feigned and lunged in the rain, with instant commentary offered by two young men squatting on the conveyor belt and peering out through the slot. 'Now first gentleman lunges and misses. Second chap responds with tight slap. *Durwans* are disengaging the combatants.' I had feared, being the largest and slowest-moving target, despite having *chhoto-mamu* at my side, that I'd somehow manage to be the lone victim of any violence. I was the only 'European' in the entire airport; again a melancholy sign of Calcutta's isolation. Finally we all climbed out to get our bags; mine were sprung open, oily and soaking. I was lucky I hadn't sent the briefcase. 'Welcome to Calcutta,' *chhoto-mamu* laughed. We had waited an hour, I had seen my first Calcutta distemper, how quickly it flared, how immediate are the irritants. And more importantly, had I known enough to consider it, I had seen the wit and improvisation that allows Calcutta to survive nearly anything.

After all the warnings about Calcutta, the drive into the city is almost a relief. Dum Dum itself is a placid village of orange-tiled roofs, ponds and dazzling green banana trees. The traveler speeds along a divided, four-lane, open-country highway known locally as V.I.P. Road, and even as he passes the herdsmen with their grazing buffalo, or the hay wagons being pulled by sun-blackened old men, he might think: *They've lied to me.* They were right to censor Louis Malle's films. If this is the worst city in the world (actually, UNESCO statistics rank it second to Karachi in dirt, disease, and general destitution), then the world's not such a bad place after all.

The real Calcutta begins with a right-hand turn off C.I.T. (Calcutta Improvement Trust) Road onto Beliaghata Main Road. It begins suddenly at a stone Kali statue a few feet off the roadway, permanently lit and garlanded, and permanently worshipped by a small mob of kneeling women. It is tropically dark now, but not so late that the streets have emptied. It is the market hour all over Calcutta. The air is coarse with smoke and waste, blurring the street lamps, bare bulbs at best. *Chhoto-mamu*'s company jeep follows the tram tracks in the middle of the road. Crowds surge, cows stray stupidly in our path, and human rickshaws clang their warnings, never breaking a jogging stride.

We are between monsoon showers and the bazaar crowds have choked off the road, moving from stall to stall. They must lift their saris and *dhotis* as they walk, for the road surface is half a tire underwater. A nameless dread sets in. The street is passable only in the center, over the tracks; rain and pedestrians have turned a wide avenue into a single rutted lane for trams and two-way traffic. Cars peel off, inches from collision: never slowing, honking, nudging themselves into the crowd. The pedestrians without looking behind them yield up the inches to allow the car to pass. We plunge into the crowd, shoppers shear off the jeep as though both body and bumper were positively charged. Their ranks seal behind us, like water.

This sudden unwanted equality with the pedestrian is part of the dread; you are hardly moving faster than he is walking, you are sitting while he stands above you; you hear the aimless tunes he hums walking past you, you pick up on a thousand scraps of conversation from couples brushing just past your cheek, your shoulder, the canvas flaps. In Calcutta the pedestrian is King. On the sidewalks (called 'footpaths') the merchant is Prince, and in the gutters, cows are Queen. Cars are not part of the nobility, they are another addition to the elastic roadway, the latest addition. The human rickshaws with their *lungi*-clad Bihari pullers and their human cargo of fat women shoppers, or *babus* from the office, or stern old men in *dhotis* under an umbrella, have the true priority. They move around the crowds and cannot see behind them as they run (miss a step, stumble in that unlighted, potholed street, and they could easily crack a leg or run themselves over); cars must follow them and pedestrians must know how to look behind them when they hear the rap of the metal clapper against the iron frame of the 'rick.'

And one realizes, too, on that first dizzying arrival, that the cows which had never really materialized in Bombay are present in hordes everywhere in Calcutta. Cows are an ancient sign of holiness, and a sentimental sign of gentleness, but they are even more clearly an indication of urban collapse. Calcutta, among many other things, is the world's largest outdoor garbage heap, and the refuse of its streets supports hundreds of thousands of human scavengers, in precisely the way it supports millions more cows, dogs, and crows. Cows cannot survive where garbage is picked up, or where traffic flow demands priority. Things move by human muscle in Calcutta: the enormous racks of hay, the rickshaws, the handcarts. Even double beds and refrigerators can be seen perched on the heads of four men, running in step down the middle of a busy street. A stumble, a missed beat, and disaster. One merely adopts a new definition of garbage, or else he flees Calcutta in horror. For us, garbage is what we have no further use for, and our society permits the luxury of pinching off a resource chain at a fairly refined level. True garbage is what *no living creature* has further use for. And by that definition, Calcutta is a lot cleaner than Montreal.

Months later, alive to the streets, I would walk through such a district in the dark, carrying my tape recorder with the microphone open, just to catch these noises – horns, shouts, songs, snatches of transistor music, and the debased, guttural Hindi and Bengali of the beggars and country people thrown onto the city's streets, as well as the occasional, anonymous and ceremonially polite *'Good evening, saab!'* that would erupt from the dark. But that first night I wasn't charmed and I wasn't amused. I was sick and pale as soap, white-knuckled, in the belly of something I wished I hadn't started.

This is the most confined exterior in the world. The sidewalk braziers belch coal and cow dung fumes, and one feels there must be a fire ahead, a barrier, a sagging roof overhead, gases building up, a wall of people trying to escape. Police constables stand on platforms at the major intersections, permitting turns that would otherwise take all night. The constables are in white with white gloves, but they are guarded by three soldiers in khaki, with rifles. When they shout to us, and when *chhoto-mamu* answers, the language is Hindi. What alienation, I remark to myself, when the policemen don't even speak your language! When I ask about it, *chhoto-mamu* explains that no Bengali would be a simple constable. For that they get Biharis.

One begins choking on people. Such diversity seems ominous; even in their innocence they strike me as a mob. Each block driven without an incident seems a minor miracle; not to crush a child, not to sideswipe a rickshaw, not to be crushed by a tram. Or, not to be killed for having honked once too often and reminded the poorest, most politicized, and perhaps most excitable urban dwellers in the world that you happen to have a car, a driver, and an impatience with their presence. The streets are pumping people, the alleys and sidewalks are hemorrhaging. Beliaghata Main Road is like a puddled river bed, surged over by the evening crowds as from an unseen, broken dam. Our car, brushed casually by frail youths squeezing past, rocks just enough to tip my baggage. In an accident we could just as casually be plucked from the shell of the car and drowned underfoot.

Bengalis love to explain Calcutta; the identification with the city is so complete that the standard question put to an outsider — 'What do you think of Calcutta?' — is a shorthand way of asking,

'What do you think of Bengalis? What do you think of me?' *What are you thinking, Clark?* chhoto-mamu asked on that first nighttime trip through Sealdah Bazaar, then finally down Chittaranjan Avenue to the center of the city. He must have known that of all the spectacles Calcutta can offer, the crowded streets in the evening are, finally, the most impressive. 'What about the soldiers guarding the constables, *chhoto-mamu*?' I asked: What am I doing in a city where even the policemen need protection? 'Why *three*, for heaven's sake?' 'To protect,' he answers. 'They discovered that one guard, then two, then three, were not enough to protect the constable. Calcutta will always require three policemen to guard every traffic constable.'

Calcutta on a summer night between monsoon showers: dark, smoky, loud, bewildering. We are passing the landmarks now: Dodoo's first factory, the Statesman Building, the Indian Airlines downtown terminal. Even here, on the busiest streets, the placid bulk of scavenging cows. The slow pace, the muscle pace of Calcutta life, is made up for with frantic activity. Buses hurtle by, packed with young men clinging to the outside of windows, to the hoods, tire mountings, and roof. It is we who confuse slowness with gentleness.

We were sitting in Trinca's, on Park Street, a onetime Swiss confectionery, now a glamorous restaurant on Calcutta's raciest street. I was having a furtive rare steak, and we were enjoying cocktails after a grueling tour of Loreto House with some of Bharati's old teachers. By now she had made contact with her married school friends who were taking her out nearly every afternoon. My links to Calcutta were still through the family.

Trinca's is a businessman's hangout. The other restaurant in the same half-block, Kwality's, attracts women and families. Trinca's has an orchestra and singer, Kwality's has none. Trinca's is convenient for businessmen — Punjabis and Europeans often — who have come to Calcutta for a few days' stay at the nearby Park Hotel, and plan to get out as quickly as they can. The resident Bengali business establishment would prefer to lunch in the various downtown clubs, and Marwaris (the joke goes) would bring a few stale *rotis* and some *dal* from home. And so the atmosphere of Trinca's is definable: a little loose, a little tacky, dark and musty and moistly air-conditioned. 'Jenny,' the Goan singer, was liquefying a familiar medley into the mike: 'I Never Promised You a Rose Garden,' 'Killing Me Softly,' 'Those Were the Days,' some Flack, some Baez, some Fitzgerald, mixed with Hindi songs from the year's big hit movie, *Bobby*.

A young man with mutton chops and shoulder-length hair came out of the dark back room. 'Excuse me, could you possibly be Clark Blaise?' he asked in a very British accent. 'And are you Bharati Mukherjee?' We admitted we were. 'No rush, then,' he said, 'but when you have finished your rare steak, would you care to come back to the bar and join Mr Chattopadhaya and me for drinks?'

Bimal Chattopadhaya was the magazine editor I had written to from Bombay. I'd had several weeks to grow nervous about that letter; knowing that Chattopadhaya had been posted in a number of Western capitals, I'd affected my breeziest tone, and revealed myself, I now feared, callow and impudent. He hadn't answered, which could only mean he'd judged me an arrogant pup, best left to forage for myself. Thereafter, in letters, I'd been dignified and professional, an easier mask to assume.

The young man who fetched us was a copy writer, on his third quart of beer. Bimal was a gray-haired, well-tailored man in his mid-fifties, resplendent in an ascot and regimental mustache. The effect was of cultivated excessiveness, a man attuned to adventure, while doubting it would be worth his effort.

He had a position to maintain; he did it by not answering our questions too directly. 'You went to Loreto House, I assume?' he asked Bharati. 'You must have gone to school with, ah, Mira Sen? No? Her younger sister, then, what *was* her name, the one with the unfortunate set of eyebrows, you *know*, who married that chap from Indian Tobacco, the one whose father was convicted for fraud... yes, yes, *Gayatri*, of course, dear sad Gayatri Sen. Then you must have run with the British Council crowd, debating with that wretched little chap who later went to England and wrote those pathetic pornographics... no? You don't say? Which Mukherjee family *are* you from — Asutosh Mukherjee? Obviously not Sir Biren's family, they're all so bloody awful to look at... Not Ajoy either? Now that is a puzzle, obviously rich and obviously Westernized...' He rattled off half a dozen possible Mukherjee families which might have explained, logically, a product like Bharati. He could not have guessed the truth.

Bimal Chattopadhaya's protection lay in being just slightly outrageous, yielding points on accuracy (because it was a game, a competitive game) in order to draw out unguarded rebuttals and unintended confidences. Upper-class British irony, a game of high polish, whereby social occasions are an opportunity to expose your opponent as a fraud and hypocrite. Extra points are scored if your opponent doesn't realize — till later — that he had done it himself. In this he won. Our conversation that lunch hour, over beers, and then that night in his Ballygunge apartment revealed far more about me than about him.

As much as a liberal Westerner may fight it, he still makes the same mistakes; I began by making the V. S. Naipaul error. Because Chattopadhaya affected British ways, I assumed his life in Calcutta was unoriginal and imitative (that he was, in short, one of Naipaul's ex-colonial 'mimic men'); I also assumed he must be alienated from Calcutta, still nostalgic for the West. He'd edited a popular rotogravure magazine in London, a fashion magazine in Paris, and an educational supplement in New York. When I asked him about racism in England, he answered simply that if one seeks racists and grants them their opportunities, he will suffer from it. On the other hand, if one has money, he simply buys a sound address and membership in a club ('Reform Liberal,' he said, 'not the

Notting Hill Working Men's Recreational Lounge') that will remove him from the possibility of harassment. Bigots are everywhere, he added, though the pointedness of the remark escaped me till later.

Did I want him to admit some horrible degradation? Did I want him to say, 'Yes, I was perfectly wretched in England.' I think that was part of it; he played a drawing room smugness so perfectly that I rushed in to vandalize it. 'I shouldn't accept being a displaced person anywhere,' he said rather icily, indicating that like us, he didn't expose himself to any more squalor in the West or in Calcutta than he could comfortably bear, and indicating further that *we* — me in India, Bharati in Canada — were displaced persons without even acknowledging it. I asked him, again assuming that the various losses were too great to contemplate, what he missed most about the Continent. 'Well,' he began, appearing to consider it seriously, 'with Gorgonzola at sixty-five rupees a kilo...' Just like us he missed the theater, wines, and cheeses, and *still*, I couldn't take his answers seriously. Surely he must miss the working conditions, the stimulation of big-time papers, the worldliness of London, Paris and New York. I was not yet able to tolerate his satisfaction with Calcutta, his ironies with the West. Yet *here I was*, as Bharati would later remind me, a foreigner in Calcutta asking a native-born Calcuttan who had come back to his home in order to rise to the top of his profession, about his disappointment and dissatisfaction. (And for me to have snickered, during the ten years of our marriage, when visiting Bengalis would ask the same of Bharati in Montreal. 'What have you given up? Is it worth it?' For the next year, I was to hear her answers, and it has shaken our marriage to its core.)

I wanted the dirt, the low-down, from a man I perceived as a journalist; what I got were evasions and flippancies. The Calcuttan has known for a hundred years how to parry an English question, how to turn a question around. I asked about the Bihar Tenancy Act, Punjab land grabs, the power cuts, the corruption — all items that had come from Calcutta papers. He nodded at each abuse, and then answered in just the tone of realpolitik that closes all discussion: 'The peasants never had electricity and never knew they were supposed to have it until anxious little politicians anxious for their votes told them they had to have it. They don't have anything to plug in, but they have electricity. And because five thousand villages had to be electrified, industrialized Bengal — which means middle-class Calcutta — had to pay. You come here wondering why the peasants don't stir themselves and throw the rascals out? Wouldn't it be uncomfortable for all the lovely friends we have and all the gentle Loreto House girls we all know and appreciate, and for the nice life we have made for ourselves if they ever learned they weren't supposed to starve and suffer? What if they ever found out that it was stupid planning and corrupt politicians and manipulations of their ignorance that was the cause of their suffering? What would they do? You're in the East, my good man, and don't ever forget it. What would happen to them — *what would happen to any of us* — if we didn't take it all passively? We'd die together. Don't make the mistake of writing that I don't recognize injustice and that I don't feel just as strongly as any high-minded Westerner on a two-week visit. But I thank God those people on the street and in the villages are as abysmally ignorant of their rights and of my privileges as they were at the dawn of history. The alternative is too horrible to contemplate.'

We went out for dinner to his favorite restaurant. We were polite and witty. He pointed out the families at various tables, dealing on their biographies, entanglements, black money dealings, sex lives, directorships, pending court cases, attachment to one, or two, political parties, with all the authority of the classic, cynical journalist. All Calcutta is his city-room if he chooses. But he is a publisher, not merely a reporter; he is of two worlds and has chosen discretion over disclosure.

Like the young man he had been drinking with that afternoon, he was close enough himself to being a *box-wallah* to know
that lie could not belittle them as unthinkingly as Naipaul had.
English had replaced Bengali as his natural literary expression;
he even recognized a small absurdity, in certain eyes, in his
position. But why demean him as a *box-wallah*, somehow less than
his 'pure culture' Bengali counterparts and certainly less fortunate than his Western colleagues? Such a man in the West,
so brilliantly adept in an acquired tongue, and so attuned to a
second culture, while being intimately involved in his own,
would hardly be pitied, or patronized, especially not by people
like me. How sophisticated he'd seem back in Montreal, for
example. Perhaps he was not quite the noblest example of the
Westernized Bengali intellectual (for that one should look to
Nirad C. Chaudhuri, a resident of Oxford), but because of his
self-awareness, his detailed knowledge of Calcutta, his personal
taste and standards, his privileges, his scorn of hypocrisy, his
position has become potentially tragic, should he choose not
to yield to the new 'Emergency Measures.' Or, should he bow,
he has become an emblem of the frailty of Westernization in
contemporary India.

On the way back from the restaurant, turning to face me
from the front seat of his sports car, he asked me — not for an
answer, but as a speculative notion — how it was that all whites in
India, like Ronald Segal (*The Crisis of India*), assumed an unassailable
superiority. What was it, did I think, about their training that
made them feel that their standards, their judgments, were all
clearer, sharper, and more just than the local's?

For my part, I stayed up very late that night, writing an
essay. Part of it I have used here, most of it was too defensive.
I have no interest in playing his sport; it's too rough, the rules
are far too complicated. I'll probably never fully recover from
my anger ('Gorgonzola, indeed!') and my shame (I will always
hear Bharati saying to me, 'In the future you might ask yourself
why it's so very strange to you that a Bengali journalist should

be satisfied to be an editor of a Calcutta magazine'). It was my first encounter outside of the family. Aggressive journalist that he was, he had not waited for my second letter, my inevitable phone call. He had sized me up from Trinca's bar, plucked me from my rare steak, and he'd played me like a sportsman until he'd grown bored and decided to cut me free.

from

Tithidore

BUDDHADEV BOSE

translated from the Bengali by Ketaki Kushari Dyson

SVATI SAID AT ONCE, 'NO, I'M GOING AS WELL.' She ran indoors, wrote a brief note for her father and pushed it into the hand of Ram's mother, changed her dress and footwear, grabbed a handbag, and when she was out in the street with Satyen Ray the first thing she noticed was that the day was still as happy, lovely and radiant as before.

The bus filled even before it reached Kalighat. Nevertheless more and more people kept boarding it: male and female college students, schoolboys, shopkeepers, the unemployed, young men who spent their days chatting to one another. The congestion was stifling. But Svati's seat, one of those reserved 'for ladies', was safe, and she was sitting by the window, looking intently outside. The streets were crowded — as if the time was late afternoon. Gangs of schoolboys were walking, but without making a racket; elderly people were wandering around as if they had nothing to do; before each shop that had a radio on there was a crowd; and at street corners there were crowds of people hoping to get on a bus or a tramcar. Cinema posters were pasted over with black paper; the doors were closed. Women, their hair down, babies in their arms, were standing in balconies or by windows, watching the street as much as they could. Today all eyes, all minds were focused on the street.

Clouds gathered, and by the time they reached the Chowringhee, rain came down. But when the bus stopped at the Esplanade, it was bright and sunny again. And in that soft-moist light Svati saw an amazing swirling of people, amazing even for the Esplanade: office executives in suits, lawyers in black coats, middle-aged gents with umbrellas in their hands, slim young clerical workers, Englishmen, Chinese, Madrassis, Christian priests, Parsis. People were rushing from every direction to every other direction – Chowringhee, Dhurrumtola, Curzon Park, Corporation Street – but it was as if they were not quite sure where they were going, as if they had somewhat lost their sense of direction. Many seemed to have forgotten what they knew by heart – that as soon as the office was closed, one had to head for home. However straggling they may appear, Calcutta's crowds are never aimless; everyone knows whither he is bound and why; but today all people had lost their goals, the certainty of their destinations, which is why these crowds were amazing, extraordinary.

Someone was standing erect and staring straight ahead; another was wandering up and down aimlessly; another seemed to make up his mind suddenly and take a few steps, then stopped again; yet another was standing, reading a newspaper, while a few others read over his shoulders. A special issue of a newspaper arrived and was an immediate sell-out.

Satyen, sitting behind Svati, stretched out his hand and bought a paper. He just glanced at it once and gave it to Svati. Svati gave it one glance and placed it on her lap. The fifteen-ish girl sitting next to her picked it up, without even a 'may I?', and as her eyes moved from the top to the bottom of the page, her tears dripped on the black print, rubbing off some of the ink which was fresh from the press.

At Jorasanko* the bus almost emptied. Everyone ran towards Dwarakanath Tagore Lane, but Satyen, about to cross the street, suddenly paused. He had seen a barrage of people — what had happened to them? Why was no one about? 'Taken away already?' — the words slipped from his lips.

'Yeah, been taken away — if you want to have a look you have to go to College Street —' said someone as he passed by.

Svati had never visited Chitpore before; amazed, she was looking at the traffic of trams and buses pushing through that narrow lane. There were lanes within lanes — twisted and dark; tall buildings jostled against each other, shutting out the sky; the pavements were marvellously crowded and were selling the most amazing wares. She nearly forgot why she was there, when Satyen's words reminded her of it: 'Been taken away. Let's go to College Street. You'll be able to walk fast won't you?'

Fast and silent, the two of them began to walk, avoiding the pushing and shoving crowds on that pavement that was a pavement only in name. After a few minutes they turned left into Muktarambabu Street. To Svati these areas of Calcutta seemed to belong to another country, another world; here the light, the air, even the smells were different. She tried to cast her glances around her, but couldn't see anything very well, so fast was Satyen babu walking.

The long, dark, curving Muktarambabu Street ended in Cornwallis Street; and in a little while the junction of College Street and Harrison Road appeared.

On reaching the covered pavement of the College Street Market, Satyen stopped and climbed the steps of a shoe shop. Many more were standing there, most of them college students. 'Coming any minute now' was the message passing from mouth to mouth.

'Was the walk too much for you?' asked Satyen.

'N-no.'

* Editor's note: Area in Chitpur in North Calcutta, where Tagore's ancestral house is located.

'Are you wishing you hadn't come?'

'No.'

Their exchange of words stopped there, and once again they fell silent. On the opposite side, on the roof of a one-storeyed shop – without any railings, dangerously unsafe – a few were standing with their cameras ready; the adjoining first-floor balcony was packed with women and children; there wasn't a single window in the area from which three or four faces weren't looking out; and no one was walking on the street, everyone stood still. Once again Satyen experienced the pressure of that waiting, that dumb waiting.

'Coming... coming...' a murmur rose in the crowd.

Svati had imagined a procession – long, slow, solemn, bowed, overwhelmed, stupefied; but it was just a handful of people who came bearing the burden on their shoulders, seemingly in a hurry, going from north to south, with a few straggling followers behind them. The sight flashed like lightning in front of Svati's eyes and disappeared; long white hair and a huge, pale, tranquil, meditative brow gleamed in the sun. That was all Svati could glimpse; she could see nothing else.

Satyen saw that Svati was standing rigid and straight, her hands clenched, lips tightly pressed; saw the trembling in her throat and lips, the deep colour of her cheeks; saw how her bright black liquid eyes became brighter, became twin shining mirrors, how then the mirrors broke, turned liquid again, overflowing, while the head was bowed.

And seeing that, Satyen felt a new tightness in his throat, a blurring in his eyes, and was ashamed of himself in his own eyes. For this death did not solicit weeping; this sorrow, this grand, precious sorrow, this final jewel of eighty years of supreme toil – was it something to be wasted frivolously in tears?

'Come now,' said Satyen.

Svati did not try to hide the fact that she was crying. She wiped her eyes with the end of her sari, coughed once, and said in a slightly husky voice, 'Let's go.'

But the trams and buses were choked. Along various streets, following various routes, everybody was rushing towards Nimtola.* The two of them stood helplessly; they stood so long that their legs ached.

Svati said, 'Hadn't we better walk? Perhaps if we went ahead a little —'

'Going ahead a little won't make any difference. Only if we could get to the Esplanade—'

'Is the Esplanade very far?' asked Svati, unsure of the geography of this region.

'Not that far,' said Satyen with some enthusiasm. 'One could go via Chittaranjan Avenue. Will you walk then?'

'OK then.'

No sooner had they crossed Kolutola and reached Chittaranjan Avenue, than the sky darkened and suddenly the rain came down once more. They took shelter under a portico. The rain was heavy, poured with a clatter, and getting wet in that downpour, a group of Chinese went by, calm and quiet, solemn and slow, each with bowed head and bare feet.

Svati stared at them as long as she could see them. Then she said, 'How beautiful they are!'

Satyen nodded in assent.

'Where are they going?'

'To Nimtola, surely.'

Svati had heard of Nimtola, so understood. 'Aren't you going?'

'I would have — but —'

'Can't I go there?'

'You could, but I wouldn't take you there.'

'Why not?'

'You can't imagine how crowded it's going to be.'

Svati didn't like that reply. She felt Satyen babu was being too cautious, too circumspect, too rule-bound even on a day like this. Meanwhile the rain did not cease.

---

* Editor's note: Major cremation ground.

Another group came along: European priests, bearded and elderly, in long white robes, flowers in their hands, peace upon their faces, prayers in their eyes. They walked through the rain, getting wet.

The rain slackened, then ceased. When the rain was still dribbling, they started walking once again, drops of rainwater falling on their hands, lips, heads. The sun came out; the oblique yellow light of the late afternoon shone on the wet black street, shimmered in the soft-moist wind.

Satyen said, 'If you are feeling tired, say so. I think we could get on a bus here.'

Svati said, 'I'm quite enjoying the walk.'

No sooner had she spoken than she felt regret and guilt. On a day like this, at a time such as this, was one allowed to 'enjoy' anything? Or even if one did, should one say it out loud? Timidly, out of the corner of her eyes, Svati gazed at Satyen Ray's face, but the grief-stricken lecturer seemed not to notice the unseemliness at all, but rather, said in a cheered voice, 'Well then, nothing to worry about.'

Quietly they went on walking, but not as before, when, disappointed in Jorasanko, they had walked silently along Muktarambabu Street. Then their pace had been fast, the lane had been narrow, and their minds had been anxious, whereas now they faced the straight expanse of Chittaranjan Avenue: a huge broad generous road, uncrowded, without tramcars, the motor cars gliding along quietly, as if they were floating. On either side of the road there were tall buildings, but the sky here was vaster, higher up, and the road was so spread out that the buildings appeared lightweight, as if the piles on the two sides belonged to two separate neighbourhoods. And above the road's entire stretch trembled, swung and shone a film — that of the rain-washed yellow-green late-afternoon's fine transparent radiance. They walked slowly, for there was no hurry now. The high-water mark of time had happened when they were standing on the veranda of the College Street Market shoe shop: it had now passed. The mind's bow, drawn so taut before, from ear to ear, was now slack. Now there was time to look at the afternoon, to gaze at the light, at the bright, beautiful sky. Svati felt a vague sense of happiness within her; a little later all her feelings of guilt vanished as well. But it was as if she did not herself take in the news of this change of weather within her own mind. She didn't think about it, didn't think much, just sank slowly into a new consciousness of happiness. And Satyen — a man mad about poetry, a Tagore fan since childhood — he too felt an obscure sense of happiness, just as at that very instant in Tagore-less Bengal, over Calcutta overflowing with grief, the flag of blueness flew on the sky's incorruptible gateway, so too in his mind the green of the living moment, of the here and the now, covered the deep black tomb of historical grief: and it all happened so easily that he himself did not take it in. Both of them quietly accepted this blurred sense of feeling good, he his, she hers, and each the other's as well. Before this they had been quiet because they had nothing to say, and now they were quiet because there was no need to talk.

Reaching the Esplanade, they once more faced the screeching of wheels, the whirl of the crowds, the impact of humanity rushing about. They had to stop several times when crossing the road. On the Chowringhee, Satyen said, 'Would you like some tea?'

'You haven't had a bite all day, have you,' said Svati, remembering.

'If you think it'll delay you — '

'Not that much more.'

'You mean, it's very late already?'

These words made Svati realize that all this time she hadn't once thought of home, of returning home, of her father. What was Father thinking? How long had she been out? What was the time now? She tried to look at the clock on Whiteaway Laidlaw, but from where she stood it was difficult. Never mind. 'Which one would you go to?' she asked.

All the little restaurants in rows were absolutely packed with people. In the middle there was a large English hotel, with frosted glass panes facing the road, ensuring privacy, and rubber matting on the steps. Satyen took Svati into that one. From the turmoil of lights, crowds, noises they were suddenly transported into a smooth, silent, solemn, spacious darkness, Once again Svati sensed a new smell, a smell that was kind of English — dry, light, warming — unfamiliar, yes, but good — it was good!

Walking along the edges of several empty tables, they were making their way towards a corner table, when suddenly someone seated at a table said, 'Hi there!'

Satyen stopped, raised his hands in greeting. Without returning the greeting in any noticeable way, the gentleman said, 'From where? Nimtola?'

'No, didn't get that far — Svati, haven't you recognized him?'

Svati had indeed. Dark, dishevelled, gloomy, Dhruba Datta was sprawled on a chair, a cigarette between his fingers, and in the glass before him a pale brown drink like — Svati suddenly remembered in a flash — like she had seen in front of an elderly Eurasian in Chang-An Restaurant. Having noticed the futility of Satyen babu's greeting, she made no similar attempt. Through a soft expression on her face, she just tried to convey that she had had the good fortune of being introduced to this celebrity once.

But she needn't have bothered. Dhruba Datta didn't notice her presence at all. Looking at Satyen, he said, 'How did it go — the business of weeping and wailing, all that racket?'

Satyen couldn't find an immediate answer, and straight away Dhruba Datta began again, 'I am feeling sorry for Tagore. He tried so hard to die in Europe, said that so many times, and put it in writing, but in the end — "I was born in this very land, may I die in this land too"!' Dhruba Datta smiled a bitter, diminutive smile, and his voice sounded too harsh and shrill in the dimly lit quiet of that big empty restaurant. It seemed that Satyen was about to say something, but realized in an instant that this man didn't want to hear anything, just wanted to spill out all the thoughts that had gathered within him. Puffing away at his cigarette, but leaving his drink untouched, the poet continued to speak, twisting his lips a little: 'I was out, and wandered in the streets for a long time, then I couldn't take it any more and escaped here. Oh, what an opportunity! Those who haven't read any Tagore except *Katha o Kahini*, or if they have, haven't understood any of it, or even if they have understood the stuff, haven't accepted it, and all those wily smart nitwits who repeat "Gurudev" on their oily lips, yet whose entire existence is an act of opposition to Tagore, and all those countless sensation-mongers who all their lives will never know — nor want to know — what Tagore is all about, the why and the how of his being: for all such people up and down the land what a marvellous opportunity it is today! The equivalent of ten IFA matches, one hundred Kanans and Saigals singing together! What a carnival for the newspaper-wallahs, what a peak season for the meeting-wallahs, and what a chance for the top business executives to make a lot of noise, puffing out their own names! What enthusiasm, what frolicking, what fun! Those people to whom it makes no difference whatsoever whether Tagore is alive or not — those are the very people who are the most drunk on this grief's Holi! Ha!'

Pausing, deliberately weighing every word, thus did the successor deliver the funeral oration of his predecessor in a shrill, harsh, severe voice. After the last sound of his voice he stopped at the right spot, bent forward and stretched his hand, partook of his drink a little, then leaned back on his chair to clarify that he had nothing further to say on that subject.

from

Autobiography of an Unknown Indian

N. C. CHAUDHURI

CALCUTTA GREW ENORMOUSLY DURING THE THIRTY-TWO years I lived in it, and became amorphous. Since 1942 it has received hundreds of thousands of additional immigrants and, according to old residents, is no longer recognizable as its familiar self. I have not seen Calcutta after this recent adulteration, but even in 1910 it was not one city. In certain of its quarters a man could easily fancy that he was in China. Other parts looked like *mohallas* torn out of the cities of upper India, and, in fact, till recently Calcutta had the largest Hindi-speaking population of any city in India. Along the Chowringhee and south of Park Street the city had an appearance which probably was not materially different from that of the European adjuncts of Chinese, Malay, or Egyptian ports, but even here it did not exhale mere commerce, club life, sport, and turf. Those who were historically conscious could sense these parts of Calcutta to be very perceptibly breathing the spirit of the builders of the British Empire in India. The rest of the city was purely Bengali.

Between the European and the Bengali parts, however, there always was a Eurasian and Muhammadan belt, very characteristic in appearance and still more so in smell. One of the typical sights of these quarters were the butcher's shops with beef banging from iron hooks in huge carcasses, very much bigger than the goat carcasses to whose size we the Bengali Hindus were more used. These wayside stalls were redolent of lard, and were frequented by pariah or mongrel dogs of far stronger build and fiercer looks than the dogs of the Hindu parts of the city. These animals always reminded me of the dogs in the butcher's shops of the *Arabian Nights*. All the components of Calcutta had personality and character, but the foreign elements seemed to be even more particularly assertive. In spite of the numerical preponderance of Bengalis the city was, and perhaps still is, an international concession, once flourishing but now moribund, on the mud-flats of deltaic Bengal.

Even when we first came to it Calcutta was vast. At the same time it was very close-knit and compact. It was not broken in relief like Rome with its Seven Hills, nor scattered in space like Delhi with its seven historic sites. That did not mean, however, that from a height the city had a smooth appearance. Looked at from the top of the Ochterlony Monument, or even from the roof of a high private house, the house-tops of Calcutta seemed in their crowded and untidy rows to bid the most solid and the ugliest imaginable defiance to the sky. They made a deep impression on me when I contemplated them with the newly acquired sense of being a citizen, immediately after our arrival in 1910. Our house, which was in the Bowbazar quarter, was a four-storied building, and as we went up to its roof an amazing confusion met our eyes. There was an immense expanse of house-tops fading away on all sides into the smoky horizon, but no two house-tops were alike in shape, height, colour or arrangement. If one had a parapet, another had a wooden or iron railing, and a third nothing. The levels were nowhere uniform, nor even rising or falling in any discernible pattern of tiers, banks, or terraces. Another extraordinary thing we noticed was that the roofs seemed to be the favourite dumping ground for lumber and waste of all kinds, from broken furniture to smashed earthenware and pieces of torn canvas or sack. The irregular upper surface of Calcutta was made more jagged still by the edges and points of this junk.

The only place where the skyline appeared to suggest architecture was the extreme west. There we could see in one ample curve the tops of the well-known public buildings of the Esplanade and Dalhousie Square. The line began with the cupolas, small and big, of the new building of Whiteaways and ran through the tower of the High Court, the flat dome of the Government House, the square tower of the old Central Telegraph Office, the high dome of the General Post Office, the leads of the Writers' Building and the statues on its cornices, to the steeple of the Church of St. Andrew. The scene gave the impression of an ugly sea of tossing brickwork contained along a clearly marked line by an architectural breakwater. If the view of Calcutta from above was ever softened it was only by its own appalling domestic smoke and the not very much more pleasant mist rising from the river to the west and the marshes to the east.

But three special features of the top face of Calcutta must also be mentioned, not only because they somewhat redeemed the squalid general effect, but also because they could not have been missed by anybody looking at Calcutta from an elevated point in the years following 1910. They were, first, chimneys and church spires. Two of each could be very prominently seen from the roof of our house. To the south-east rose the very tall chimney of the sewage pumping station at the Entally end of Dhurrumtollah Street, and the other was the ornamental chimney of the municipal waterworks on Wellington Square. Both the chimneys have now disappeared. The church spire nearest to us was that of the Roman Catholic church at

Bowbazar-Sealdah corner, but we could see the taller spire of the church on Wellesley Square almost equally distinctly. In Calcutta of those days no temple or mosque rose into the air. If any bells rang they were church bells. The people of Calcutta were so used to church spires that they gave the distinctive name of Bald Church to a steepleless church in our locality. In my time the church had disappeared, but it had bequeathed its name to the quarter.

The second landmark in the Calcutta sky was the group of five cranes on the site of the Victoria Memorial, then in the course of construction. These impressive architectural ancillaries were not less decorative and monumental than architecture itself, and for many years these magnificently arranged objects, imprinted as they were on the southern sky of Calcutta, created the illusion of a vast Brangwyn etching overhanging the city or some colossal ghost ship working its derricks in the upper air. When with the completion of the building the cranes disappeared, with them also disappeared one of the most vivid and poetic associations of my first years in Calcutta.

The third feature we noticed has also become rare, if it has not disappeared altogether. Every thousand yards square or so of the top face of Calcutta had a bamboo mast bearing on its head a bird-table, consisting only of a trellised frame, for pigeons to sit on. At the foot of the mast crouched a watchful man with an upturned face; he held a long and thin stick in his hand and from time to time prodded the birds with it. The birds at first tried to avoid the stick by changing places; then one or two began unwillingly and lazily to ascend with laboriously flapping wings; but as soon as three or four had gone up the whole flock rose with a whirr and began to fly to and fro over an orbit of about a quarter of a mile, keeping the trellis at the centre. They flew in one direction to begin with, and then took a complete right-about turn towards the other direction. At the turning points they wholly melted away in the atmosphere, but as soon as they had taken their turn flashed back into vision like silvery scales on the blue-grey sky. After about half-a-dozen turns in this fashion they came back to their frame and began to drop by twos and threes on it, and with a little jostling and elbowing settled down for the time being, to be prodded up again after a while by their keeper. Eight, ten, or even a dozen flocks were seen flying at the same time, and they gave a feathery and shot effect to the Calcutta sky. This sky was never gorgeous, but it had at times a pearly tenderness, and to this softness the flying birds added not only a suggestion of the pastel shades of the pigeon's throat, but also a turtledove sensibility. The contrast of such a sky with what lay spread out below was very marked. It seemed as if a crowd of misbehaved and naughty children were showing their tongues and behinds to a mother with the face of Michelangelo's *Night*.

Within a few days of my coming to Calcutta I learned with astonishment from my new school-fellows that the pigeons, and, even more so, their keepers were held in the worst possible disrepute by the human beings of the city. I casually mentioned to some of my school-fellows that I used to keep pigeons at Kishorganj. They looked with scandalized incredulity at me, because I had already given proof in the class that I was clever at books, and in my general behaviour, too, there was nothing to suggest a keeper of pigeons to these Calcutta boys: I showed no obvious signs of the moral degeneration which pigeons were supposed in Calcutta to bring on mankind. Fortunately, the boys took my former pigeon-keeping as the oddity of an East Bengal boy and did not report to the teachers. In the case of a Calcutta boy a cry would have arisen: 'Sir, this boy flies pigeons,' and at that cry the cane would have descended mercilessly on my back.

On the ground Calcutta presented a very impressive façade. But it was a façade which looked inwards, like the amphitheatre on the arena. The arena was formed by the famous Maidan or, as it is called in Bengali, the Field of the Fort, and the city stood in a rough arc round it like the inner face of the Coliseum.

The parallel is not as correct for the two wings of the façade of Calcutta as it is for the eastern or Chowringhee section, for both the wings – the first from Hastings to St. Paul's Cathedral and the second from Esplanade corner to Outram Ghat – were leafy. To the north, the Government House was all but hidden by the trees which stood trunk to trunk along the low white balustrade which formed its outer boundary wall, and towards the river the long line of the beautiful *polyalthia longifolia* of the Eden Gardens hid the High Court and the Town Hall even more effectively. Only through the funnel-like opening of the road called Government Place West could a glimpse of the Treasury Buildings be caught. At this entrance a formidable group of statuary stood on guard. Queen Victoria, Lawrence, Hardinge, Canning in greenish bronze reminded everybody in 1910, even if the unobtrusive Government House modelled on Kedleston Hall did not, that he was very near the heart of the British Empire in India. To the south of the Maidan there was a similar line of trees along Lower Circular Road, and although there was not in that quarter the same reminder of British power in India as there was to the north, there was at least a reminder of British sickness, both civil and military. For one set of the buildings which could be seen through the trees constituted the British Military Hospital and the other the Presidency General Hospital. The first was reserved for British soldiers and the second for British civilians.

Although the wings of the façade of Calcutta were leafy, the brick work on the eastern side was long, high, and solid enough to obliterate all sylvan atmosphere. This front would not have stood the scrutiny, building by building, of an architectural designer, but, seen from the distance and as a whole, it was not unimpressive. The skyline, though not absolutely uniform, was not unbalanced by any pronounced irregularity. I once saw the Chowringhee from the River Hooghly, when going to the Botanical Gardens at Sibpur in one of the Port Commissioners' ferry service steamers, and the familiar line of buildings beginning with the Army and

Navy Stores and ending in Whiteaways was estranged to my eyes by the beauty shed on it by the distance.

The central point in this façade of Calcutta was certainly the high pile of the Indian Museum, rather dull-looking from the outside but always enlivened by the thought of what it contained within. There was no place in Calcutta, unless it was the zoological gardens of Alipur, of which I was more fond. The huge galleries, each at least one hundred feet long, forty feet wide, and as many high, were always reeking of the sweating upcountry men who visited the museum as a matter of duty and trudged through the galleries as solemnly and steadily as my Kishorganj peasants marching to the field of Id prayers. They never stopped before anything unless they saw some visitor taking particular interest in one or other of the exhibits or comparing something in a book with the objects. Then they crowded round that visitor and asphyxiated him with their body odour. It was, however, impossible to get angry with them. They were as natural and primitive as the exhibits, though not as monumental. In the entrance hall were the bull and lion capitals of the pillars of Asoka, in the hall to the right were the highly ornamental red sandstone railings of the Bharhut Stupa, and in the hall to the left the Siwalik fossils together with the skeletons of the huge Hasti Ganesa or *Elephas Antiquus Namadicus Falc.* of the Nerbudda valley. It could be said that in these galleries of the Indian Museum were represented all the previous empires in India from that of the gigantic prehistoric elephants to that of Asoka the Buddhist and Samudragupta the Vishnuite.

Facing the Indian Museum across the Maidan stood Fort William, equally silent from the outside but busy and humming like a beehive within with sun-helmeted British soldiers. It was impossible for any person endowed with the consciousness of history to overlook the correlation of the museum with the fort. It was as if those who were living for the time being in Fort William were saying to those who had been housed for all time in the Indian Museum — 'Hail, dead emperors, emperors about to die salute ye!' In

1911, unknown to all of us, the shadow of death had already fallen. I still remember my father reading with his friends the news of the transfer of the capital to Delhi. The *Statesman* of Calcutta was furious, but was thinking more of the past than of the future and was not inspired to prophecies like Cassandra. We, the Bengalis, were, but not in the spirit of Cassandra. We were flippant. One of my father's friends dryly said, 'They are going to Delhi, the graveyard of empires, to be buried there.' Everybody present laughed, but none of us on that day imagined that although the burial was the object of our most fervent hopes it was only thirty-six years away.

Only one section of the façade of Calcutta had depth, and that was the section between Park Street and Lower Circular Road. The interior here was like the front, only quieter and more spacious. To walk down Middleton Street, Harrington Street, and Theatre Road was to walk into an area of large, still houses standing in their own grounds planted with *lagerstroemia indica*, canna, and ixora, and of wide silent streets shaded by *gul mohurs*, and cassias, and an occasional *lagerstroemia flos-reginae*. All these flowering trees and shrubs blossomed from April to September, making a gorgeous blaze of colours — scarlet, vermilion, pink, purple, lilac, blue, white, and golden yellow, in the midst of which the houses looked dull and ordinary. They did not, however, jar with any obtrusive ugliness. The majority were impressive by reason of their size and solidity, although not by their architecture. But a few had style. They were old buildings in the modified Georgian manner of the East India Company. Here too, as in the façade, it was the effect as a whole and not the details which constituted the attraction, and in this attraction space and silence were the principal elements. The whole area was very much like the old cemetery at its centre, where Landor's Rose Aylmer lies buried.

> *Ah, what avails the sceptred race!*
> *Ah, what the form divine!*

What every virtue, every grace!
Rose Aylmer, all were thine.

Rose Aylmer, whom these wakeful eyes
May weep, but never see,
A night of memories and sighs,
I consecrate to thee.

The inhabitants of the locality prized the silence greatly, and they wrote angry letters to the newspapers against the tooting of horns by taxis prowling for fares at night.

For us Bengalis one street of the area came to acquire a dreaded notoriety. It was Elysium Row. This was an inviting name, to which the great Bengali barrister, Sir S. P. Sinha, the first Indian member of the Viceroy's Executive Council, and later to become Under-Secretary of State for India and the first Indian peer and Governor of an Indian province, who lived in the street, added greater lure. But the pleasantness of the name and the pride evoked by the association with Sinha were wholly smothered for us by the fear inspired by Number Fourteen, the headquarters of the Special Branch or the political police. There were few Bengali young men with any stuff in them who did not have dossiers in Number Fourteen, and many had to go there in person, to be questioned, or to be tortured, or to be sent off to a detention camp. After the passing of the Defence of India Act of 1915 we began to think of Elysium Row more in connexion with the police than with Sinha. To have been in Elysium Row came to be regarded as equivalent to being branded on the forehead or having a ribbon on the chest, according to the standpoint or courage of the dragooned visitor. My younger brother as a young man of eighteen was taken there, questioned by third-degree methods, and then photographed in full face and in profile for future identification. That did not, however, prevent his identity being mixed up in the mind of the police with quite a different person's, and this confusion caused no small amount of harassment to my brother. I did not have to go there at any time of my life, but at a late stage I had a dossier. In my school and college days I did not come in the way of the political police nor did they come in my way, and I never walked through Elysium Row. Therefore, the spaciousness, the silence, and the flowers remained my only impressions of this part of Calcutta.

The rest of the Chowringhee façade was only skin-deep, and the hinterland was a strange world whose strangeness was not felt by us only because everybody took it for granted. Russa Road at the southern end of Chowringhee led into the old and respectable Bengali quarter of Bhowanipore, best known for its lawyers, and through Bhowanipore to the less wealthy but more religious quarter of Kalighat; Bentinck Street at the opposite end was famous for its Chinese shoemakers; Dhurrumtollah, which was at the same end, was itself a street of shops, bazaars and Eurasians, but it was also the ingress to the main Bengali parts of the city. An observer could stand at the Chowringhee ends of Dhurrumtollah and Russa Road and watch men coming out between nine and ten in the morning and going in between five and six in the afternoon like ants out of and into their holes. The Bengali parts of Calcutta, both north and south, sent them out in the morning for office work and sucked them back in the evening. These were the men to whom Calcutta belonged by birthright. They loved Calcutta as nobody else did. They lived in it like deep-sea fauna in the depths of the sea. Most of them would have preferred death to being removed from Calcutta.

Their Calcutta, which was also my Calcutta for thirty-two years, was an immense maze of brickwork cut up by streets and lanes. It was not labyrinthine like the Indian quarters of the cities of northern India, and it did not bring on that claustrophobia which impels newcomers to those cities to rush out into open spaces in order to breathe easily. Nor did it have that putrid squalor which makes the inhabitants of the same upper-Indian cities feel like living in the intestines of the Leviathan. Also, there was not that accumulated dust, to try to remove which was equivalent to raising only more dust. All these unlovely features of urban life in upper India, our part of Calcutta did not possess, but there was no limit to its architectural meanness. Walking along the ever-lengthening streets and lanes of these quarters one expected at every turn and step to come upon some spot of handsomeness and repose, for instance, a fine building, a spacious square, a wide vista, or at least a colourful bazaar. These expectations were never fulfilled. The more one trudged, the more one felt like swallowing an endless tape of shabbiness.

On account of this all-pervasive inelegance even the wider streets gave no impression of being straight, although they were straight in layout. The awry fronts on either side, taken with the erratic skyline and the unfinished surfaces, checked the growth of any impression of symmetry and harmony. Three or four times every hundred yards the skyline would be falling down abruptly from sixty to ten feet and changing its outline from that of the straight parapet of a flat-roofed brick house to that of the sloping roof of a mud-walled and tiled *bustee*. For the same distance the street front would be presenting three or four incongruous patches: a gaping shed, a solidly built wall pierced by small windows, an unglazed shop window or, rather, a mere opening, and a house with venetian blinds. There was not a single inviting front-door anywhere. The Bengalis of Calcutta seemed to have a particular aversion to attractive entrances. One of the two entrances to a particular house I knew had a new door. But it had its attractiveness, which in truth was no more than that of newness, reduced if not wholly suppressed by an infelicitous attempt on the part of the owner at being helpful to his visitors. What welcome the door offered was rendered unwelcome for persons with a sensitive verbal taste by a signboard bearing in English the inscription: 'Female Entrance.' Even where the interiors were luxurious the front door was made to disguise the fact as completely as possible. This particular aspect of the architectural dowdiness had its counterpart in the insensitiveness often displayed in Calcutta in the naming of persons. 'Demon', 'Goblin', 'Owl', 'Idiot', 'Tuppence', 'Snub-nosed', were quite common names for men and women there. In fact, through a whimsical affectation of Calcutta ways my eldest son came to acquire, to the great disgust and indignation of my father, the nickname of 'Imbecile'. Of course, these names never bore any relation to the appearance or abilities of the persons so named. When upon the announcement of such names you would expect the emergence of a corresponding physiognomy, a very handsome man indeed might step into your room. In regard to names the trick was meant to avert the Evil Eye or befool evil spirits, but I am unable to account for its extension to the design of front-doors, unless it happens to be a legacy from the days of Muslim rule when rich people did not care to give any outward expression to their affluence for fear of attracting the attentions of the tax-farmer.

To this morphological dinginess the Bengali parts of Calcutta added the ebbs and flows of a functional dinginess: the first daily, the second seasonal, and the third yearly. The Bengalis wash (*i.e.*, rinse in plain unsoaped water) their cotton *dhotis* and *saris* at home every day, and the Bengalis of Calcutta are even more fond of this daily washing than other Bengalis. Actually, the afternoon toilet of Calcutta women passes under the name of 'washing' in thoroughbred circles. Thus, at least twice a day, and sometimes more often, an immense amount of washing has to be hung up to dry. The front veranda, if there is any, or the roof is the place reserved for this purpose. In some houses there are a number of clothes-lines, in others the *dhotis* and *saris* are simply let down from the parapet or railing with the top ends tied to a pillar or rail. When wet they hang heavy and straight, dripping water on the footpath below, and when dry they flutter and twirl in the wind. As each piece is at least fifteen feet in length and forty-four inches in width, the houses when the washing is drying have the appearance of being draped in dirty linen. In addition, there always are subsidiary lines carrying the children's shirts, frocks, vests and drawers, and the napkins and sheets of the very large number of babies that there always are in these houses, and on most occasions the exhibition of cotton garments is reinforced by bedclothes — mattresses and quilts, large and small, wetted by the children and the babies.

The gathering up of these articles in the afternoon is almost a ritual, like the hauling down of flags on warships in the evening. Except in the houses of the rich this is in the hands of the girls of the family. In the afternoon two or three comely persons appear on the veranda or roof, as the case may be, advance to the railing or parapet, and, leaning on the one or the other, carry out a composed survey of what is going on below. If anything particularly interests them they rest their chins on the rail or wall and contemplate it with wide open, round, solemn eyes. There never is any mobility or change in their expression, but suddenly a face is tossed up and an electric glance flashed towards the window across the street, where the presence of a lurking admirer is suspected. But this ripple passes away as soon as it makes its appearance. The face relapses into the usual immobile placidity, and the girls go on gathering up or pulling down the *dhotis* and *saris*, normally in a very unconcerned manner, but sometimes screwing a puckered mouth in undoing the knots. They move up and down, piling up the clothes on one of their shoulders or arms, and when at last they walk away they look like huge washerwomen.

Another source of untidiness in our parts of Calcutta was the inexplicable but at the same time the most complete non-co-operation between the domestic servants and the municipal sweepers. In Calcutta of olden days the municipal sanitary service was not haphazard as it has grown recently. The streets were regularly watered, swept, and even scrubbed. But while the street-cleaning ended by about six o'clock in the morning and three in the afternoon, the kitchen-maids would begin to deposit the offscourings exactly at quarter-past six and quarter-past three. Nothing seemed capable of making either party modify its hours. So little piles of waste food, ashes, and vegetable scraps and peelings lay in individualistic autonomy near the kerb from one sweeping-time to another sweeping-time. During this interval, however, the refuse deposit was respected like an archaeological deposit, and was never trampled on or kicked about. All Bengali Hindus are very particular about left-over food, which they consider to be very unclean; therefore they never go anywhere near it. A small boy I knew used to take the most intelligent conceivable advantage of this prejudice in order to escape punishment for his naughtiness. He would make straight for the garbage heap before his house and stand on it. Then there was nothing else to be done but for his elder sister to throw away all her clothing, go up to him, retrieve him, and, dragging him inside, give him a scrubbing under the tap and have an untimely bath herself. The prejudice did not, however, extend to fruit rinds. They were thrown indiscriminately on the footpaths to be trampled on by all and sundry. To slip on a mango or banana skin and have a sprained ankle was a very common mishap in Calcutta.

The contribution of the seasons has now to be considered. It was in Calcutta that I learned for the first time that the seasons could uglify no less than beautify. At Kishorganj, Banagram, and Kalikutch every season added something to the attraction of the world around us. The summer sun, hot as it was, shed more happiness than discomfort, for besides being white and clear it had a life-giving quality. This, we used to say, is the sun to ripen the mango, the jack-fruit, and the melon, and it did ripen not only the fruits but also the earth, which became seasoned and mellow like an old violin. To this heat, there was an extraordinarily harmonious accompaniment of sound, a sound so intense and energetic and yet so mild and musical, that one could imagine its having been produced by the revolving top that our earth is. It was the crickets which converted the earth into a humming top. They began at about ten o'clock in the morning, just as the earth and the trees also began to feel warm to the touch. They constituted the Grasshopper's Green Herbarian Band. We hardly ever saw the brown little creatures, but we could call up before our eyes an immense string orchestra madly scraping, bowing and fingering, swaying and stretching. The *Yatra* parties had made us quite familiar with the movements of violinists. This rilloby-rilloby rilloby-rill went on till about five in the afternoon and then suddenly ceased. As dusk fell, there began the gorgeous outings of the fireflies in clustered nebulae of phosphorescent light in the midst of the darkened foliage.

These were my summer associations in the country, but on coming to Calcutta I saw that the summer heat could only produce stench more quickly, and make the streets even more messy than they normally were. They would now be strewn with empty coconut shells, whose milk is the favourite summer drink. The only thing which in our parts of Calcutta redeemed the summer was the cool evening breeze from the south and the sea. Without this breeze, I believe, the *embonpoint* of all denizens of Calcutta, who in their inordinate fondness for *ghee*, sweets and starchy foods take immense quantities of them daily, would have rotted away in sleep and the bodies begun to emit stench like the tight carcasses of dead bullocks. It may have been some instinctive fear of this kind which made all wealthy citizens of Calcutta keep the electric fan on all through the night.

The winter was not pleasanter. The temperature never went down low enough to make the cold bracing, but it became just cold enough to make people catch cold. There was grime everywhere, and, in addition, an accumulation of dust which, if it was not as overwhelming in quantity as the dust of upper-Indian cities, was worse in quality, for it was a dishonest half-breed between honest coal and honest earth. The winter mornings in the city were never refreshed for me by the dew I was accustomed to in the country, where to walk through the grass at dawn was to crush a mass of diamonds. The only evidence of dew that I saw in Calcutta was the damp surface of the footpaths. But, the worst thing was the smoke and the combination of smoke and mist in the evenings. At Kishorganj the mist hung over the landscape exactly like a veil of fine muslin. In Calcutta both the smoke and the mist spited each other. The mist would not allow the smoke to go up, and the smoke would mix itself up with the mist as it came down. We could never determine how much of the dark mixture we saw all around us was mist and how much smoke, but it was so thick that we could fancy beating it up with a stick. In any case, we were suffocated, and the gas-lamps in the streets looked reddish yellow. It was only on those rare evenings when a strong cold wind blew from the north that the atmosphere was swept clean of this dirt and the street lamps in their long lines took on the appearance of an endless and wavy festoon of soft greenish light. But in these evenings no true son of Calcutta came out willingly into the streets. He stood in mortal fear of catching pneumonia. He preferred to die of consumption in his dovecote.

But drab as the summer and winter were in Calcutta, in order to measure the full power for uglification of the seasons it was necessary to live through the rains. I have already described the rainy season at Kishorganj, but I might recall one or two impressions to bring home the contrast which Calcutta presented. The sheet-like downpour at Kishorganj had the quality of crystal, drizzle was opaline, and both were set off by a shining green. The clouds varied from the deepest collyrium blue to soft pearly shades, and apart from this infinite graduation from dark to white, they burnt in piled-up masses of gold, orange and red, or blushed in equally immense masses of pink, at sunrise and sunset. On moonlit nights, if the sky was lightly clouded, a ring with rainbow colours appeared round the moon; if there were those beautifully diapered cirro-cumulus clouds, their rippling outlines would be edged with amber. I never saw any of these things in Calcutta. The buildings hid the lower sky, and all the finer shades of the portions overhead were blotted out by the smoke and the lights of the city. For most of the time we could see only an unbroken shroud of grey.

The grey on the ground was worse. In Calcutta of those days tarmacadam was reserved for the so-called European quarters, and we, the Bengalis, had only rubble and earth on our streets. This mass decomposed during the rains, became thin and watery enough to be capable of being splashed head-high, but even in that diluted state lost none of its stickiness. This mud, as it lay on the flagstones of the footpaths, converted them into grindstones for our shoes. Thus it happened that those of us who could not go about in carriages were always down at heel and bespattered on the back during this season. Those who went about in carriages spared themselves but made the lot of the pedestrians harder. Fortunately, nobody minded anybody else's appearance, since it was taken to be the normal aspect of mankind during the rains. As for the houses, they looked worse. There were very few of them which did not wear a thoroughly bedraggled and miserable air. The trees, though washed of the dust which normally lay thick on them, did not look bright or refreshed. At Kishorganj, even after a violent gale, they looked as if they had had only a bit of wild horseplay, but in Calcutta they appeared as if they had undergone a ducking.

Sometimes the rains were so heavy that instead of the usual mud we had floods in the streets. The sewers of Calcutta were never equal to coping with the rains. The difference between their highest capacity and the demand made on them during the rains could be stated only in astronomical figures of cu.-sec.-s. I had once to go into the subject, but have forgotten all about it except the esoteric abbreviation I have used. The tangible fact was that after even a moderate shower certain streets and crossings were inevitably flooded, and heavy showers converted them literally into canals and ponds. I have seen collapsible boats brought out in the streets. People who piqued themselves on their wit used to say that such and such a street in Calcutta was flooded if a dog raised its hind leg. The water was of the dirtiest shade of brown, with all the floatable elements in the garbage afloat, and all the soluble elements in solution. It was knee-deep at certain places, at others even deeper. Some carriages and motor cars would be ploughing their way through it, leaving swirling wakes and backwashes behind, but the trams would be completely held up. The anxious inspectors would be wading about, with their trousers tucked half-way up the thigh, taking soundings with their own lower limbs. The sweepers stood at attention at regular intervals like statues, each at his manhole, after having opened it to let the water pass down into the sewers quickly. Even then the water did not subside for three or four hours. Sometimes even a whole day or night was required. It was being Venice with a vengeance.

Tagore began a famous political speech of his with a reference in his characteristic style to these immemorial floods. 'No sooner has the smallest pluvious wind blown,' he declared, 'than the floods rage from our lane to our main street, the wayfarer's pair of footgear is borne aloft over the head like his umbrella, and at least the denizens of this lane are seen to be no better adapted to life than the amphibians — these are the things I have been observing from our veranda year after year from my childhood till my hair has grown grey.' Tagore attributed it half to foreign rule and half to the fatalistic resignation to evil and authority of his countrymen. His countrymen attributed it wholly to foreign rule. The Calcutta Corporation attributed it to a number of causes which it was difficult to understand without a considerable knowledge of irrigation and sanitary engineering combined. But whosoever's the fault, the fact indeed was that those of us who cared for our shoes did wade through the streets with the precious pair in hand. I did so on a few occasions, but the universal spectacle of men going about shoes-in-hand sometimes drove me to attempts at originality. I tried to walk in my shoes. It was worse still. There was more unpleasantness in having them on, for the water was clammy enough by itself, and to have equally clammy leather round the feet, and to feel and hear the water in the shoes squirting in and out noisily at every step were sensations even more unbearable. So our wading shoes-in-hand was not wholly parsimony, it had in it an aesthetic impulse as well.

Last of all I must refer to the yearly accumulation of shabbiness. The house-owners in Calcutta had no notion of maintenance, and even though the preservation of their own property was involved in it considered expenditure on such things as annual repairs and painting utter waste. It would be only after a sustained campaign of complaints and dunning on the part of the tenants that they would send a workman or two to give the house a coat of dirty whitewash inside and a dirty coat of paint outside. Thus the general run of houses in Calcutta, even at their best, looked as if the sharp edge of their cleanly appearance had been rubbed off. This dinginess accumulated from year to year till the general effect became one of mottled grey.

To go out of the city into the suburbs or the countryside did not offer better prospects or aspects. The immediate outskirts of the city were squalid and congested beyond description. They were full of mean and insanitary sheds and *bustees*, built wall to wall, and separated only by dusty roads when not by narrow and evil-smelling lanes. All the bigger roads had open drains on both sides, running with coal-black sewage, and this drain had to be crossed and recrossed every time when one wanted to go into or come out of a house or a shop. None but the inhabitants of these localities could go about in them without handkerchiefs to the nose.

Little relief awaited me even when I broke my way through the suburbs, for the countryside just around Calcutta, though open, seemed to have been poisoned to death. It lay like a mangy bandicoot bitten by a snake. The trees did not thrive there, the grass had a burnt-up look, the cottages were exact replicas of the suburban *bustees*. These parts brought desolation into one's heart.

The next ring was chlorosis-stricken. Here too the trees did not flourish. They were pallid. The houses, both brick-built and thatched, wore a deserted appearance. It was not till one had moved twenty-five miles away that the earth seemed to be its old self. I noticed these concentric rings of different atmospheres and effects whenever I had to come to Calcutta by train.

So, ultimately, one had to work one's way back towards the Chowringhee front in search of repose and order. As long as I lived in Calcutta, I kept up the habit of walking down to the Maidan as far as the Victoria Memorial, or to the Eden Gardens and the riverside between Outram and Prinsep's Ghat. But my yearning for fine architecture was never destined to be satisfied. Domestic architecture was, of course, inconceivable, but even the public buildings I scrutinized in vain. Some of them were presentable, some even imposing and handsome to my unformed taste in architecture. But I soon learned that they were all imitations. The High Court was a copy of the Cloth Hall of Ypres, the Government House of Kedleston Hall; Writers' Buildings and the Revenue Office were passable imitations of the style of the French Renaissance; certain other buildings were pseudo-Greek—Doric, Ionic, or Corinthian. The Cathedral, which had a western window of stained glass after designs by Burne-Jones, was in very pinchbeck Gothic. The Military Secretariat built for Kitchener, although ambitious, was so devoid of true character that in the medallions on its façade the heads of Venus could hardly be distinguished from those of Mars. Nowhere was there anything authentic or original. Only in 1921 did Calcutta get a genuine specimen of architecture, in the Victoria Memorial. It has faults of design, but still it is the only thing to redeem the City of Palaces architecturally. Yet it is extraordinary to relate that the Bengali citizens of Calcutta, who are totally unconscious how many of their pre-existent public buildings are imitations, regard the Victoria Memorial as such. They think that it is an unsuccessful imitation of the Taj Mahal. Let alone Emerson, the designer of the memorial, even if Brunelleschi, Bramante, Michelangelo and Wren had appeared in person and sworn otherwise, they would not have convinced these scoffers.

from

Thy Hand Great Anarch!

N. C. CHAUDHURI

Town and Country in Bengali Life

B UT NOT ONLY ATROPHY, SOMETHING WORSE — FOSSILIZATION, has come over the mind of Hindu Bengalis on account of the separation of their life from its natural environment, which was brought about by the partition of 1947. For present-day Bengalis, Bengal is nothing but Calcutta as it is now, and such a city cannot support either happiness or creativity. The most serious loss is severance of contact with the waters of Bengal, and more especially with three great rivers which have made Bengal what she is geographically. These are the Padma (the main channel to the sea of the Ganges at the present time), the Brahmaputra (locally known as the Jamuna or Jabuna), and the Meghna. All three are now in the new state known as Bangla Desh.

Of course, Calcutta still stands on a river, and that is a branch of the Ganges. Although known in English as the Hooghly river, its Sanskrit name is Bhagirathi, and the Bengalis have always called it simply Ganga (the Ganges). In the past this branch was the main outlet to the sea of the waters of the Ganges. In the early part of the nineteenth century it discharged so much water into the Bay of Bengal that Bishop Reginald Heber, when coming to Calcutta in a sailing ship in October 1823, found that even at a distance of one hundred miles from the mouth of the Hooghly his ship was struggling against the current of that river. As he wrote: 'The mighty Ganges ran like a millstream at a fathom or two underneath, against which nothing but a very powerful gale could contend.' Even near Diamond Harbour, about forty miles below Calcutta, the river, Heber wrote: 'was still of vast width and rapidity.' The pilot informed him that the tides in it ran at a rate of 10 to 11 knots.

Moreover, in its lower reaches up to the sea the Ganges retained its sacred status only in this branch. The Padma had none. What was even more important, it was on the two banks of this branch of the Ganges, known locally as the Bhagirathi, that the culture which could be regarded as the distinctly Bengali form of Hindu culture, arose and flourished. Thus the traditional Bengali culture was a riparian culture. It had even a religious sanction behind it. For all Bengalis, to die in the waters of the Ganges was like receiving the extreme unction of the Roman Church, and therefore dying men and women were carried to the river even over distances of forty miles on the shoulders of their relatives. So it happened that the strip of territory of this width to the east and west of the river delimited the homeland of Bengali culture laterally, and all Bengalis tried to remain in touch with it socially, and culturally as well. The rest of Bengal lost cultural and social standing to a lesser or greater extent according as the areas receded farther and farther from these two lines.

But the cultural importance of the Bhagirathi has become a thing of the past. The river began to shrink and silt up even before the end of the nineteenth century, and has been kept navigable for ships in its lower reaches by continuous dredging. With the growth of Calcutta, it lost its cultural status and became only a channel of commerce, except for traditional Bengali Hindus who went to bathe in it as a religious duty. The modern Bengali culture which was created in Calcutta had no association with the river on which the city stood. Both the physical and cultural decline of the river is symbolic.

Fortunately, I did not have to live in Calcutta after the partition of Bengal in 1947, and so I have not been exposed personally to the general decadence of Bengali life. But even before the fatal partition, life in Calcutta was felt to be stifling by all sensitive Bengalis, because, in spite of being the centre of all intellectual activity among Bengalis, it eroded sensibility and feeling. This was felt, above all, by Rabindranath Tagore, the great poet and the greatest Bengali that has lived.

But Tagore had the means to live away from Calcutta. For Bengali writers of ordinary means there could be no escape from the crushing weight of its drabness. They had to live in it in order to carry on their writing, earn their livelihood, and yet deal with the ever-present problem of saving what they wrote from the city's polluted, corroding, and asphyxiating atmosphere. As a rule, when they wrote poetry or fiction, the only strong and lasting products of the Bengali literary effort, they drew on their experiences in the villages. But they could not raise their own life as lived above the material squalor imposed by the city and their very inadequate means of living. No one visiting their houses and observing their way of living could ever have imagined that they could be capable of such flights of imagination and feeling as they often displayed in their works. I know their life, and I myself have lived it, although I have never acquiesced in the material squalor of that life. But that rebellion, in its turn, has alienated me even from Bengalis of my class.

from

White Mughals

WILLIAM DALRYMPLE

WHEN WILLIAM HUNTER SAILED INTO CALCUTTA FOR the first time to take up a job as a Junior Clerk in the Company at the very beginning of the nineteenth century, he wrote home: 'Imagine everything that is glorious in nature combined with everything that is beautiful in architecture and you can faintly picture to yourself what Calcutta is.' And this wasn't just because (as one cruel commentator has suggested) he was in love — and had arrived fresh from Peckham.[1]

In 1806 Calcutta was at the height of its golden age. Known as the City of Palaces or the St Petersburg of the East, the British bridgehead in Bengal was unquestionably the richest, largest and most elegant colonial city in India. Here a Nabob like Philip Francis could boast in the 1770s that he was 'master of the finest house in Bengal, with a hundred servants, a country house, spacious gardens, horses and carriages'. Francis's 'wine book', which survives in the India Office Library, gives an indication of the style in which such men lived: in one typical month, chosen at random, Francis, his family and his guests drank seventy-five bottles of Madeira, ninety-nine bottles of claret, seventy-four bottles of porter, sixteen bottles of rum, three bottles of brandy and one bottle of cherry brandy — some 268 bottles in all, though part of the reason for such consumption was the noxious state of the Calcutta drinking water, and the widespread belief that it should always be 'purified' by the addition of alcohol — and especially by a little tot of brandy.[2]

Nor was it just the British who did well and lived extravagantly: Bengali merchant dynasties also flourished. The Mullick family, for example, had rambling baroque palaces strewn around the city, and used to travel around Calcutta in an ornate carriage drawn by two zebras.

If Calcutta impressed and surprised the British who sailed out from Georgian London, it amazed Mughal and Persian travellers, for whom it combined the splendour of scale with the novelty of imported notions of European urban management and Palladian architecture.* Khair un-Nissa's cousin, Abdul Lateef Shushtari, first saw Calcutta in 1789 and could not believe his eyes: 'The city now contains around five thousand imposing two or three storey houses of stone or brick and stucco,' he wrote.

> *Most are white but some are painted and coloured like marble. Seven hundred pairs of oxen and carts are appointed by the Company to take rubbish daily from streets and markets out of the city and tip it into the river. All the pavements have drains to carry off the rain water to the river and are made of beaten brick so as to absorb water and prevent mud forming. Houses stand on the road and allow passers-by to see what is happening inside; at night camphor candles are burned in upper and lower rooms, which is a beautiful sight. Grain and rice are plentiful and cheap...*

---

* Though even at the best of times, town planning was never one of Calcutta's more obvious virtues: as early as 1768, Mrs Jemima Kindersley thought it 'as awkward a place as can be conceived, and so irregular that it looks as if all the houses had been thrown up in the air, and fallen down again by accident as they now stand: people keep constantly building; and everyone who can procure a piece of ground to build a house upon consults his own taste and convenience, without any regard to the beauty or regularity of the town'. Mrs Jemima Kindersley, Letters from the East Indies (London, 1777), p.17.

There is no fear of robbers nor highwaymen, no one challenges where you are going nor where you have come from; all the time, big ships come from Europe and China and the New World filled with precious goods and fine cloths, so that velvets and satins, porcelains and glassware have become commonplace. In the harbour at Calcutta there are over 1000 large and small ships at anchor, and constantly the captains fire cannons to signal arrival or departure...[3]

If Calcutta was a city of trade and business, it was also a place of swaggering excess, famous for being as debauched and dissolute as any port in the world. Forty years earlier, Robert Clive had written that 'corruption, licentiousness and want of principle seem to have possessed the minds of all the Civil Servants'; and he spoke from experience. British Calcutta was a uniquely introverted, self-obsessed and self-regarding society, a little island of Britishness with remarkably few links to the real Indian India beyond. In his decade in the subcontinent, Philip Francis, for example, never ventured more than a mile or two outside Calcutta, and as late as 1793 the artist William Hodges, travelling up the Ganges and Jumna, could express it 'a matter of surprise that a country so closely allied to us should be so little known. Of the face of the country, of its arts and crafts little has yet been said.'[4]

The hundreds of Company servants and soldiers who arrived annually in Calcutta – typically, penniless younger sons of provincial landed families, Scots who had lost their estates or their fortunes (or both) in one of the Jacobite uprisings, squaddies recruited from the streets of the East End, down-at-heel Anglo-Irish landowners and clergymen's sons – were all prepared to risk their lives and travel thousands of miles to the impossible climate of Bengal's undrained marsh and steaming jungle, hazarding what would very probably be an early death, for one reason: if you survived there was no better place in the world to make your fortune.

More clearly and unequivocally than those elsewhere in India, the British inhabitants of Calcutta had come east to amass a fortune in the quickest possible time. For the politically

ambitious in the East India Company too, this was the place to
be: here, by the side of the Governor General, was somewhere
you could make your name, find yourself quickly promoted up
the ranks, and, all being well, return home with a Governor's
cocked hat and an honour which would allow you to match your
elder brother's inherited title. Few in Calcutta seem to have
had much interest in either the mores of the country they were
engaged in plundering, or in the social niceties of that which
they had left behind.

By 1806 William Hickey was an attorney working for Henry
Russell's father, the Chief Justice of Bengal. He had been in
Calcutta for thirty years now, but was still appalled by the excesses
he saw around him every day in the taverns and dining rooms
of the city. In his celebrated diaries he depicts a grasping, jaded,
philistine world where bored, moneyed Writers (as the Company
called its clerks) would amuse themselves in Calcutta's punch
houses* by throwing half-eaten chickens across the tables. Their
womenfolk tended to throw only bread and pastry (and then only
after a little cherry brandy), which restraint they regarded as the
highest 'refinement of wit and breeding'. Worse still was

> the barbarous [Calcutta] custom of pelleting [one's dining companions]
> with little balls of bread, made like pills, which was even practised by the fair
> sex. Mr. Daniel Barwell was such a proficient that he could, at a distance,
> snuff a candle and that several times successively. This strange trick fitter
> for savages than for polished society, produced many quarrels... A Captain
> Morrison had repeatedly expressed his abhorrence of pelleting, and said that
> if any person struck him with one he should consider it intended as an insult
> and resent it accordingly. In a few minutes after he had so said he received
> a smart blow in the face from one which, although discharged from a hand
> below the table, he could trace by the motion of the arm from whence it
> came, and saw that the pelleter was a very recent acquaintance.

---

* 'Punch' being of course an Indian word, arriving in the English language via the Hindustani
panch (five), a reference to the number of ingredients for the drink, which traditionally were
(according to *Hobson Jobson*) 'arrack, sugar, lime-juice, spice and water'.

He therefore without the least hesitation, took up a dish that stood before him containing a leg of mutton, which he discharged at the offender, and with such well-directed aim that it took him upon the head, knocking him off his chair and giving him a severe cut upon the temple. This produced a duel in which the unfortunate pelleter was shot through the body, lay upon his bed for many months, and never perfectly recovered.[5]

With only 250 European women to four thousand men, and with little else to spend their money on, the young Writers tended to wander the streets of Calcutta, whoring in the city's famous brothels and debauching in its taverns. Even the otherwise admiring Shushtari was horrified by the number of bordellos lining the Calcutta backstreets, and the health problems this caused:

Brothels are advertised with pictures of prostitutes hung at the door... Atashak — a severe venereal disease causing a swelling of the scrotum and testicles — affects people of all classes. Because so many prostitutes are heaped together that it spreads from one to another, healthy and infected mixed together, no one holding back — and this is the state of even the Muslims in these parts![6]

Even his own cousin, he admits elsewhere, caught something of the sort in Calcutta, 'an itching skin disease called *hakka o jarb* common in Bengal... It spread to cover his whole body and the itching allowed him no rest, so that he had to employ four servants to scratch and scrub him continually; this they did so vigorously that he often fainted; and he was no longer able to eat or sleep.'[7] That such social diseases were rampant was due at least partly to the fact that the manners and morals of Calcutta's European élite left much to be desired, at least to Shushtari's Persian eyes. It wasn't just the phenomenal consumption of alcohol that worried him: 'No-one eats on his own at home whether by night or by day, and people who know each other go to each others' houses and debauch together... No man can prevent his wife from mixing with strange men, and by reason of women going unveiled, it is quite the thing to fall in love...'[8]

All this was, in a way, hardly surprising. The Writers who made up most of the Company's Calcutta employees were little more than schoolboys, sent out from England as young as fifteen. After a dull and uncomfortable six-month voyage they were let loose from the holds and found themselves free from supervision for the first time. One traveller commented how 'the keeping of race horses, the extravagant parties and entertainments generally involve the young Writers in difficulties and embarrassments at an early period of their lives', while according to another observer, 'the costly champagne suppers of the Writers' Building were famous, and long did the old walls echo to the joyous songs and loud rehearsing tally-hoes'.

Joyous songs was clearly about as sophisticated as British Calcutta's musical scene got. In 1784 a Danish player of the newly invented clarinet turned up in the city, seeking employment. Joseph Fowke, regarded as one of the more cultured citizens, was appalled: 'This Clarinet D'Amor [is] a coarse instrument,' he wrote in his diary, 'worse to my ears than the grunting of Hogs.' As for the new music of Haydn that the clarinet player had brought with him from Europe, Fowke was quite clear that it was not fit for public performance: '[This] Noisy modern music...' he wrote. '[Haydn is] the Prince of Coxcombs.' A John Bull conservative down to his square-toed shoes, Fowke continued, 'Fashion governs the world of Music as it does in dress — Few regulate their taste on the unerring principles of Truth and good Sense.' [9]

Certainly not, so it would seem, the Calcutta clergy. According to Hickey, the army chaplain Mr Blunt, '[an] incomprehensible young man, got abominably drunk and in that disgraceful condition exposed himself to both soldiers and sailors, talking all sorts of bawdy and ribaldry, and singing scraps of the most blackguard and indecent songs, so as to render himself a common laughing stock'.* Even the Calcutta Constabulary were far from paragons of virtue: W.C. Blaquière, the startlingly effeminate police magistrate throughout the 1780s, being a noted cross-dresser who used to leap at any opportunity to adopt female disguises.† Wellesley had made some efforts to reform this dissolution, and in one of his more far-sighted moves had set up Fort William College in an attempt to educate the cleverer of the Writers in the Indian languages that they would need to administer the subcontinent. But the social reforms and stricter Victorian morality that began to establish themselves from the 1830s onwards were still far away, and in 1806, when Khair un-Nissa first arrived in Calcutta, this was still a city of Hogarthian dissipation.

Endnotes

1. Denis Kincaid, *British Social Life in India up to 1930* (London, 1930), pp.22, 95.

2. David Burton, *The Raj at Table: A Culinary History of the British in India* (London, 1993), p.208.

3. Sayyid Abd al-Latif Shushtari, *Kitab Tuhfat al-'Alam, 'Dhail al-Tuhfa* (written Hyderabad, 1802; lithographed Bombay, 1847), p.427.

4. Quoted in John Keay, *India Discovered* (London, 1981), p.22.

5. William Hickey (ed. A. Spencer), *The Memoirs of William Hickey* (4 vols, London, 1925), Vol. 2, p.187.

6. Shushtari, p.434.

7. Ibid, p.137.

8. Ibid, p.301.

9. *The Oriental & India Office Collection (OIOC), Fowke Papers, Mss E6.66, Vol. XXVII, J. Fowke to M. Fowke, Calcutta, 12 December 1783.*

* Blunt was part of a long tradition of dubious English clergymen exported to India after failing to find a living at home. The curate of Madras in 1666, for example, was described as 'a drunken toss-pot', while his counterpart in Calcutta twenty years later was 'a very lewd, drunken swearing person, drenched in all manner of debaucheries, and a most bitter enemy of King William and the present Government'. Back in Madras, Francis Fordyce, padre to the Presidency throughout the 1740s, turned out to have fled his post as chaplain at St Helena after having debauched a planter's daughter. In Madras he fared little better, quarrelling with Clive and being called before the Council to justify his conduct. He refused to attend, but it was declared in his absence that he vowed he would 'pull off his canonicals at any time to do himself justice'. See Henry Dodwell, *The Nabobs of Madras* (London, 1926), pp.19–20.

† So comely was Blaquière's appearance that when Zoffany came to paint a Leonardo-style *Last Supper* for the altarpiece of St John's church in Calcutta he chose him as the model for the traditionally effeminate-looking apostle John ('the apostle Jesus loved'), and posed him with his long blond tresses tumbling over Jesus' breast. Jesus himself was modelled by the worthy Greek priest, Father Parthenio', while according to Mildred Archer, the auctioneer William Tulloh, who had disposed of James Kirkpatrick's Electrifying Machine, 'was far from pleased to find himself as Judas'. It is certainly an unusual reworking of the familiar scene: as a contemporary critic pointed out, 'Peter's sword hung upon a nail on the wall is a common peon's *tulwaar* [scimitar]: the water ewer standing near the table is copied from a *pigdanny* [a Hindustani spittoon]: and there is a *beesty* bag full of water lying near it.' See Mildred Archer, *India and British Portraiture 1770–1825* (London, 1979), p.158.

from

The Calcutta of Begum Johnson

IVOR EDWARDS-STUART

ALTHOUGH SHE HAS LEFT NO MEMOIRS WE LEARN FROM contemporaries that Frances Johnson prided herself that she kept up all the old customs to the last except that as she got older she forwent her early morning drive. As of old she would dine at three or four o'clock, take her siesta after dinner and then take her airing in her carriage. On her return home her house in Clive Street would be lit up and thrown open for the reception of visitors. All who were on visiting terms were expected to come without invitation, and a few who had been previously invited to stay to supper and cards. As Sleeman recounts of these evenings, 'the male visitors were not men who had risen at six o'clock in the morning, and were worn out with business or office work, but lively gallants, fresh from the afternoon siesta, and ready for a little supper, as people would be who dined at one or two; and of course, they talked, laughed, flirted, sang, danced and played cards till midnight, as people can do who have slept away the afternoon.'

It is related that at home Frances was waited upon by a number of nubile girls who ministered to her every want. Slavery, it may come as a surprise to learn, was rife in British India in the 18th and early 19th centuries.

Most of the slaves in Calcutta were Bengali who apparently came from two sources — they were either Bengalis captured by the Mugs of the Arakan on their frequent raids on the coastal villages, or they were children sold by their parents who could no longer afford to keep them. This type of slave was mainly employed by local Bengali magnates.

Of course the import of slaves into India had been going on for centuries as Carey reports: 'The slave trade, formerly carried on by Muscat, from Zanzibar to Scinde, in Hubshys (Africans) and Abyssinians, was so considerable, that six hundred young people, of whom three-fourths were girls, were imported into Kurrachee every year; Georgians were occasionally imported for the harems of the rich. The price of an Abyssinian girl was sometimes as high as two hundred and fifty rupees; boys were sold at from sixty to a hundred rupees. The slave trade was entirely abolished after Scinde came under British rule.'

It is a matter of interest as to whether some of these African slaves made their way south or whether there was another direct source of supply, because by the 18th century in Calcutta many Europeans kept slave boys to wait on them at table, and there seems to have been a very strong market for Africans who were called Coffres ('Kafirs', after the word for unbelievers). The Calcutta papers carry numerous advertisements for such slaves. For instance, an advertisement in 1781 read: 'To be sold by private sale: two Coffree boys, who play reasonably well on the French horn; about eighteen years of age; belonging to a Portuguese Padre lately deceased.' And another for two Coffree boys who can play the French horn, who dress hair and shave, and wait at table. And so on.

It would also appear from one advertisement quoted by Busteed that the Europeans not only bought and sold slaves but like the plantation owners of the deep south of America, were not averse to buying slaves for the purpose of breeding. The advertisement quoted is for 'three handsome African ladies of the true sable hue, commonly called Coffresses, between fourteen and twenty-five, for marriage with their fellow countrymen.'

As Frances kept to a strict Calcutta routine we can follow her normal daily routine through the writings of Mrs Sherwood:

> She is called some time before sunrise, and her ayah brings her every article of dress, completely clean, fresh from the dhoby. She is enveloped, over her morning wrapper, in a splendid Cashmere shawl, and she is then carried out to take the air, whether in a carriage or open palanquin. Soon after sunrise she returns and, having taken some coffee, she goes to bed and, if she can, sleeps soundly for an hour or two. She is roused before the family breakfast hour, in sufficient time to go through a somewhat elaborate toilet: not that she uses the smallest exertion herself, but goes through every process of bathing, hairdressing, and so on under the hands of one or two black women.

> The lady's toilet being finished, she issues from her apartment into the hall, where a breakfast is set out in the most elegant style, and where many gentlemen soon drop in. The meal is a public one, and continues some time, during which much polite conversation is carried on; the company then disperses, and she withdraws to some elegant room, where she reads a little, does a little fancy work, receives or writes a few notes, or receives some lady visitor. On occasion she returns a visit in her carriage. She knows a good deal of gossip of the Europeans, but little of the ways and habits of the natives.

> A little renewal or change of dress is made again before tiffin, at which time the table is set out with the same display as at breakfast; and the vacant seats are again occupied by guests. This is the best meal of the day, and much wine and pale ale is drunk. The party does not often sit after tiffin, and our lady withdraws to her own suite, takes off her outer dress and ornament, and lies

*down, remaining asleep or perhaps reading till the heat of the day is past,
and the sun low. Then follows a still more elaborate process of dressing,
with an entire change of every article of wearing apparel, and the lady goes
forth to take air in her carriage, generally on the course, where she meets
all the great people of Calcutta, and has the opportunity of smiling on her
female friends and receiving the bows and compliments of the gentlemen.
On her return she adds a few jewels to her dress, and sits down to dinner
with her husband, after which she most often goes out to a ball or assembly,
for which a last and still more magnificent toilet must be made.*

The afternoon siesta was a must in old Calcutta not only for
the Europeans but also for the Indians and from about midday
until sunset the streets were deserted.

But at sunset the whole of Calcutta became alive as with
one accord both European and native went to 'hawa khana'
or eat the air. From the great houses rolled out the carriages.
The belles of the town such as the Misses Sanderson, Emma
Wrangham, etc. would be seen driving their smart phaetons
usually accompanied by their young beaux mounted beside them
on their prancing horses. These would wind their way to the
Course, the only drive then in existence, but the dust raised
did not add to the enjoyment. At the Course a band would be
playing and the gentry would draw up their carriages to listen to
it and chat with friends. Those who preferred a more peaceful
and dustless excursion would proceed to the river where they
would enjoy outings in pinnacles or budgerows. For those who
could not afford carriages there would be walks amongst the
shrubs and trees surrounding the great tank.

There were also many places of entertainment in old Calcutta
of which the most famous was the Harmonica Tavern. Of this
Mrs Fay wrote in 1780: 'I felt far more grateful some time ago
when Mrs Jackson procured me a ticket for the Harmonica
which was supported by a select number of gentlemen who,
each in alphabetical rotation, give a concert, ball and supper,
during the cold season, I believe once a fortnight.'

Boating parties were another form of entertainment mainly between Calcutta and Garden Reach. The boats used were called snake boats or marpunkies. Of these Stavorinus wrote in 1770:

> *Another boat of this country, which is very curiously constructed, is called a mourpunkey; these are very long and narrow, sometimes extending to upwards of a hundred feet in length, and not much more than eight feet in breadth; they are always paddled, sometimes by forty men, and are steered by a large paddle from the stern, which is either in the shape of a peacock, a snake or some other animal; the paddles are directed by a man who stands up and sometimes makes use of a branch of a plant to regulate their motion, using much gesticulation and telling history to excite either laughter or exertion. In one part of the stern is a canopy supported by pillars, on which are seated the owner and his friends, who partake of the refreshing breezes of the evening. These boats are very expensive, owing to the beautiful decoration of painted and gilt ornaments which are highly varnished and exhibit a considerable degree of taste.*

Horse racing was introduced early to Calcutta. A race course existed at the end of Garden Reach and the present race course was laid out as early as 1810. Hicky's *Gazette* mentions race meetings and race balls in 1780 and the Bengal Jockey Club started as early as 1803.

The racing took place in the morning and was followed by breakfast and music in tents erected for the purpose. There were normally only three races each morning each being contested by only two ponies. A race ball would be held during the course of the meeting, for dancing was the main enjoyment of Calcutta society. It went on irrespective of the weather and Lord Valentia wrote: 'I attribute consumption among the ladies to their incessant dancing...' A small quiet party seems to have been unknown in Calcutta. A ball in India was a very different affair from the same scene in England. As Carey wrote:

In the first place the company includes no old ladies at least, of the softer sex, for doubtless there are the usual proportion in breeches. The absence of elderly persons in Indian society, is one of the first things that strike a new arrival. At a certain age, people usually leave the country, and thus there is always a degree of youthfulness about the company one meets. But, strange to say, young unmarried ladies are as scarce as old ones, and naturally more in demand: consequently, a lady's dancing days last as long as she remains in India, and a man has the satisfaction of seeing the mother of his six children as much in request, even among young sparks, as before he married her, while any damsel not yet wedded has as many partners on hand as she could accommodate in a week. Hence the light fantastic toe has enough to do, and has to keep up the steam to the end of the chapter. Fortunately the ball rooms are expressly adapted for such efforts, being lofty, spacious and airy, windows open on every side, and ventilation facilitated by a hundred-punkah power. A white cloth coated with French chalk, covers the floor and affords a smooth surface for the feet. Among the male portion of the company there is a great predominance of uniforms, while the toilettes of the ladies are of the most expensive kind and, there being no lack of lights, the whole forms a brilliant scene.

The ladies of the settlement, at first only a few in number, may be placed in four categories. First there were those who came out to India with their husbands and, as a junior writer's pay was ridiculously low, these would normally only be the wives of the most senior of the Company's servants either civil or military. Second, there were the daughters of such senior officers who were either born and bred in the country such as Sophia and Frances Croke or who had been left in England and came out to join their parents or, as was the case of Margaret Maskelyne, an elder brother. The third type, only a few in number, as leave was a very rare occurrence, were those who became engaged or married to a Company servant on leave and had either returned to India with him or joined him at a later date to be married. Fourth and last were those, who came out to stay with friends or relations with the objective of finding a husband, and their numbers would increase rapidly as time went on. These young ladies were irreverently known as the 'fishing fleet' and the custom survived until the outbreak of the Second World War.

The experience of the young girl landing in India for the first time must have been rather nerve-racking for she was quickly put on show by the hosts with whom she resided and for several nights the house would be beset by streams of callers of the unattached males who had so far failed to find suitable partners. Marriages, once arranged, were concluded with haste, the only requirement being the licence issued by the Governor-General for without it no marriage was legal. If this showing off of the new arrival did not have the desired effect, church going on Sunday gave another chance to any aspiring suitor, as Miss Goldborne relates: 'I have been at Church in my new palanquin (the mode of genteel conveyance) where all the ladies are approached by sanction of an ancient custom by all gentlemen indiscriminately, known or unknown, with offers of their hands to conduct them to their seat. Accordingly, those gentlemen who wish to change their condition (which between ourselves are chiefly old fellows) on hearing of a ship's arrival make a point of repairing to this holy dome and eagerly tender services to the fair stranger.'

And what was the aim of these hopeful maidens? Carey explains in a well-known anecdote:

> One of the prizes held out to a young lady on reaching India, as open to all comers, was 'three hundred a year, dead or alive' which passed into a proverb and was stamped on the damsel's brow as plain as print. The meaning was that by marrying a member of the Civil Service, she secured a husband with at least £300 a year, and at his death, would be entitled to a pension from the Civil Fund to the same amount. The latter provision, however, was contingent on the husband having served a certain period; and, on one occasion, this fact was communicated to a lady at a grand dinner just after her marriage, when she could not

conceal her disappointment, but called across the table to her husband —
'John, John, it's a do after all: it is a do.'

It may be wondered why the young ladies turned their attentions towards the older members of the civil service rather than to the handsome young officers in their glittering uniform. There were three good reasons for this state of affairs which persisted up to the end of the 18th century.

First, there was the question of pay, which to say the least, was meagre and inadequate and less than received by the King's officers. Yet the Company expected their officers to maintain certain standards.

Secondly there was the question of home leave for which the Company had made no provision at all. If, for any reason, such as urgent family affairs, a need for a change of climate or ill-health, an officer wished to return to England he must first resign his commission and hope, that when the time came that he wished to return to India he would be reappointed, a hope that was seldom realised.

Thirdly there were no pension rights. The officer, unless he had private means or had been fortunate enough to be able to make money outside his profession (and this became more and more difficult as time went on) had to carry on until ill-health or wounds received in battle forced him to leave India and return to his native country in a state of abject poverty. For even the most successful of the Company's officers could not rise above the rank of Colonel and only very few of such appointments existed.

But as more and more King's troops arrived in India to reinforce the Company's troops a much more important cause for grievance arose. A King's officer of the same rank as a Company officer, irrespective of his age, seniority or experience always took precedence.

It was only after 1795 that furlough on pay for three years was conceded and full pay for life after twenty-two years of service, less any command or additional pay being drawn at the time of retirement, which reduced it considerably. But in order to return home with an adequate pension it was necessary to achieve the Colonelcy of a Regiment and this could take from thirty-five to forty years. Later the Company also granted retirement on half pay to those officers who had served thirteen years in India. The Company's officers' pay was brought into line with that of the King's officers and pensions were also awarded to those with mutilated limbs, severe wounds or loss of sight. Officers could now reach higher rank and only one office on the Indian establishment was denied them — that of Commander-in-Chief India and this office would not become within their reach until after the Mutiny when the East India Company rule came to an end.

Considering the small number of ladies in the settlement Calcutta appears to have had more than its fair share of beauties. We have already met the graceful and charming Marion Hastings, the bewitching Catherine Grand and will later meet the lovely Rose Aylmer. Of the senior officials two were the possessors of wives of great beauty — Sir John Day and Sir Robert Chambers.

Lady Chambers was, according to Miss Fay writing in 1780, 'the most beautiful woman I ever beheld — the bloom of youth; and there is an agreeable frankness in her manner that enhances her loveliness and renders her truly fascinating.' She was one of those ladies celebrated for driving gaily caparisoned horses on the Calcutta Course and for her 'attendant beaux, both as to smartness and variety yield to no-one.' Frances Wilton had married Sir Robert in 1774 when she was only sixteen. Her father was a respected Royal Academician.

Lady Day was another who was gifted with great beauty as can be seen in her portraits by Romney and Gainsborough. She was a Miss Benedetta Ramus, her father being an old and trusted retainer of the King. Before leaving for India, Mr Day, as he then was, went to pay his compliments to St James's. He was received by His Majesty who knighted him, a circumstance that occasioned a witticism in the newspapers from it having occurred in the month of September. The facetious George Selwyn, seeing in the *Gazette* that Mr Day was made a knight, exclaimed: 'By God, this is out-Heroding Herod. I have long heard of the extraordinary power His Majesty exercised, but until this moment could not have believed that he could turn Day into Knight, and make a Lady Day at Michelmas.' Of the unmarried girls in Calcutta there is no doubt that the greatest beauty of them all, according to contemporaries, was Miss Sanderson. Wherever she went the young admirers surrounded her like a swarm of flies but she encouraged all and encouraged none. She must have had a great personality and a sweetness of temper combined with a great sense of humour that proved irresistible. On one occasion, it was told, before a grand ball at Government House, she let it be known privately to a number of young men, who were all given the information with a vow of secrecy, that she would convey her favours on the one who turned up at the ball in a special livery that she had invented herself. When the great night arrived no fewer than sixteen young aspiring suitors came to the ball in identical outfits of a pea-green hue trimmed with pink lace. But umbrage was not taken and she danced with all her young beaux in turn and, when the ball was over, they all accompanied her home marching by the side of her palanquin. Alas for all these young hopefuls the delectable Miss Sanderson married Richard Barwell and died in Calcutta in 1774 after only two years of marriage.

Her successor as the belle of Calcutta was the famous Emma Wrangham. She was the daughter of William Wrangham, a member of the Council at St Helena, and had come out to Bengal to stay with some friends of her father. Not only had she a good figure, attractive looks and a graceful manner, but she was a tom-boy to outdo all tom-boys. As William Hickey wrote:

> *Her natural flow of spirits frequently led her into extravagances and follies of rather too masculine a nature, instead of seating herself like other women on horse-back, she rode like a man astride, would leap over*

any hedge or ditch that even the most zealous sportsmen were dubious of attempting. She rode several matches and succeeded against the best and most experienced jockeys. She was likewise an excellent shot, rarely missing her bird; understood the present fashionable service of pugilism, and would without hesitation knock a man down if he presumed to offer her the slightest insult; in short she stopped at nothing that met her fancy, however wild or eccentric, executing whatever she attempted with a naivety and ease and elegance that were irresistible.

Emma was obviously the centre of much gossip and speculation in Calcutta society and we find constant mention of her in Hicky's *Gazette* either in her own name or under various pseudonyms such as 'Turban Conquest', 'Hooks Turban' and the 'Chinsura Belle'. Under 'Racing Intelligence' in the *Gazette* she appears as the famous filly St Helena. But the scurrilous Hicky must have had a soft spot for her for he relates that at a ball in Chandernagore 'many very graceful minuets were walked by the beauties of the age, amongst whom the inimitable Miss W... excelled in every step and motion of her foot.'

Emma Wrangham finally married on 27th May 1782, at Chinsurah, John Bristow, a senior merchant who settled on her £40,000. She presented him with four children who were her pride and joy. She left India to return to England in 1790.

One other beauty must also be mentioned and that is Mrs Wheler, the wife of a member of the Supreme Council, who arrived in Calcutta in December 1777. She was one of the guests of honour at the grand ball given by Francis at which he finally fell in love with 'la belle Catherine'. He wrote: 'She appeared in public for the fast time at our ball in wonderful splendour. At the sight of her looks all our beauties stared in envy and admiration. I never saw the like before.' Unfortunately for the beaux of Calcutta she soon succumbed to the Indian climate.

A description of the ladies of Calcutta would not be complete without mention of the 'bibis' or Indian mistresses of whom most bachelors had at least one. Not only did they give comfort where it was needed in bed, but through them many young writers and officers gained a greater insight into the customs and usages of the country, together with a knowledge of the native language, than they otherwise might have done. They were accepted as part of life throughout the whole of the eighteenth century and in a number of cases the children of such liaisons were sent home to be educated. No eyebrows would have been raised to see the following advertisement in 1792: 'A neat compact and new-built garden house is advertised for private sale for 1500 sicca rupees. It is pleasantly situated in Chowringhy, and from its contiguity to Fort William peculiarly well calculated for an officer; it would like-wise be a handsome provision for a native lady or child.'

Calcutta was not, however, all enjoyment and pleasure. The nearness of the mass of jungle to the settlement and also the number of foetid jheels was presumed to account for the prevalence of a disease, called pucka fever during the eighteenth century. According to Carey, Mrs Kindersley wrote of it 'as the illness of which most persons die in Calcutta; it frequently carries off a person in a few hours – the doctors esteem it the highest degree of putridity.'

The general state of sanitation in Calcutta however, makes one wonder not at the deaths that took place but rather at the number that survived. In a letter to the *Bengal Gazette* in April 1780 a correspondent wrote with regard to the condition of the main supply of drinking water – the great tank in Lall Diggee:

> *As I was jogging along in my palanquin yesterday, I could not avoid observing without a kind of secret concern for the health of several of my tender and delicate friends, a string of pariah dogs, without an ounce of hair on some of them, and in the last stage of the mange, plunge in and refresh themselves very comfortably in the great tank. I don't mean to throw the least shadow of reflection upon the sentinels, as the present condition of the palisades is such that it would take a Battalion*

> at least of the most nimble-footed sepoys to prevent them. I was led insensibly to reflect upon the small attention that is paid by people in general, to a point of such unspeakable importance to their health and longevity as the choice and care of their water, the great vehicle of our nourishment.'

Another correspondent writing on the subject of sanitation says:

> Would you believe it, that in the very centre of the opulent city, and almost under our noses, there is a spot of ground measuring not more than 600 square yards, used as a public burying ground by the Portuguese inhabitants, where there are annually interred upon a median not less than 400 dead bodies; that these bodies are generally buried without coffins, and in graves dug so exceedingly shallow as not to admit of their being covered with much more than a foot and a half of earth, in so much that, after a heavy fall of rain, some parts of them have been known to appear above ground; that when the pressure of the atmosphere happens to be at any time diminished, and the effluvium arising from the accumulating mass of corruption has room to expand, the stench becomes intolerable and sufficient to give the air a pestilential taint! Moreover the quantity of matter necessarily flowing from it, assimilating with the springs of the earth, can scarcely fail to impart to the water in the adjacent wells and tanks a morbid and noxious quality, laying by this means the foundation of various diseases among the poorer sort of people, who are obliged to drink from it; nor can those in more affluent circumstances, from the natural indolence and deception of servants, promise themselves absolute exemption from it.

Again from another source we learn that 'the dead bodies of indigent natives were dragged naked through the crowded thoroughfares to the river, into which they were thrown; and sometimes a corpse in a state of putrefaction was left lying in close proximity to some crowded bazaar, until the distressed neighbours would liberally fee the haris or scavengers charged with the duty of removing it. The country around the city was very insalubrious and epidemic diseases often devastated the settlement.'

But sanitation was not the only problem suffered by the people of Calcutta for both robbery and dacoity were rife and here again we turn to Carey:

> *Murders and robberies were of very frequent occurrence in the heart of the city: and, in the suburbs, armed gangs of these marauders sometimes boldly paraded the highways by torchlight. Within the city, where offences against life and property were perpetrated more cautiously, craft took the place of effrontery. The single thief committed his nightly depredations, having his naked body smeared over with oil, so that it was next to impossible to hold him… The dacoits infested the Sunderbands, and the river leading to and from Dacca. We hear of them coming in bands of seven, fourteen and twenty-four boats, and attacking Europeans as well as natives, and stripping them of their goods, and when opposed adding murder to their misdeeds.*

Mr Burgh, on his way to Calcutta, was killed and thrown into the river on 3rd November 1788; two European gentlemen proceeding towards Dacca, were the next day attacked and left without even their clothes; and on that evening Mr Willes proceeding from Sylhet, fell in with the same party and though he escaped into the jungle, his boats were plundered.

from

Original Letters from India, 1779-1815

ELIZA FAY

Letter XV   Calcutta, 22 May 1780

MY DEAR FRIENDS,
    I may now indeed call for your congratulations since after an eventful period of twelve months and eighteen days, I have at length reached the place for which I have so long sighed, to which I have looked with innumerable hopes and fears, and where I have long rested my most rational expectations of future prosperity and comfort.

Calcutta, you know, is on the Hoogly, a branch of the Ganges, and as you enter Garden-Reach which extends about nine miles below the town, the most interesting views which can possibly be imagined greet the eye. The banks of the river are as one may say absolutely studded with elegant mansions, called here as at Madras, Garden-houses. These houses are surrounded by grass and lawns, which descend to the waters edge, and present a constant succession of whatever can delight the eye, or bespeak wealth and elegance in the owners. The noble appearance of the river also, which is much wider than the Thames at London bridge, together with the amazing variety of vessels continually passing on its surface, add to the beauty of the scene. I was much pleased with the snake boat in particular. Budgerows somewhat resembling our city barges, are very common — many of these are spacious enough to accommodate a large family. Besides these the different kinds of pleasure boats intermixed with mercantile vessels, and ships of war, render the whole a magnificent and beautiful moving picture; at once exhilarating the heart, and charming the senses: for every object of sight is viewed through a medium that heightens its attraction in this brilliant climate.

The town of Calcutta reaches along the eastern bank of the Hoogly; as you come up past Fort William and the Esplanade it has a beautiful appearance. Esplanade-row, as it is called, which fronts the fort, seems to be composed of palaces; the whole range, except what is taken up by the Government and Council houses, is occupied by the principal gentlemen of the settlement — no person being allowed to reside in Fort William, but such as are attached to the Army, gives it greatly the advantage over Fort St George, which is so incumbered with buildings of one kind or another that it has more the look of a town than of a military garrison. *Our* fort is so well kept and everything in such excellent order, that it is quite a curiosity to see it — all the slopes, banks and ramparts, are covered with the richest verdure, which completes the enchantment of the scene. Indeed, the general aspect of the country is astonishing; notwithstanding the extreme heat (the thermometer seldom standing below ninety in the afternoon) I never saw a more vivid green than adorns the surrounding fields — not that parched miserable look our lands have during the summer heats; large fissures opening in the earth, as if all vegetation were suspended; in fact, the copious dews which fall at night, restore moisture to the ground, and cause a short thick grass to spring up, which makes the finest food imaginable for the cattle. Bengal mutton, always good, is at this period excellent — I must not forget to tell you that there is a very good raceground at a short distance from Calcutta, which is a place of fashionable resort, for morning and evening airings.

from

Show Your Tongue

GÜNTER GRASS

Fᴵʀꜱᴛ ᴛᴏ ᴛʜᴇ ᴛᴇᴍᴘʟᴇ ᴏꜰ Kᴀʟɪ, ɪɴᴛᴏ ᴛʜᴇ ʜᴏʟʏ ᴏꜰ ʜᴏʟɪᴇꜱ. Next, Daud Haider leads us to Calcutta's oldest bathing and cremation facility, right beside the pier for the ferry to Howrah on the other side of the Hooghly River: the Nimtallah Ghat. Just as many Bengalis are not bashful about pushing up close to us, wanting to see, to touch everything, showing no fear of body contact except within their caste system, so now, too, they let us watch as they bathe, are massaged, and burn their corpses. But without Daud along, we would not have risked entering the temple, moving in among the bathers, drawing close to the pyres.

All three sites have old garbage and fresh garbage in common. Kali, a bogeywoman in black granite, adorned by the priests with gold glitter and flowers, is showered by more and more glitter and flowers as the pilgrims, who have been standing in long lines outside, are finally led into the orbit of the 'Terrible Mother.' The temple attendants guide and push the neverending throng, collecting money at the various entrances. With all the others, we too walk barefoot over mangled flowers. Shove, are shoved, slip on slick soles. From our feet, mounting nausea, horror. We've had enough; but Daud (laughing) wants us to watch. The odor of stale flowers clings to us with persistence. In front of the temple: beggars, prostitutes, booths full of devotional kitsch, the bustle of shopping.

At the bathing facility, a fat man's back is being walloped by the knees of a masseur while the fat man bites on a stick that many before him have bitten. On the steps down to the river, people sit, waiting, the brackish brew still ahead of them. The slow movements of the bathers, slowed as if by dream. In the loamy yellow water of the Ganges drift fecal matter, floral wreaths, single blossoms, charred wood. Set distant now by a river breadth, the industrial plants of Howrah. Sky daubed with smoke banners and monsoon clouds. In the anteroom of the bathing area: towel recital, betel vendors, also opium pipes on display next to head scarves, plastic bowls.

The crematorium has a special department for electrical incineration. Two corpses wrapped in cloths — a young man, an old woman — surrounded by family. In an adjoining building, which serves as an inn, groups are crouching, some sleeping, waiting their turn. As everywhere on Calcutta's north side, the architectural style of the buildings is Victorian, with an admixture of Indian detail. Someday Nimtallah Ghat will be protected by landmark status, even if it takes the assistance of the World Bank.

In one of the crematory courtyards, all of them open to the river, a male corpse burns within a pile of wood. Two other pyres give off labored, smudgy smoke, because the wood is still wet from the recent floods. Reinforcements of brushwood, kerosene. The smoke, indolent, loiters. Along with his helpers, the Brahman, a grimy bald man, keeps trying to fan the fire. On a pyre farther down, an old woman, not yet covered by the crisscross of wood, lies amid the farewells — howls that begin and end abruptly — of her daughters and grandchildren. Sticking out from under the shroud, head, shoulders, the feet. Because they are rubbed with ghee, clarified butter, the exposed limbs and the fleshless skull-like head glisten. More garlands thrown on. The flat smoke of the neighboring fire drifts slowly, very slowly, down to the river.

Not even the ceremonial howling dampens the workaday, almost cheerful mood. Along the front of the row of bathing and cremation buildings are booths, tea kitchens, and huts where prostitutes wait. Among the shifting throngs, fidgety goats and cows. Behind them, the tracks of the Circular Rail, and freight trains moving. On the other side of the railroad — the crossing safeguarded by a double gate — narrow slum, leaning against factory walls, runs parallel to the tracks. Daud Haider explains that more and more slums are forming along railroad tracks since there is no other place for them.

Behind the track crossing, where Nimtallah Ghat Street begins, and towering above the huts of the slum, piles of stacked wood for sale as fuel for cremations. As I sketch, I find order in the tangle of timber. Bald branches, pale flayed trunks. The wood is weighed out on metal scales. Only the rich can afford sufficient wood. The free-market economy, death as an overhead expense, like everywhere else.

Off to Alipore, where the rich reside and the consuls with their spouses have cloistered themselves for ease of social visits. The suburb dates back to Warren Hastings, who built his villa here and had the marble for his staircase brought from Benares. We visit the National Library, the former residence of the British viceroy. Over a million books, all exposed to Calcutta's special climate, the director jokes, and points to air-conditioned quarters in the new annex.

The Victorian reading room: stalwart tables, reading lamps of antiquarian charm, comfortable chairs, as if colonial power intended to stay on forever and ever. And everywhere (as everywhere in the world) students: suggestive of application, of interest, even. During their student days, Daud, his friend

Sourav, and Sourav's wife, Tripaty, who have joined us, found all their sourcebooks on Indian and Western literature here. (All in English. Neither Daud nor Sourav, who is also a writer, can read poems written in Urdu or Tamil.)

In the spacious stacks, through whose channels we are rapidly towed, six underpaid library employees lead the battle (defeat already conceded) against the mold-producing climate, frequently interrupted by the consumption of tea or preparations for their next strike.

On to the modern annex — which, lacking Victorian trimmings, needs no commentary on its international ugliness — where rare, often unique, books, scrolls, and manuscripts have found rescue in climate control. We look at Tamil script etched on narrow strips of palm leaf.

In an institution tended so carefully for reasons of state, the filth, strewn about or in piles, is particularly eye-catching. Just endure it: the primal stench of the men's toilet right next to the cafeteria. But what compels the studious young ladies of Bengal, always fresh as blossoms in their saris, to throw their sanitary napkins on the floor of the women's toilet? There are piles of them, Ute reports, and her eyes, all Pomeranian censure, pursue the graceful daughters of the ambitious middle class.

Later, Daud leads us to the Behala Manton slum on the city's west side. Within its small quarters, perhaps sixty by two hundred yards, live more than six thousand people, four thousand of whom are children. In stalls roomier than the huts, booths, and sheds, stand about a hundred black milk cows in resident swarms of flies. The slum and the cows belong to a man who lives outside Calcutta and exacts between fifty and a hundred rupees per month per hut. Barely eighteen inches wide, the passageways between the huts are open sewers that empty, to the right, into a long canal filled with the torpid cloacal tide. I see only one water pump; I'm told there is a second, by the cows.

Only one child, who is proudly displayed to us, goes to school. A quarter of the adults have found employment: as sweepers or ricksha pullers. An invitation, energetic but friendly, to look inside the hovels. Six, seven people to a shack. Because of the daily danger of floods during the monsoon season, the beds — or, rather, the common bed — is raised on bricks. It takes up most of the room. Under the bed, beneath a patchwork blanket, and in a lean-to nook lie, hang, are piled the paltry possessions: shiny aluminum pots, water jugs, storage jugs. Everything emphatically clean, the stamped clay floor swept, the pillows on the family bed, five or seven of them, neatly lined up. And always attended by divinities, in brightly colored pictures. I would maintain that these wretched asylums, Calcutta's millions of slum huts, are cleaner than the rest of the city's chaotic checkerboard: a desperate cleanliness, wrested from misery.

When, shortly before Durga Puja, virtually every quarter of the city stood under water, the Behala Manton slum was also evacuated. Only a few of the huts collapsed, they tell me. But the passageways, the open sewers between the rows, and the main lateral lanes are still nothing but a morass. Yet crowds, hordes of children, water bearers, all sorts of burdens carried on heads, burdens that, no matter how bulky and projecting, manage to make it past one another. Above all this, the acrid smoke of open fires fed with cakes of dried cow dung.

As everywhere else in the city, the women and children here too follow in the wake of the cows, collect the dung, dump it into tubs, mix it with chopped rice straw and coal dust, make a paste, and from the paste make cakes that are pressed to dry on the walls. Each cake imprinted by fingers, the fingers of women and children. In every quarter of the city, even near Park Street, on the walls of the old English cemetery, on culverts tall as men, next to the subway construction sites, a gigantic ruin that feeds its contractors — everywhere, but especially on fire walls or walls around villas, which are embedded with broken glass to prevent access and ward off the evil eye, those cakes are drying, and all of them, as though works of art, are signed with three fingerprints.

And so once more, beauty intrudes in some purely utilitarian, ad hoc item. All framed and pedestaled works of art should be forced to compete with such scenes from reality. I saw walls filled with dung cakes that marched in stirring order to the left, to the right, yet leaving space for Calcutta's murals, the hammer and sickle, the Congress hand, and other party symbols — as if tolerating politics.

... and whatever the time of day, as if there were no time, old women squat on curbstones and rinse out bottles, or wait, with nothing in their hands, for the day to pass.

The two of us at night, with books under the mosquito net, as if searching for footing on the old fat tomes. Ute knows what comforts her. We have to stay up late, reading *Joseph and His Brothers*, a legend both strangely relevant to India and yet so out of place.

And each evening the pavement dwellers, who, if they have work, are often sweepers in nearby middle-class households, sweep their own spot for sleep on the cracked pavement, the broom — their hallmark — always with them. There they lie, as if sloshed from a bucket.

In a semi-ruin in the Moslem quarter, near the Great Mosque. There, in holes that were once rooms, are quartered six, seven young medical assistants, earning five hundred fifty rupees — less than fifty dollars — a month. They are friendly, ask questions, hardly wait for answers, bring me a chair, a piece of cardboard so I can sketch more comfortably (from the fifth floor) noonday nappers on the roof terraces nearby. The young doctors regret they cannot offer tea; all their water has to be drawn in buckets from a hole on the ground floor.

On every flat roof, in every direction, shops, shacks, family hovels, piles of trash. I count with my pen, as though having to establish a lasting inventory: tin pipes, tires, scrap wood, jute sacks stuffed with paper, baskets, earthen pots, bicycle parts, snarls of wire, bottles being sorted...

Later Daud pushes us down side streets and through narrow passages into areas that seem forgotten. Inner courtyards, where men from Orissa — only men — live, they have found work in Calcutta, far away, in place and time, from their families. Then past an Anglican church, waiting in cool classicism for Sundays to come; then through the Armenian cemetery, where among the many gravestones, one declares that long before Job Charnock built his first shed on this accursed spot (and called it Calcutta), Armenian merchants had set up trade.

Later, suddenly, in the midst of this thickly settled decay, we find ourselves standing before a huge, grandiose synagogue, alien and earnest, maintained intact and clean by its remnant congregation. Behind the iron grating of the gate, steps free of weeds lead to the locked temple.

from

In Clive's Footsteps

PETER HOLT

B Y THE NEXT MORNING THE TRAIN HIT THE OUTSKIRTS OF Calcutta. I stood in the corridor and talked to one of Calcutta's citizens, an engineer called Barun who was returning from working on an irrigation project in Tamil Nadu.

Barun knew a thing or two about water, particularly the water in Calcutta. 'Calcutta is an unhealthy place,' he advised. 'Do not even dream of drinking from a tap. Brush your teeth with cola if you have to. I got jaundice from the water so I should know. Anyone who can afford it drinks bottled mineral water.'

Clive had actually visited Calcutta once before to recover from a bout of fever he had picked up in Madras. After the stifling humidity of the south, Calcutta was popular as a health cure in the cool months of October and November. Listening to Barun drone on, and gazing out of the train window at the fume-laden sky, modern Calcutta did not seem much like a health resort.

I remembered a sad tale I had just read in my newspaper. A youth called Mohamed Nausad bought something called a puchka from a street vendor in the centre of Calcutta. After devouring the last morsel, he complained of stomach pains and was admitted to hospital. Death followed soon afterwards.

'What is a puchka?' I asked Barun.

'It is a snack with a lot of very hot spices,' he said. I vowed not to go within a dozen paces of a puchka.

We pulled into Howrah station and I exchanged farewells with the Kerala communists. They had eager looks on their faces and couldn't wait to exchange views with their Marxist colleagues. Barun wished me well. He had warmed to the puchka theme and had got onto the subject of which antibiotics to take in case of amoebic dysentery.

Howrah station has been described as hell on earth, full of diesel fumes, filth and noise. It is a place where you cannot move without tripping over a beggar, a seething mass of homeless all there for the specific purpose of hassling arriving and departing passengers for money.

But the station was surprisingly relaxed. I had known worse chaos at rural bus stands in Tamil Nadu. A surly porter grabbed my bag and we pushed through the throng of people with none of the sleeve-tugging and cries of 'money, master' that I had been led to expect. There was no problem finding a taxi and I asked the driver to take me into the city centre. All in all, a comparatively painless experience.

In the streets outside the station it was another matter: a fantastic confusion and anarchy that is Calcutta's masses. The number of people in the city is one of the East's great mysteries. The official government figure is 1.1 million. Locals talk of over 20 million. The number climbs alarmingly when food stocks run low in rural West Bengal and peasants advance on the city looking for work. On one day alone you might find 80,000 new residents moving in from the villages. Even in Clive's day there were 400,000 people in Calcutta, with only 2,000 Europeans.

AFTER MORE THAN A MONTH IN CALCUTTA I DECIDED, ON
the basis that things couldn't get much worse, that it was a city
in urgent need of a disaster. Perhaps a calamity like a plague,
famine, flood or earthquake might stir the inhabitants to
positive action for once in their lives.

Calcutta was founded on 24 August 1690, one hundred
years before Clive's first visit. She was the creation of Job
Charnock, an English merchant affiliated to the East India
Company. Charnock recognised the value of three small
villages — Sutanati, Govindour and Kalikata — as an ideal
location for 'quiet trade'. Calcutta takes its name from the
last of these villages, which in turn was named after the black
Hindu goddess Kali. The dreadful Kali is the wife of Shiva,
and is portrayed as a bloodthirsty, axe-wielding psychopath,
dripping in blood, with the heads of her victims hanging on
string around her neck. In normal circumstances the likes of
Kali would be taken in for police questioning. But in Calcutta
she is revered as the city's patron goddess. The similarly evil
appearance of Calcutta must be more than mere coincidence.
The forces of Hindu destiny at work again?

Job Charnock was a godly man. He distinguished himself
by rescuing an Indian widow, who was about to commit suttee
and burn herself on her husband's funeral pyre. Charnock
whisked her away and married her the same night in a Christian
ceremony. She was a great beauty and Charnock loved her
dearly. He was distraught when she died twenty years later.
Thereafter, on each anniversary of her death, he sacrificed a
live cockerel at her tomb.

By the time Clive reached Calcutta the city was beginning
its social climb that would make it the London or Paris of the
East. Merchants were on a relentless crusade to make money.
Grand Italianate mansions were going up on the banks of the
Hughli River. Crates of claret and hock were brought in to
water the thirsty inhabitants. Food stores on a level with Mr
Fortnum's and Mr Mason's Piccadilly Emporium were importing

delicacies like Durham mustard, pickled oysters and reindeer tongue. It was *de rigueur* for Europeans to have a large retinue of servants and everyone competed for the lavishness of their carriages.

Behind the palatial front lines in the native quarter of 'Black Town', it was a different story. Clive might have seen sights that were splendidly described half-a-century later by Reginald Heber, Bishop of Calcutta: '...deep, black and dingy, with narrow, crooked streets, huts of earth baked in the sun, or of twisted bamboos, interspersed with ruinous brick bazaars, pools of dirty water...a crowd of people in the streets, beyond anything to be seen in London, some dressed in tawdry silks and brocades...religious mendicants with no clothing but their long hair and beards in elf locks, their faces painted white or yellow, their beads in one ghastly lean hand, and the other stretched out like a bird's claw, to receive donations... a constant clamour of voices, a constant creaking of cart wheels, which are never greased in India... add to all this a villainous smell of garlic, rancid coconut oil, sour butter and stagnant ditches.'

The ungreased cart wheels are still there, but they have been joined by the internal combustion engine. And it is the traffic in twentieth century Calcutta that gets to your senses first.

The taxi, a battered yellow crate, lurched out of the station at breakneck speed. The driver seemed unconcerned that he was in charge of a machine with the aerodynamics of a house brick. Then came the mammoth traffic jam that is daytime Calcutta. The driver sharply decelerated and we crawled over potholes. A multitude of people scurried about their business like deranged locusts. We dodged marauding cows, who seemed to have developed a traffic sense, and goats, who had not. The driver leaned out of his window to shoo the creatures away.

We crossed Howrah Bridge to the east bank of the Hughli. Bicyclists wobbled dangerously in the middle of the road until trucks forced them onto the verge. Policemen in grey-white uniforms blew whistles and tried vainly to look official. You hardly noticed the traffic lights. A grimy layer of dirt covered the bulbs so that they emitted only a dull glow.

The rear bumpers of the buses were decorated with demonic figures and slogans like 'Danger. Use Horn'. This was unnecessary advice in a city where honking your horn is as natural as a West Ham fan shouting encouragement from the terraces. A fire engine, bells a-ringing and firemen clinging grimly to the sides, added to the cacophony. And at the core of this madness were the trams. Long, stately trams, proceeding confidently down the tracks. They set the pace of the traffic and were treated with great respect by motorists and pedestrians alike. A Calcutta tram does not stop for anyone.

The Paragon Hotel was typical of the cheap lodgings in Calcutta's tourist ghetto of Sudder Street. 'Drug addiction prohibited', cautioned a sign in the lobby. The aroma of cannabis wafted from the dormitories. The Paragon was packed with young European backpackers, who insisted on wearing hippy garb like harem pants and embroidered waistcoats over bare chests. All very Jimi Hendrix *circa* '68. The mode of attire must have seemed quaintly old-fashioned to the youth of Calcutta for whom the height of trendiness was a permed, crinkly, slicked-back Michael Jackson haircut, stone-washed denims, fake Lacoste sports shirts, and trainers allegedly made by Reebok, but probably copies knocked up in a Bombay sweatshop.

My first night in Calcutta I shared a room with a Frenchman called Pascal. He lived in Hong Kong where he worked as a film extra playing Westerners in Chinese kung fu movies. His other occupation was smuggling. 'Maybe pocket TVs from Singapore or gold from Hong Kong. It pays for my travelling…and my head.' Pascal tapped his large Gallic nose. He was using heroin and was now considering running narcotics into Europe. I thought he was excessively stupid. He couldn't have looked more like a smuggler, a customs officer's dream. He wore a silk hippy waistcoat over a bare chest. A thin pigtail ran down the back of his neck. Above his ears, the sides of his head were shaved to a fine stubble, leaving a bushy, black thatch on top. He might as well have gone through the green channel at an airport yelling: 'Hey boys! Look at me. I'm a drug runner.'

Pascal was ill. He had become addicted to heroin while bumming around Thailand and now his habit was taking up an increasing amount of his time. I first met him by the entrance to the Paragon. He was going through cold turkey, sniffing and shivering, waiting for one of the many Sudder Street dealers to return with a gram of the low-grade Pakistani heroin that is known as 'brown sugar'. The bulk of India's heroin comes from Pakistan, a country where twenty per cent of the male population is alleged to be addicted to the drug.

My room-mate was not a happy person. The dealer was already three hours late. More than anywhere else in the world, perhaps, it must be a nightmare being addicted to heroin in India. Unpunctuality is the norm; business appointments are seldom met on time and dope dealers are no exception. If the man says he'll be on a street corner at, say, midday, you can reckon on 2 pm. Judging by Pascal's ashen pallor, Bengali black marketeers were worse time-keepers than most. He was shaking and coughing and spitting phlegm into a grubby handkerchief. By mid-afternoon, the dealer had returned and the Frenchman was a lot more cheerful. I found him in our room lying on his bed having smoked some of the brown powder. He looked tediously vacant and would not be good company. I left him and set out to explore the city.

In the alleyway outside the Paragon the filth by the side of the road was worse than at the end of an overcrowded party in a small London flat. Rubbish was piled high. A man threw the murky contents of a bucket into my path, splashing my trousers. A mother sat by a vegetable stall picking lice out of her child's hair. The child cried in pain. The gutters brimmed black with water that seemed to scream, 'Cholera!' The World Health Organization has reported that 'the Calcutta area... forms the starting point for a long distance spread of cholera.' The city's health officials claim the disease is presently in check. This can be only by the grace of God.

In Sudder Street a group of Indians were crowded around an elderly monkey, which had somehow found its way into the centre of Calcutta. I reckoned it must be a pretty senile monkey to want to leave rural Bengal for life in the city. Considering the Indians' often cruel treatment of animals, I didn't give much for the monkey's chances. At Calcutta Zoo, for example, it is considered great fun to poke the animals through the bars with long sticks. But this monkey was attracting a surprising amount of compassion. Its fur was tatty and it was obviously very hungry. A beggar threw an orange. The monkey pounced on the fruit and quickly devoured it. A small boy, keen to show off his macho side in front of his elders, threw a stone at the animal. The crowd rounded on the boy and loudly ticked him off. Perhaps they thought their visitor was an incarnation of the Hindu monkey god, Hanuman. Monkeys are revered in India. The superstitious believe that they were once men, but were given tails and hair for their laziness.

Monkeys have also played a traditional part in sorting out village feuds. Rather than demand satisfaction, an aggrieved party waited until he knew the rains were coming. Then he climbed on the roof of the house of the man who had insulted him and poured rice all over the tiles. From their perches in the surrounding trees the monkeys could see the tempting morsels. They descended on the roof and devoured the rice, much of which had fallen in the cracks between the tiles. The monkeys solved this problem by pulling up the tiles, thus unroofing the house. Then the rain came and the water poured through. The trick was to leave the rice scattering until the last moment before the monsoon broke. If the moment was judged properly, you could ruin your neighbour's property in a matter of minutes.

I left the crowd and walked along Sudder Street dodging hawkers selling Punjabi oranges. 'Yaagh-yaagh,' they shouted. I could not work out whether 'yaagh' meant orange in Bengali or whether the salesmen suffered from a speech defect. I passed kerbside barbers shaving their customer's hair in the light of street lamps; pools of soapy water lay around their stools. Sugar cane juice salesmen were squeezing the cane through huge mangle contraptions to which were attached bells. Each time the wheel turned it jangled as if to let customers know that juice was being served. Regiments of cab drivers muttered, 'Want taxi?' to any reasonably affluent-looking passer-by.

I turned into one of the small cafés dotted along Sudder Street where I ordered a banana milkshake. The café's owner lent me his copy of the Calcutta newspaper *The Telegraph*. The paper included a 'Barter Bank', a column where Calcutta's young readers could advertise items they wanted to swap. 'Aquarium, novels and mini soft drink bottles', announced Ajay Gupta from the suburb of New Alipore. 'I offer an aquarium in good condition, two P. G. Wodehouse novels and five Campa Cola mini bottles in exchange for fifty posters of Samantha Fox on roller skates or anything of corresponding value.' Perhaps fifty posters was slightly excessive, and how could the value of Miss Fox begin to correspond with that of Mr Wodehouse? But I liked the roller skates idea.

Was Ajay Gupta typical of Calcutta youth? A party of male students sat on the next table chatting noisily. One of them turned to me and asked the usual questions. Where was I from? How old was I? Was I married? Why not? His name was Vinod, and he had just started studying medicine.

He then asked me a question that I had heard many times already in India. How could he go about getting a job in Britain? He was a young, bright man of twenty-two and he was desperate to leave Calcutta.

He talked about his life in the city. 'India is the black hole of Asia, Calcutta is the black hole of India. There is no future here. I have been trying to get a good job for a year, but no luck. There is too much unemployment.

'When I talk like this to foreigners they ask why I want to leave India. They say I will not like it in the West. There is too much rudeness, it is a bad way of life, they say.' Vinod laughed bitterly. 'It is easy for them to say that. They can leave India whenever they want and go home to good jobs and roads without holes in them and cities where no one sleeps on the pavement. I hate these foreigners for their arrogance. They see India as nicely old-fashioned and polite. I would rather have the rudeness of the West and a good job and maybe a car. Here, if I am lucky, I will have a car by the time I am forty.

'It is easy for foreigners to say there is no need for material possessions because they have them back home. It is easy for them to talk. When they are forty they will have cars, homes of their own and gardens where their children can play. I will not.'

Depressing stuff. I left the café and began my quest for Clive's Calcutta, the city where at least *he* made his fortune. I walked up Sudder Street, negotiated the ferocious traffic on Chowringhee and crossed over to the sprawling expanse of open ground that is the Maidan. This is the two square miles of parkland that has been the site of countless political rallies and where, on weekends, up to ten thousand young Calcuttans turn out to play cricket. Here also is Calcutta's military bastion, Fort William, partly built by Clive and still in use as an army base. The original fort was in a severely dilapidated state when Clive first arrived. It was as Governor of Bengal, on his last visit to India, that he supervised the construction of the present ramparts and barracks.

I moved on to the Victoria Memorial, a lump of solidly early twentieth-century British building standing at the southern end of the Maidan. A statue of Queen Victoria at her grimmest looks down on tourists entering the surrounding gardens. Beautiful is not a word that springs to mind when describing the Victoria Memorial, although it looked quite attractive under night-time floodlights. The Vic is what British rule was all about. It was built with a firm, stately hand and a curious, heavy mix of classical European design with local influences. The man behind its conception, the viceroy Lord Curzon, saw it as the British answer to the Taj Mahal. Needless to say, it goes wide of the mark.

Inside the VM was one of the few statues of Clive still left in India. Until an upsurge of Indian nationalism in the late 1950s there were busts of Clive all over the sub-continent. Bearing in mind that he had been chiefly responsible for laying the foundations of the British Empire in India, the government of Jawaharlal was understandably sensitive about prolonging his memory. The statues had to go. Clive's sculpture in the Vic is a marble replica of the original bronze by Tweed that stands in London. Very imposing it is too, depicting the man as his usual doom-laden self, weighed down by responsibility and nagged by ill health.

I walked until early evening and returned to the hotel via Park Street where the rich have their apartments, a fact that was difficult to believe. It was just like everywhere else in the city: broken sewers spewed filthy water down what remained of the gutters at the side of the wide boulevard; a regiment of beggars stuck out their bowls for alms. You were just as likely to see a beggar, both legs missing, sores covering his body, lying on the pavement outside the entrance to an expensive block on Park Street as in one of the worst slums.

Back at the Paragon, the Frenchman Pascal was still in a semi-comatose state. He planned to take the train next morning to Varanasi, India's holiest city. 'It will be better for my head than Calcutta,' he explained. Bearing in mind his condition, I agreed that he was probably right.

I slept fitfully my first night in Calcutta. Even after a shower, the humidity and grime clung on obstinately. Outside my window in the early hours came the sounds of a series of dog fights; incredible canine battles that sounded as if the One Hundred and One Dalmatians had drawn against the Hound of the Baskervilles — and some of the Hound's mates. There was a savage barking and roaring with yelps of pain from the vanquished. At 3 am I left my room to peer into the alleyway behind the hotel. Three dogs, whose ancestry owed much to the Airedale, had set about an animal, whose ginger coat might have been quite elegant were it not covered in mange. Ginger had a torn ear. The smell of blood enraged his attackers. A fight to the death was prevented only by a local resident who threw a flower pot at these canine hooligans. The dogs gave up and fled into the night.

Back to the reason why Clive was in Calcutta in 1757, the year that was to establish British rule in India. It was his task to avenge the deaths of the Europeans who had died in the infamous Black Hole.

English schoolboys will tell you that the Black Hole of Calcutta was the single most important event in Anglo-Indian history. You will hear that on 20 June 1756, the wicked, debauched and French-backed Nawab of Bengal, Siraj-ud-daula imprisoned 146 Europeans overnight in Calcutta's Fort William in a cell no larger than 250 square feet. You will also hear that by the next morning 123 of the prisoners were dead from suffocation.

Worse. A lady was among the prisoners. An English lady at that. Mary Carey survived the night only to be dragged off to Siraj-ud-daula's harem, thereby adding charges of abduction with an intent to rape to the Nawab's already unimpressive record of murder on 123 counts. Shocking stuff. Englishmen were up in arms. They wanted the Black Hole avenged and Clive was the man for the job.

Contemporary historians say the Black Hole story was an example of eighteenth-century British propaganda at its best. According to Mark Bence-Jones the figures are poppycock.

The myth was based on the writings of a survivor, John Zephaniah Holwell, described by Bence-Jones as a 'talented but not always truthful propagandist'. When one considers the size of the cell, Holwell's figures have to be mathematically impossible, and it is now thought that anything between thirty-nine and sixty-nine people were incarcerated, with eighteen to forty-three deaths. But, as Bence-Jones puts it, 'Even for this lesser number it would have been horror enough to spend one of the hottest and most sultry nights of the Bengal June crowded together in a room fourteen feet by eighteen, unventilated but for two small barred windows.'

Whatever the death toll, the whole sorry affair seems to have been one huge cock-up that started after Siraj-ud-daula was taken not unexpectedly drunk after a twenty-four-hour alcohol and opium binge. Well, wouldn't you celebrate if you'd just captured a fort? The Nawab's exasperated captain of the guard shoved the prisoners into the first cell he could find. In the euphoria of victory everyone was screaming and shouting, and how was the captain to know the room was a bit on the small side? Only acting on orders, guv'nor.

The tag 'Black Hole' is also misleading. Far from being exclusively concerned with events in Calcutta, prison cells in military barracks all over Britain's colonies were, until only one hundred years ago, known as black holes. The London newspapers were also outraged by the detention of Mary Carey, who was described as an English woman. In fact, brave Mary was a foreigner, who only ended up in the cell because she refused to be separated from her English husband. Would the British public have been so concerned about her fate had they known she was a Portuguese half-caste?

Despite the fuss back in Britain, Siraj-ud-daula, chief baddie of the piece, was not in the slightest concerned about his actions. A few days later he was back in his capital of Murshidibad organising an elephant fight and tiger hunt. Anyone who can go big-game hunting after annoying the enemy to the point that they are about to totally disrupt your life has to be quite cool. A case of sod politics, let's bag a tiger.

These days Indians certainly aren't taught in school about the Black Hole. A London-based Calcuttan friend of mine says he never even knew the incident had taken place until he arrived at Eton. Nor is the Indian Government keen on the story. The site of the cell, on which now stands the GPO building in Dalhousie Square, was first marked by a stone memorial erected by our outraged propagandist Mr Holwell. After years of neglect during the nineteenth century the structure collapsed and was replaced in 1902 by a forty-five-foot-high stone obelisk engraved with the victims' names and commissioned by the viceroy Lord Curzon. In 1940, to show willing and appease Indian sensitivities, it was moved to St John's Church, a few hundred yards from Dalhousie, where it remains today.

St John's, modelled on St Martin's in the Fields in London, was built after Clive's time in 1786. But it stands on the site of St Anne's, Calcutta's first church, where he would have worshipped. Having walked the streets all morning, I sought the sanctuary of a taxi to take me there. The driver, a young Sikh, had a fine sense of understatement. 'Calcutta...no discipline,' he remarked as a rickshaw, its coolie oblivious to all danger, slewed in front of the car.

The churchyard was certainly suffering from a lack of discipline. A group of small boys were kicking a football around the overgrown graves. Much of the grounds — a sizeable area considering this was in the heart of Calcutta — were taken up by a vegetable patch and an encampment of shacks where the gardeners lived with their families. But at least attempts had been made to grow a lawn and new bushes had been planted.

The Black Hole memorial was streaked with bird's mess. A dead dog lay nearby, its body covered in flies. Grass grew up around the base of the obelisk. It stood in a corner of the churchyard near an ugly clutter of corrugated iron fencing and in the shadow of the tall church spire. I got the feeling that someone had decided to place this embarrassing and none too beautiful testimonial to British sacrifice as far out of sight as possible.

A little way from the memorial were the tombs of Calcutta's founder, Job Charnock, and Admiral Charles Watson, the man who helped Clive recapture Calcutta. The admiral died soon afterwards in a terrible epidemic that claimed the lives of nearly two hundred Europeans and many more Indians.

The church was surrounded by towering pillars that supported the roof above the verandah. It was on the wide steps outside the main entrance that two hundred years ago the bachelor clerks of the East India Company would have viewed the latest talent arrived from England. Starved of female company, the lads would check out the new girls as they walked into Sunday service with their chaperones. Young ladies, who were prepared to undertake the hardship of the seven month voyage from England, were for the most part seeking a husband with good prospects. There were plenty of eligible young men in Calcutta, who were on their way to making decent fortunes.

I walked inside St John's. It was not a lively, airy church like St Mary's. The windows were smeared with city grime so that the daylight struggled to shine through; three electric lamps above the altar emitted a depressing, blood-red glow; the floor was of gloomy, grey marble.

A lonely communion service was in progress. The congregation numbered one man, the verger, who was being administered to by the vicar, the Reverend John Stevens. Tiny congregations were, sadly, nothing new to St John's and it was surprising that the place had survived at all. The only time the church was full was in November when Calcutta's Diplomatic Corps crowded

Once, two hundered years ago, the trader came
    Meek and tame.
Where his timid foot first halted, there he stayed,
    Till mere trade
Grew to Empire, and he sent his armies forth
    South and North
Till the country from Peshawur to Ceylon
    Was his own.
Thus the midday halt of Charnock — more's the pity! —
    Grew a City.
As the fungus sprouts chaotic from its bed,
    So it spread —
Chance-directed, chance-erected, laid and built
    On the silt —
Palace, byre, hovel — poverty and pride —
    Side by side;
And, above the packed and pestilential town,
    Death looked down.

But the Rulers in that City by the Sea
    Turned to flee —
Fled, with each returning spring-tide from its ills
    To the Hills.
From the clammy fogs of morning, from the blaze
    Of old days,
From the sickness of the noontide, from the heat,
    Beat retreat:
For the country from Peshawur to Ceylon
    Was their own.
But the Merchant risked the perils of the Plain
    For his gain.
Now the resting-place of Charnock, 'neath the palms,
    Asks an alms,
And the burden of its lamentation is,
    Briefly, this:

'Because for certain months, we boil and stew,
    So should you.
Cast the Viceroy and his Council, to perspire
    In our fire!'
And for answer to the argument, in vain
    We explain
That an amateur Saint Lawrence cannot cry: —
    '*All* must fry!'
That the Merchant risks the perils of the Plain
    For gain.
Nor can Rulers rule a house that men grow rich in,
    From its kitchen.

Let the Babu drop inflammatory hints
    In his prints;
And mature — consistent soul — his plan for stealing
    To Darjeeling:
Let the Merchant seek, who makes his silver pile,
    England's isle;
Let the City Charnock pitched on — evil day! —
    Go Her way.
Though the argosies of Asia at Her doors
    Heap their stores,
Though Her enterprise and energy secure
    Income sure,
Though 'out-station orders punctually obeyed'
    Swell Her trade —
Still, for rule, administration, and the rest, Simla's best.

from

City of Joy

DOMINIQUE LAPIERRE

A CRUMBLING OLD BUILDING, WITH A STAIRCASE THAT STANK of urine and filled with a confusion of silhouettes in *dhotis* wandering about, the Calcutta customs office was a classic shrine to bureaucracy. Brandishing like a talisman the notice for his parcel of medicine, Stephan Kovalski swept into the first office. Once inside, however, he had no sooner taken a step before his commendable enthusiasm deserted him. Seized by the spectacle before him, he stopped in his tracks, transfixed. Before him extended a battlefield of old tables and shelves, sagging beneath mountains of dog-eared files, spewing out yellowing paperwork tied vaguely together with bits of string. There were piles of ledgers all of which appeared to be chewed by rats and termites, and some of which looked as if they dated back to the previous century. The cracked cement of the floor was likewise strewn with paper. From drawers that were coming apart bulged an infinite variety of printed forms. On the wall Kovalski noticed a calendar for some year long past, which sported a dusty effigy of the goddess Durga slaying the demon-buffalo, the incarnation of evil.

A dozen *babus** in *dhotis* were seated in the middle of this chaos, beneath a battery of fans which throbbed out a veritable sirocco of moist air and sent the papers into a whirl of confusion. While some scrambled to catch documents as if they were chasing butterflies, others jabbed a single finger at antique typewriters, pausing after each letter to verify that they had actually managed to hit the right key. Others were talking on telephones that didn't appear to be connected to any line. Many of them seemed to be engrossed in activities that were not, strictly speaking, professional. Some were reading newspapers or sipping tea. Others were asleep, with their heads propped up on the papers that covered their desks, looking like Egyptian mummies on a bed of papyrus. Yet others, seated in their chairs in the hieratic position of yogis, looked as if they had attained the ultimate stages of nirvana.

On a pedestal near the entrance, three divinities from the Hindu pantheon, bound together by a tangle of cobwebs, watched over the enormous office, while a dust-covered portrait of Gandhi contemplated the chaos — with supreme resignation. On the opposite wall, a yellowing poster proclaimed the glorious virtues of teamwork.

The entry of a foreigner had not aroused the slightest bit of interest. Eventually Kovalski's eye fell on a little man with bare feet who happened to be passing with a teapot. The employee stabbed his chin in the direction of one of the officials who was typing with one finger. Stepping gingerly over stacks of files, the priest reached the man in question and handed him the slip he had received in the post. The *babu* in glasses examined the document at length, then, taking stock of his visitor, he inquired, 'Do you like your tea with or without milk?'

'With,' replied Kovalski, somewhat taken aback.

The man rang a bell several times, until a shadow emerged from among the pyramids of files.

* Originally a term of respect, now used to designate lesser officials in the civil service.

He ordered a tea. Then, fiddling with the document, he consulted his watch.

'It's nearly lunchtime, Mr Kovalski. Afterwards, it'll be a bit late to find your file before the offices close. Please, come back tomorrow morning.'

'But it's a question of a very urgent consignment of medicines,' protested the priest. 'For someone who could die.'

The official assumed a compassionate air. Then, pointing to the mountain of paperwork that surrounded him, he said, 'Wait for your tea. We'll do everything we can to find your parcel as quickly as possible.'

With these words, enunciated with the utmost affability, the *babu* got up and withdrew.

Next morning at precisely ten o'clock, the time when all the administrative offices in India open, Kovalski was back. A line of some thirty people preceded him. A few minutes before his turn came up he saw the same official with the glasses get up and leave, just as he had done on the previous day. It was lunchtime. Kovalski rushed after him. Still with the same courtesy, the *babu* merely pointed to his watch with a grave expression. He made his apologies: it was midday. In vain Kovalski pleaded with him; the man remained inflexible. The Pole decided to remain where he was and await the *babu's* return. But on that particular afternoon the official did not reappear in his office.

As luck would have it, the next day was one of the two holiday Saturdays in the month. Kovalski had to wait until Monday. After three more hours of lining up on the steps of the betel-stained staircase, he found himself once more before the *babu* with the glasses.

'Good morning, Father!' cried the latter amicably, before the inevitable, 'Do you like your tea with or without milk?'

This time Kovalski was full of hope. The *babu* began by popping into his mouth a wad of betel that he had just made up for himself. After several efforts at mastication, he got up and headed for a metal cabinet. Straining at the handle, he had to make a number of attempts at opening it before he actually succeeded. When the door finally did turn on its hinges, the cabinet expelled an avalanche of files, ledgers, notebooks and different documents, almost burying the unfortunate official altogether. Had there not been a human life at stake, Kovalski would have burst out laughing, but the urgency of the issue preserved his calm. He rushed to the victim's rescue, bent on extracting him forcibly from his ocean of papers and procuring the immediate surrender of the parcel of medicines. He was not quite familiar with the sometimes subtle ploys of local bureaucracy. In his haste, he tripped over a coconut that another *babu* had deposited on the floor next to his chair, to quench his thirst during the course of the morning. Fortunately there was no shortage of papers to soften the Pole's fall.

As it happened, the incident had a positive effect. The official with the glasses began to thumb through the pages of several ledgers that had spilled out of the cabinet. Kovalski watched him for a while, fascinated. The man was running his fingers down a confusion of boxes and columns in search of some cabalistic *mantra* scrawled in almost illegible ink. Suddenly he saw the *babu*'s finger stop on a particular page. He leaned forward and could hardly believe his eyes. In the midst of all this geological subsidence of paperwork and records, one single entry brought all the chaos back into touch with a living, palpable, indisputable reality. What he read was his name. This bureaucracy was not quite as ineffective as even the Indians themselves claimed.

The discovery propelled the official in the direction of another section of the sea of papers that looked as if it might totally engulf him at any second. With all the dexterity of a pearl fisher, he fished out a yellow-covered file on which Kovalski deciphered his name for a second time. Victory! A few more moments of patience and Bandona's protégée could have her first injection of the life-saving serum. However, as if exhausted by the effort of his find, the *babu* straightened himself up, consulted his watch, and sighed, 'Father, we'll continue after lunch.'

That afternoon the *babu* looked more forbidding. 'The information on the ledger does not correspond to that on the slip you were sent,' he announced. 'It'll have to be verified in other ledgers.'

'Only the expression of sincere regret on the official's face prevented me from bursting into a rage,' Kovalski was to say.

The sixth and seventh days passed without their being able to find the correct ledger. On the eighth day, the *babu* claimed forty rupees from the priest to assign two additional employees to the search for the right references. Another whole week went by. Bureaucratic disaster was systematically swallowing up even the very best of intentions. Stephan Kovalski had given up all hope when, after six weeks, he received by post a further notice inviting him urgently to come and clear his parcel. By some miracle Bandona's protégée was still alive.

The *babu* received his visitor with all the transports of affection befitting an old friend. His joy at seeing Kovalski again was very real. He asked for another thirty rupees for the purchase of revenue stamps and took charge of a pot of glue and a brush with four remaining bristles. Liberally he brushed the place reserved for the stamps, but in the meantime the stamps, caught up in the whirlwind from the fans, fluttered away. Kovalski was compelled to produce another thirty rupees for three new stamps. Then he was invited to fill in a series of forms to establish how much duty he was to pay. Working this out, and also computing the amount owed for the various taxes took nearly all day. The final sum was exorbitant: three hundred and sixty-five rupees, three or four times the declared value of the medicines. But then there was no price to be put on a human life.

'Even then my difficulties weren't altogether over,' the Pole would sigh. 'The customs office wasn't permitted to receive direct payment of the duty it prescribed. The duty money had to be cleared by the central bank which would then issue a receipt. This meant one more day wandering from counter to counter in that tentacular establishment.'

At last, clasping the precious receipt to his chest, Kovalski ran back to the customs office. By this time he had become such a familiar figure that everyone welcomed him with a cheery 'Good morning, Father!' His *babu,* however, displayed an unaccustomed reserve. He refrained from even examining the document and instead asked the priest to accompany him. Together they went down two floors and entered a storeroom where mountains of parcels and crates from all over the world were piled high on shelves. The *babu* asked one of the uniformed customs officers to go and fetch the package of medicines. Moments later, Stephan Kovalski at last confronted the precious dispatch, a box hardly bigger than two packs of cigarettes. 'It was like a mirage, a vision of life and hope, the promise of a miracle. The long wait, all that time spent in fruitless activity, all that desperate effort was at last going to result in the saving of a life.'

He held out his hand to take possession of the parcel.

'I'm sorry, Father,' apologized the uniformed customs official. 'But I can't let you have it.'

He pointed to a door behind him on which hung a sign with the words 'Goods incinerator'.

'The date for your medicines expired three days ago,' he explained, making for the door. 'We're obliged to destroy them. It's an international regulation.'

The *babu* who until now had remained silent, intervened swiftly, grabbing hold of the tail of the man's shirt.

'This Father is a holy man,' he protested. 'He works for the poor. He needs that medicine to save the life of an Indian woman. Even if the date has run out, you must give it to him.'

The uniformed customs officer surveyed Kovalski's patched shirt.

'You work for the poor?' he repeated respectfully. Kovalski nodded. Then he watched as the customs officer crossed out the word 'perished'.

'Father, don't say anything to anybody, and may God bless you.'

Despite the medicine, Bandona's protégée died four weeks later. She was twenty-eight years old, a widow, and she left four orphans. In an Indian slum, such a qualification didn't really apply to any children. When parents died, and God knows that happened often enough, they didn't leave orphans behind; other members of the family — an elder brother, an uncle, an aunt — or in the absence of any relatives, neighbours would adopt them at once.

The young woman's death was very quickly forgotten. That was another characteristic of the slum. No matter what happened, life went on with an energy and vigour that was constantly renewed.

Wrong Side of the Tracks

ADRIAN LEVY & CATHY SCOTT-CLARK

THE TRAIN MEANDERS TOWARDS CALCUTTA'S HOWRAH station. We had boarded the Kalka Mail in the Indian capital at dawn the day before, and now, 24 hours later, everyone in the carriage is feeling fractious. Ajay Kumar, a bank manager from New Delhi, has a tale to tell. 'I brought my nephew here once to visit his grandparents and lost him in the chaos. He jumped off before the train was even at a full stop. Engulfed in the hurly-burly, he was. We didn't see him again for four years. We thought he was dead. He was only 12... But then he suddenly came back home, sent by the Calcutta police, and all the boy would say was that Howrah station was a terrible place and that he would never go back there again.'

'Too right,' pipes up Mr Vijay. These are the first words that he has spoken for the entire journey. 'My neighbour's son ran away to Howrah station never to be seen again. He told me he came here to search for the kid and found nothing but wild children. All of them had become thieves. Their fingers were like vipers, he told me, slithering into all your nooks and crannies.' He gathers his bags to his chest.

It seems an incredible story, to lose a child in the crush of a railway station for years, or for ever, but everything about Indian railways is larger than life: 37,000 miles of track, 7,000 trains running daily, serving more than 3.7 billion passengers yearly, the world's largest employer, retaining more than 1.6 million staff. Every one of its major termini is a disorientating world for a newcomer. And Howrah station is in a different league. Imagine King's Cross, St Pancras and Euston all lumped together. Like every station the world over, Howrah attracts a steady stream of the rootless and homeless. But, unlike other stations, Howrah's twilight society is a vast metropolis in itself that spills out of the concourse and down to the banks of the Hooghly river, a world that is overrun by tribes of lost children.

'Howrah is populated by little devils.' Mrs Dutta, a widow cocooned in her white sari, weighs in with the authority of a local. The entire carriage is now animated as we pull into the largest station in Asia. 'The children who live here are like the locusts sent by the God of Abraham to destroy the pharaoh. Don't feel sorry for them. My advice is that once you get off this train, fly from Howrah like a garuda [a fabulous, winged human of Indian myth]!'

Ajay Kumar grabs a copy of the *Telegraph* from a newspaper-seller jogging beside the carriage window. 'Look at this, look at this.' He reads aloud a headline: 'Whiff of Death, Life of Crime: kids dragged into theft trap by the train tracks.'

The Metro section of the *Telegraph* of Calcutta is focusing on one of its favourite topics. It reports how the previous day four boys aged between 10 and 12 appeared before Calcutta's juvenile court charged with 'pilfering luggage'. A police investigation estimates that Howrah station is now home to up to 3,000 children, some of whom came of their own volition. Others were abducted or mislaid. The vast majority were apparently addicted to glue or heroin and ensnared by gang bosses who forced them into committing crimes. 'We are being overwhelmed,' D. P. Tarenia, superintendent of Howrah's railway police, told the *Telegraph*. 'The adult ringleaders are very clever. They base themselves outside the station, using the kids as couriers and thieves. They know that the kids' new-found habits ensure that they don't roam too far.'

A charity working with street dwellers had written to us a month before describing the scale of Howrah's problem. The Society for Educational and Environmental Development (Seed) said that thousands of lost children aged between four and 12 were drawn to Howrah from somnolent villages all over India by the thrill of the track, by dreams of life in Asia's largest and most riotous station. 'Many of those who end up in police custody can no longer remember from where they have come,' a Seed worker wrote. 'Some have forgotten their parents' names and even their own.' Because the state government of West Bengal has scant resources, all of the lost children are forced to rely on their wits, thieving from the 3.5 million passengers who pass through the station every day.

As the Kalka Mail slides towards platform eight, battalions of railway coolies with their brass licence badges and crimson, green or orange workshirts hurdle over the tracks, sprinting to claim a coveted position at a carriage door. Behind them, we notice an indistinct scuffle of inky elbows and matted hair, a phalanx of children moving at such ferocious speed towards our train that it is nearly impossible to make out who or what they are.

Even before the Kalka Mail has lurched to a standstill, a pervasive smell of sweat tinged with ammonia fills the carriage. Hands dart around us, on the floor and in the parcel racks. Looking down, the debris of the past 24 hours is seething with ragged children – fighting over water bottles and discarded palm-leaf plates of rice and dhal. A crusty kid whoops as he retrieves a sticky 10 rupee note (about 12p) from the crease of a seat. A child dressed in rags, a glue-filled sock clutched to his face, howls as a pot-bellied babu from the home ministry in Delhi stamps on his hand.

Only when the public-address system announces the early arrival of the Amritsar Mail at platform six does the human torrent recede into the vastness of the station's concourse. Psychedelic speak-your-weight machines and tell-your-fortune booths give it the appearance of a West Bengali steam fair and above the mêlée we can see Mrs Dutta flying like a garuda from the station with her bags held high above her head.

Standing proud in the middle of the concourse is the Railway Protection Force (RPF) booth. Inside, police officer Jahid is holding back a deluge of complaints: 'pockets rifled'; 'bags filched'; 'carriage doors picked'; 'tiny thieves'. In a lull, he briefs his men about a success from the night before, telling them how colleagues at the city's Tangra police station are holding one of Howrah's most notorious criminals, an ambidextrous hitman and bomb-maker known as the Skeleton. He was picked up on Calcutta's Gobinda Khatik Road on his way to a killing, and confessed that he had been paid to assassinate the local leader of the Trinamul political party.

'You all know the Skeleton from his baby face,' officer Jahid lectures his force gravely. The men also know the Skeleton for another reason – the feared hitman is 4ft tall and only 12 years old. His real name is Raju Das and – like those who plundered our train and the dozens of pairs of eyes we can now see staring out from the deep, dry recesses beneath the platforms – his home is Howrah station.

'I have been a thief, a liar, a beggar and a card cheat. I've ridden the Gitanjali Express to Mumbai to run on Chowpatty Beach. I've taken the Coromandal Express to Chennai to swim in the Bay of Bengal. I've sat on top of the Amritsar Mail all the way to the Golden Temple and jumped on the Dehra Dun Express to see the Himalayas – all before I passed 10 years old. And I never once paid for a ticket.' Bablu Das, the pint-sized top dog of platform nine, is in his stride, fingering the ominous tumour on his cheek, bragging to a crowd of even smaller gang members sitting crosslegged and in awe, every one of them absent-mindedly scratching the ringworm whorls that mark their elbows and feet.

'Prick!' A heckler disrupts Bablu's oratory. Bandana Boy, his main rival, shouts from the tracks below: 'Who was it who found 3,000 rupees [£50], yaa? On the floor of the Coalfield Express, train number 3029, from Ranchi? I found it. Not you, man, with all your cool talk of travelling. Bablu bollocks.'

Glue Head, a gungy sock stuck to his nose and mouth, is distracted, constantly looking up the platform, waiting for fellow gang member Shyam to arrive with a new supply of Denrite, the peardrop-scented adhesive that he says 'makes me fly'. Crying Boy, perpetually snivelling, chisels away at an attaché case, beating and bashing it only to find that it contains nothing more than a sheaf of paper, which he cannot read. A boy who calls himself the Artist and his one-legged friend, Hopper, fall about in hysterics as they slip into the same arm of a pink cardigan, claimed from the first-class carriage. Only Israel and his best friend Rasheed Khan, so new that he hasn't yet got a station name, sit to one side, chewing on some droopy toast pilfered from the pantry car of the Kalka Mail. They smear it with the contents of a half-finished sachet of Fruit Kick jam.

They are all babbling in 'hotchpotch', a language unique to Howrah station, an amalgam of Hindi, Bengali, English and Telugu – representing the length and breadth of India, from where they have come. These 10 boys, the oldest of them no more than 12, represent one small gang among hundreds that roam the 24 platforms, competing to pick over the 950 suburban and inter-city trains that arrive and depart daily.

Bablu's boys continue their audit of the takings so far: 30 one-litre water bottles that can be resold for three pence a time; copies of the *Telegraph* that fetch nine pence per kilogram;

three wallets, one purse and a handbag. It is enough for each of them to eat and get high: fresh rice from a railway *darbar* costs 6 rupees (10p) a portion, and Denrite is 30 rupees a tube. A 5mg wrap of dirty brown heroin is 25 rupees.

All of Bablu's gang have an encyclopaedic knowledge of *Trains at a Glance*, a 200-page Byzantine timetable that even Mr S.K. Chakraborty, Howrah's senior station manager, struggles to keep abreast of. Chakraborty is a career civil servant whose retinue of clerks and assistants work hard to keep station life out of his air-conditioned office. 'No, no, no. No boys. No children. No problems as you will see. Everything in Howrah station is tickety-boo. This is a safe environment for passengers, with all modem luxuries,' he tells us. Chakraborty is proud of his 8,238 sq m domain, a pristine concourse swept dozens of times a day. He has the most sophisticated toilets in Calcutta, lots of them. 'How many toilets?' he barks at an aide.

'One-hundred-and-twenty for men and 29 for women, sir.'

Mr Chakraborty beams: 'We have the finest water-closets in Calcutta – and 108 drinking water fountains to boot.' But apparently no lost children and no adult gang leaders to harness them in crime.

Back on platform nine, a pantry car attendant from the Gorakhpur Express is storming down the platform. 'Who's stolen my fucking tray? Mother-chod [fucker]. Bloody bastards. Drug pushers.' The boys scatter, but Glue Head is off his face again and the attendant grabs him by his lank hair before kneeing him in the groin. Two RPF officers jog down the platform to assist, cracking the child about the head with their bamboo truncheons, screaming at him while he wails and snivels. Only a hail of spit from those boys who have shinned up on to the roof forces the authorities into retreat, but not before a policeman hurls Glue Head on to the tracks, where he crumples and vomits up the dhal and rice foraged earlier from the floor of the Kalka Mail.

We have been warned by the police not to interfere, and so we are forced to wait until they leave before joining Glue Head between the railway sleepers, stepping over piles of human faeces to reach him. Agya Hajra is his real name, he stammers. He thinks he is about 10, maybe 12, and left his village in Orissa following a cyclone in November 1999 that killed 10,000 and left one million people homeless. 'My brothers and sisters were dead. My parents were dead. My village was under water. I wandered around for weeks until I came to a railway station — Bhadrakh, I think. The trains had just started running again, and I climbed on to the roof of the first one leaving.' Agya refuels from his glue-filled sock. 'Bhadrakh to Chennai. Chennai to Mahabalipuram. I saw the Ganesh Shrine there. And then down to Trivandrum — I ate dosa and idli.'

Glue Head had bounced like a pinball across India, visiting Mumbai to catch a glimpse of Bollywood idol Aamir Khan. Then he rode on to Jammu in the troubled northwest to watch the Indian army lob shells at Pakistan. Eventually, he hitched a ride on the roof of the Jammu Express bound for Howrah station, arriving at platform seven, at 11.40am, 18 months ago after a roundabout adventure of roughly 5,000 miles. 'I was so excited about coming to Howrah. You hear such stories about it from the boys travelling the trains: rich pickings, plenty of food. But there is no welcome for a new boy here. Nobody would speak to me for a month. I slept in the daytime because so many people wanted something at night. So tired all the time. Then one of the dadas approached me. Said if I worked for him there would no more kickings. No more police truncheon. No more terrible things.'

The dadas who run Howrah's child gangs are themselves former joyriders who have graduated from the platforms to living in the slums that surround the station. Robi Chatterjee, Glue Head's criminal mentor, is the undisputed dada of platforms one to 13. 'I only had a pair of shorts and a T-shirt,' Glue Head volunteers. 'Robi gave me Denrite and told me it would keep me warm. Other boys get brown sugar from him. Beedis [cigarettes].' What did he have to do for Robi Chatterjee in return? Glue Head grins, flaps his hands and, with a flick of his filthy feet, is off down the platform.

The Artist, real name Santosh, remains behind and shyly reveals a drawing he has done of a boy sitting at a desk filling in neat columns of figures. The Artist says he is the star pupil at Howrah's makeshift Platform School, supervised by the Society for Educational and Environmental Development. It is a grand title for a charity run on a minuscule budget by local slum dwellers, many of whom are themselves bonded labourers, working for the cement factory behind Howrah. But they find one hour a day to come to the station where a bench at the far end of platform nine becomes a haven for Bablu's gang, safe enough for them to become children. And with coloured pens on used computer paper, the boys draw pictures of homes, parents, brothers and sisters.

'I am a failure,' the Artist announces suddenly, breathing out peardrop fumes, slipping his hand into one of ours. 'My parents told me that. Three years ago. I failed my school exams. My mother and father beat me and said I was an idiot. Go away, they said. There is no room in this house for a fool. So I went away and got on a train.'

One-legged Hopper bounces down the platform. 'I have a real name, too – Tiya. I lost my parents at the market in New Delhi. A man took me to the railway station. Said I should come with him to Calcutta. When I arrived, he put me in his car and tried to do things to me. I escaped.' Hopper pulls his shorts down over the stump of his leg. 'I lost it trying to jump on to the Rajdhani Express. A coolie pushed me out of the way. I fell between the train and the platform. Other boys die and the police take the bodies away.'

Another boy brandishes a deformed fist like a trophy. It is missing most of its fingers. 'The Rajdhani Express got me, too,' shouts Sapan Das, whose hand was crushed between the train and a pillar.

We wander back towards the RPF booth. Beneath an official sign declaring, 'Ticketless Travel is a Social Evil', Mr Bhattacharya cranks up his chrome Milano cappuccino machine, oblivious to the packets of Britannia biscuits that are disappearing off the far end of his stall, stuffed into grimy pockets by children. Across the shining concourse, Mr Ghosh unpacks jute bags and inflatable cushions, a must-have for the millions of third-class hard-seat passengers. To his right, Mr Majumdar, the book-seller, dusts copies of Lenin's *What is to be Done* – a bestseller in a city that has been run by a Marxist government for so many years, no one can remember it any other way.

All the traders are discussing another article on juvenile crime published in the *Telegraph* that morning. 'We are besieged by these filthy children,' they tell us. 'They steal our books and wares. They use Lenin as kindling; they sell anything for drugs. They are a threat to the society of the station. They carry disease.' But these traders are not heartless, only exasperated by the realisation that there is no solution to the problem of Howrah's lost children.

An impatient officer Jahid strolls over. 'Have you got official permission to be here?' he barks. But his anger is half-hearted, and soon he is sipping tea. 'Look, I admit it, we are drowning in lost children, bloody thousands of them. What the hell are we supposed to do? Take them all home? They become wild, and then all they understand is the stick. These kids are used by dadas to terrorise the residents of Calcutta. They traffic drugs, weapons, even kill. We cannot help it if they come from their broken homes or poor villages. We are not social workers, see? Tell me, do you know how to police poverty?'

The parents of Howrah's lost children are more often than not invisible. There are no missing posters, no one to claim the bodies crushed under the trains. But Mrs Bishwakarma, from a village in the far northeastern creases of India, told us that she never reconciled herself to losing her son. Dheeraj had started truanting at the age of seven, after an argument with his father over a stolen 10-rupee note. Their village near Makum was a rough-tough area of Assam, over-run by drug traffickers and insurgents. But as long as Mrs Bishwakarma was sure that Dheeraj wasn't hanging out with Assamese gangsters, there was no need to worry. She had three other sons to care for and a daughter with a club foot.

But then when he was nine, Dheeraj stopped coming home altogether. After three years, her neighbours pronounced him dead. 'Try and imagine what we went through,' she asks us. 'We blamed ourselves, his father and I. What had we done? Why hadn't we tried harder? India is so vast — where do you begin your search?'

In fact, Dheeraj had never intended to vanish. He had walked to the local railway station, as he had done many times before, and sneaked on to the first train. Then he fell asleep. When he awoke, six hours later, the train had stopped at the city of Dibrugarh, far further than he had ever travelled before. He was surrounded by policemen who accused him of stealing from a passenger. 'I was in the lock-up for a night — I was terrified,' he tells us. 'But then I met some other kids who told me they were going to Guwahati, the state capital. I had always wanted to see it and I thought that I would be in terrible trouble if I went home now. It was easier to keep going than to turn back.' By the time he reached Guwahati, Dheeraj was 22 hours from home.

'I spent six months in the city, working the fields and the station. I was filthy, but I never thought of myself as a street kid, see. I thought, "I'm from a nice family. I've a mother and father" — but I was too scared to go back to them.' It was only after Dheeraj spent two days without food, lying on the floor of a train, counting 49 people stepping over a biscuit, hoping that no one would crush it, that he finally realised he was truly lost. 'I kept thinking I shouldn't be scavenging. I wanted that biscuit so much. I focused on it for hours. After I ate it, I walked through the carriages crying and hitting myself — why the hell had

I left home? What had I become?' Dheeraj eventually arrived at Howrah station. 'I ate beef for the first time, pretending I was a Muslim — anything tasted good. But soon I was sprawling in the gutter and had forgotten almost everything about myself.'

For the majority of Howrah's lost children, their journeys end at the station, but one night a British charity worker found Dheeraj lying in the road. Tim Grandage, who resigned from his job as a bank manager in Calcutta to set up homes for street children, cleaned him up and sent him to school. Three years later, the teenager boarded another train — back to Assam. Walking towards his home for the first time in six years, he was terrified that his parents would reject him. He recalls thinking how small his house now seemed: 'Was this the place I grew up in? Then my mother saw me and ran over and said I would always be her son, whatever I had done and wherever I had been.'

For all of Howrah's children, a random collision of circumstances has sent their lives thundering like a runaway tender in unexpected directions. 'Even if you ride the right train, you can end up getting off at the wrong stop. I fell asleep on the journey from my village and spent six years finding my way home,' says Dheeraj as he packs his things for London, where he recently won a scholarship to art school. 'Everyone has their own reason for getting on the train in the first place, but it soon becomes like a drug, compelling us to travel further and further, running away from who we once were. Before you know it, people stop seeing you, only the rags you're dressed in.'

After the 21.55 Bhubaneswar Express from Orissa has been plundered, Howrah falls into an uneasy sleep. The dead hours. Every inch is staked out by hawkers, cleaners, coolies and travellers, bedding down to a soundtrack of bronchial coughs. Bathed in a sickly green light in which clouds of mosquitoes hover, the station dwellers wrap themselves in cotton shawls and dhotis beneath a sign pronouncing 'Cleanliness is next to goodness'.

On the concourse that now resembles a temporary field hospital, there is room for everyone, except the lost children, who are considered even more untouchable than the well-organised gangs of lepers and cripples whose flaring fires mark out their patch in the arches beneath the station forecourt. Twenty Howrah boys, those who have renounced drugs, win some respite in a nearby Seed night shelter. The rest head for the recesses beneath the platforms and the tunnels beyond the station.

We walk outside and through the slumbering taxi rank, down to the shores of the Hooghly, where in the daytime boats ferry thousands of commuters to the commercial heart of Calcutta. At night, the silent gangplanks lead to the dadas' encampment, where we have been told Robi Chatterjee sleeps. Beneath oilskin canopies, men lie spreadeagled on rope charpoys, guarded by hard-faced minders with gimlet eyes. 'What the fuck do you want?' hisses one. Is Robi Chatterjee here, we ask? 'He's out of action for a while — go back to your hotels.' Robi, we learn later, is doing time for robbery and weapons possession.

At a rickety school desk, eclipsed by the RPF booth, Mohammed Alum is finishing work. Seed's chairman and founder has spent the day questioning unaccompanied children getting off trains, adding their names to a list of new arrivals, one of the only attempts to quantify the size of Howrah's child city. He formed Seed after his own slum neighbourhood was overrun by juvenile criminals, preferring to engage rather than fight them: 'The authorities and traders rarely see beyond the rags and petty crime. We are here to remind everyone that these are, after all, children, hustling to survive.'

As we walk with him along the track, Alum points out small knots of bodies, children wedged between the railway sleepers — Bablu and Bandana, wrapped in each other's arms. 'They are drowning in a deluge of Ds: death, deprivation, deficiency, disease, disability, destitution, dropping out of school, delinquency, diffidence, drugs, din, dust and dirt. Nobody cares if they live or die, and it's at night that they can disappear.' Of those whom Alum squeezes into Seed's one sparse shelter, and among the many he takes to hospital, sexually transmitted diseases are now a recurring problem.

In the shadows of a shunting yard, a boy rocks on his haunches, only to scarper as an unmarked van pulls up: eight children lying on a siding are bundled into the back and driven away in what could as easily be an abduction as a police crackdown. Back on the concourse, a whimpering boy is hurled out from under a trader's blanket. A man who has pulled up at the taxi rank in a smart Maruti saloon prowls between the tracks, lingering over the sleeping children. No one that Alum has ever seen before, but perhaps someone who knows that there are no printed pleas by worried parents pasted to the pillars. He passes the police booth where two officers are snoring, their blankets obscuring the legend, 'We are here to protect you.' And then he disappears from sight.

from

The Last Look

SUSANNA MOORE

Calcutta, 3 March 1836

WE SAILED WITH THE TIDE, THE CURRENT RUNNING FAST, BIRDS diving in our wake. The river was brown, thick with silt. The sound of the sea grew fainter and fainter in my ears, escaping with each breath. My heart was beating fast. My feet were cold.

Harriet and I stood in a small open boat, at last done up in our finery (I could see my maid Brandt in another boat with the servants, nodding proudly at me), our feathered heads cocked like birds as we listened to the din of bells and drums coming from the temples along the shore. Lafayette, most handsome in the uniform of the 16th Lancers, whispered to us as he bounded past that it sounded like a veritable legion of devils let loose. Harriet laughed with pleasure. (Lafayette is her favorite; I'm not sure she likes Henry at all.)

When I looked to see if my darling Frolic was happy enough in his swinging basket, I saw to my horror a brown stain all around the hem of my gown. The same with Harriet's Pekin silk, the sight of which, I'm ashamed to admit, assured me that it was not something I had done to myself. All the same, it was very distressing; the stain was climbing to my knees. I lifted my skirt and saw to my relief that it was only dirty water. I had not felt it at first because of the stiffness of my crinoline. My new morocco boots were soaked through.

I touched Harriet's arm and pointed to her gown with the tip of my parasol. She stared at her skirt in dismay, her eyes near to popping. 'It is bilgewater. My boots are ruined,' I said. She held her arms in the air, fluttering them like wings, and looked in alarm to Lafayette, but he was standing at the bow and could not see her. She gathered her skirt and held it above the flooded boards, and I did the same. (Father, like Chesterton, believed that a prepossessing exterior was a Perpetual Letter of Recommendation, and I was gratified that he was not there to see us.)

There was a bend in the stream and all at once I could see the masts of ships, hundreds of them, and Fort William in the distance. Henry promises that the whole of the European community can fit inside Fort William for months at a time should it be necessary to seek refuge, although I believe its builders overlooked the necessity of a source of fresh water. I was so overcome at the sight of the ships that I could not speak.

Naked men leaned on long poles before a row of white palaces, and men squatted in the shallows, pouring river water over their heads. Bullocks with gilt horns stood chest deep in the water, and women washed their hair, their breasts bare. 'No Englishwoman has hair like that,' Harriet whispered to me. Her lisp makes her speech sound old-fashioned: 'No Englishwoman hath hair like that.' Of course she hathn't, I said to myself. Our great-aunt Winsome was known to lisp, so it is not an affectation. It is a family curse, as Maman always said.

There were schooners from America, and Chinese ships painted red, and country boats, their goods spilling carelessly into the water. Arab sailors sat in the rigging of what Lafayette said was a slave ship. One of the men swung round to shake his black hindquarters at us, and the other sailors laughed. Tiny boats holding beggar men swarmed around us. The men knelt on straw mats dotted with coins and cowrie shells, screaming and gesturing. Lafayette flung them a handful of coins, most of which fell into the river.

Harriet pointed with her fan as a perfect little pleasure barque with Gothic windows made to resemble a garden room floated past, but there was no one in it. The severed head of a goat, caught in the current, swirled uncertainly once or twice and was sucked into the depths.

I felt a sharp pain in the centre of my chest, a longing for Ravenhill and England so strong I had to grasp the rail. Without thinking, I looked around for a place to hide, but there was no hiding place. I was filled with shame at my cowardice. I said to myself, as I have said hundreds of times, that I am here because I cannot be without him. I silently recited my Milton. *So dear I love him, that with him all deaths I could endure, without him no life.*

Knowing my thoughts as always, he looked back and beckoned me closer. His sunburned neck shone with melted pomade, and I moved toward the bow to wipe his neck with my glove. Just as I reached him, the sailors threw their lines and the boat scraped noisily against a piling, nearly knocking us off our feet. Before we knew it, Harriet and I, our skirts heavy with water, were lifted into the air by a gang of chattering bearers and placed upright on the quay. I looked round for our English servants, but they were lost in the crowd. I could not see Henry or Lafayette.

I took my first step on land in four months (to Harriet's delight, my boots squeaked). My head was spinning — black faces pitched all around me. I clasped my sister's hand, and we waited in the smoke of the torches (within moments, a small circle pressing curiously around us had grown into a mob of hundreds). I caught sight of Henry, Lafayette trailing skeptically behind, as he strode impatiently up and down the steps of the quay. I was relieved to see that they too were unsteady on their feet.

There was a melancholy absence of official dignity. There was a great deal of yelling and waving of arms, but it seemed theatrical and arbitrary — no gun salutes, no keys to the city, no orphans with bouquets. Hundreds of quarrelsome green parakeets lifted themselves from the branches of a dead tree, perhaps as a gesture of welcome; a corpse bobbed in the wake of a passing boat, the legs and arms singed black, perhaps as a gesture of warning; and a tight little group of disdainful Chinamen dressed in blue refused to look at us, signifying nothing at all.

The smell of decay was so acrid my eyes began to burn. As I searched for my handkerchief, I noticed that my powder had begun to smell, too. "Do you smell my powder?" I whispered to Harriet. She was watching the women in the river and, to my dismay, waved to one of them.

She leaned toward me, the veil of her bonnet brushing my cheek as she took a discreet sniff. She shook her head. 'I smell only the river. And the charcoal fires. It makes me hungry.' She smiled as she turned away and, for an instant I minded her lack of concern. But then Harriet seldom thinks about anything.

I surreptitiously sniffed my sleeve. 'Perhaps I am imagining it, but it seems very strong. It revolts me — a mixture of sweat and dirty linen and wet dog and — are you certain? It is very disturbing. Does your powder not smell? Is this what it will be? Can you not smell it, Harriet? Tell me!'

'I promise you, I cannot smell you,' she said, her voice a trifle loud.

As I found my handkerchief, a rush of shouting street vendors and porters and beggars and fishermen seized us to cram us into a dank carriage. There was movement everywhere — native men and children black with flies swirled around us, rocking the carriage; goats and cows pushed through the crowd. A hundred black hands smacked the rumps of the aged cab horses and we lurched away, driving along the shore as the river disappeared behind the white palaces.

The sky turned quickly to black. The road was unpaved, the only light an occasional lantern on a swaying stalk of bamboo. There was a smell of rotting fruit and rotting mud. A lady who appeared to be European — suddenly it was hard to tell — drew alongside in a new barouche and leaned forward to peer boldly at us, her eyes glinting in the carriage lamps. Beneath her satin bonnet, artificial vegetables flourished in a garden of false ringlets. I know from Henry that although the Mughals once made Bengal a place of exile, it soon became the richest province in their empire, a place to revel in debauch. Although it is no longer so corrupt, thanks to East India Company, I hope for Cousin Lafayette's sake that it hasn't become too Christian; like all of us, he is here to make his fortune. With a knowing smile, the woman pulled in her handsome head and the barouche drew ahead of us as we passed beneath a towering gateway guarded by the Unicorn and the Lion, coming to a stop before a large and imposing house that was the very image of Kedleston Hall, except for the black men in white dresses and red turbans rushing down the wide staircase with torches. A rickety carriage followed us through the gates. The carriage doors flew open and Henry jumped out, his long frame bent in two, as Lafayette hurried to extract us from the crowd of native men surrounding us. For a moment my sister's fairy face was illuminated in the torches, and as the light played about her face I thought how Queen Mab-ish she looked — for better or worse, she is one of those people whose appearance matches their character. She seemed delighted by our reception.

We were led up the staircase, past a guard of native soldiers with blunt lances (Henry said the lances must have been left behind by Alexander the Great), all saluting with the left hand, and into an enormous hall with a black-and-white checkerboard floor where fifty people sat in a forest of potted palms, eating what looked to be grouse while a regiment of pipers played a reel. The ladies, fork in one hand and fan in the other, were dressed in low satin gowns with enormous sleeves (many months out of fashion, I couldn't but notice). At the head of the table, a woman of a deep orange tint with six golden arrows in the bands curling around her ears (she had that particular second-rate look of an ambassador's wife) blinked uncertainly when she saw us standing there, our mouths agape.

It was soon explained that we'd been given up for lost. The steamers had been looking for us for weeks. Sir Charles, whom Henry replaces as Governor-General, is a smallish person, the very image of his grandfather minus the revolving eye. He is rumoured to have a native companion and is exiled to Delhi. Lafayette claims they used not to mind that sort of thing here; a native mistress (Lafayette calls them bibis) was better than marrying a Portuguese widow, but it is different now. I cannot help but like Sir Charles – they say his hobby is peacocks.

Because of the lateness of the hour, we were spared the more formal ceremony of arrival. Sir Charles swore in Henry right there at the table, as Harriet looked longingly at an epergne of fruit and the ladies looked at us. As Harriet and I were bustled away like maidens at our first assembly, I looked over my shoulder and saw they had resumed eating. What they wanted in manners, they made up in appetite.

We were taken down a dark gallery piled with bundles of linen. The rare lamp smelled of rancid tallow. There were paintings on the walls – fine men in ermine robes, I suspect. Maj. Quinn, our escort, pointed to the heaps of linen and asked if we'd be so kind as not to tread on the people asleep on the floor. Harriet jumped to avoid trampling an elderly woman. We were soon separated – Harriet, with a whimper of dismay, was lured past some busts of the Caesars and carried to a wing of her own. Henry, I was assured, in answer to my question, would not be far from me. I wondered where he was – perhaps meeting with his new Political Secretary, Mr. MacGregor.

My rooms were as spare as a gibbet save for the intimate adornments of the person, presumably a woman, who was living in them. A boy lounging sleepily on a blue-striped mat gave a surprised shout when he saw me. A string tied to the boy's big toe ran across the room to a filthy flounce of white cloth suspended a few feet above a bed set in the centre of the room. The cloth looked like an enormous fluttering moth. It is a punkah fan, my new maid Rosina hastily explained, meant to keep me cool (she is a half-caste and knows these things). My first thought was that I would request a string long enough to reach the passage, where I will be happy for the child to pull to his heart's content. I do not like the idea of someone, even a servant, in my room through the night; I never have. Maj. Quinn, who appears to have a tic, said that the punkah boy is relieved every two hours. With a soft clap of his hands, a hundred servants seeped from the darkness to spirit away the belongings of my predecessor before I'd even had a chance to look at them. Three smiling men in white dresses and gold sashes arrived with trays of covered dishes (I assume it was food), but I was too tired to eat and I asked Quinn to send them away.

I wanted to stay awake lest Henry should come, but the bed, although possessed of little more than a bolster and cotton quilt, was most enticing. The gauze bed curtains were trimmed with swags of patched green netting. The legs of the bed stood in small dishes filled with water, a circle of peppercorns strewn around each dish. Brandt kindly beat the mattress for lice. Our trunks must be sitting on the quay; she was not able to replace the bedding with linen of my own.

I sent the twitching Maj. Quinn off to Harriet, and Brandt undressed me and took away my ruined gown and boots. There were raised welts up and down my sides, perhaps from the new busks in my stays (Brandt has sewn in silver ones, which will not rust in the damp), and Rosina rubbed my waist to ease the swelling. My breasts were tender, having had only the comfort of muslin these last months, but I did not let her touch me there. Brandt placed Melbourne's *Milton* and my Prayer Book next to the bed and convinced Frolic that he should climb into his basket — he is to have his own servant, whom we will meet in the morning. I insisted that Brandt and Rosina go to bed.

On looking closer, I discern that the peppercorns around the bed legs are beetles. I must ask for more candles. Now there is music outside my window, perhaps a snake charmer. Even that will not keep me awake. Nor the chatter of the servants in the yard, nor the smell of jasmine. It is my thirty-fourth birthday.

from

Calcutta

GEOFFREY MOORHOUSE

Ultimate Experience

NO TRAVELLER FROM THE WEST IS COMPLETELY PREPARED for his first experience of India. Whether he flies into the fiery dawn of Bombay or Delhi, as he frequently does, his senses will at once be shocked and stimulated and confused by the strangeness of his new landfall. He may have inklings of what to expect but he can never have more than that, for everything that is about to happen to him is on such a scale and of such magnitude as to defy and almost to dissolve all his careful anticipation. He may have been entranced once by the queer and exotic doings of snake charmers, fire eaters and gulli-gulli men at sundown in the great square of Marrakesh, which will have seemed a marvellous spectacle especially organised for the benefit of tourists. In India the traveller discovers that such things can be customary processes of living. He may believe that he has sighted the utmost poverty in the cave dwellings and hovels of Southern Italy or Spain. In India he realises that this was not so, and that something infinitely worse goes on and on, hopelessly and terribly. The traveller's confusion and the sick feeling he begins to detect in the pit of his sensitive stomach is liable to be increased, moreover, if he happens to be British. For in all this confusion and this rivetting strangeness he becomes aware of things as faintly familiar as an old coat of varnish, or a forgotten diary discovered one traumatic day under the dust in the box room. These consist of ways some people have of doing and saying things, of a sign manual casually observed upon a building, of a lingering and homely style inextricably mixed up with all the oddness. They make the traveller fairly blink with recollection as he struggles with some fresh encounter that he suspects he has had some place before. And then one day, while he is still astonished by his landfall, he takes plane again and flies on to the East; for there, he has heard, lies the ultimate in this weird and marvellous and awful experience.

If he has disdained the services of Indian Airlines and boarded someone else's Boeing, he finds that some of his reflexes have disturbingly changed. He spends much of the next three hours pondering the comforts of travel by international jet-propelled aviation. He toys with his glossified meal, complete with dainty salt and pepper shakers and real quill toothpicks wrapped in cellophane; and he catches himself wondering just how many thousands (possibly millions?) of dollars were spent in devising and developing the plastic sheet whose frictional surface is intended to stop his share of hors d'oeuvre sliding off the tray and into his neighbour's lap. He relieves himself of a few uncomfortable thoughts in the lavatory aft, where Pan American have thoughtfully provided handcream and soap (both by Morny) and after-shave lotion (by Onyx); all done up in small attractive packages which invite the traveller to pocket them, for there are plenty more where they came from and he's welcome. He chooses, perhaps, the mouthwash instead, for a bitter little flavour has been coming on and he likes to make his landfalls nice and clean. Thus revitalised and refreshed, he takes his aerial passage across India, until the

warning lights go on and the stewardess hopes he has enjoyed
his flight and he knows he is coming to earth again.

As the Boeing flexes its wings in descent, the traveller begins
to observe the details of a landscape which has changed somewhat
since his taste of Bombay or Delhi. There the ground seemed
barren and burnt from the sky but here it looks wonderfully
fertile. The predominant colour is green, sometimes vivid
and deep, sometimes nearly yellow, but always the promise of
growth. And there is water: water in craters, water in canals,
water in lakes and just over there a great gleaming swamp of
saturated fields with what looks like chickweed floating on the
top between the dykes. A city appears, enormous and sprawling
around a wide brown river which has shaped itself in a dog-
leg and which has ships hanging at anchor. Silver oil tanks
sparkle in the piercing light but there is a haze of smoke over
the city which renders a range of high dockside cranes as an
indistinct thicket of industry and a vast row of factory roofs as
a rusty sheet of corrugated iron. It could almost be Liverpool
on a sensational summer's day. But as the Boeing cants over
and skims even lower above the gleaming swamp and past the
lunar grey of some gigantic reclamation from the waters, the
traveller knows it is no such thing. For there are palm trees here
and a brown man coaxing a black bullock along a straggling
road and, gracious me, a dazzlingly white Early English church
tower poking up from jungle. Then the plane is down and as it
bounds and sways along the runway, the traveller notices that
he is about to disembark at a spanking international airport,
as new as Prague's, as inviting as Rome's. He blinks yet again,
and wonders whether rumour has lied once more. For he has
come to Calcutta. And everything he has heard about it sounds
quite remarkably unpleasant.

This, he has been told, is the problem city of the world,
with problems that not only seem insoluble but which grow
every day at a galloping and fantastic rate. This is where nearly
eight million people exist, who will have become more than

twelve millions by 1986 if the estimates of population experts are correct. Only Tokyo, London and New York contain more people than this and scarcely any of them have a conception of how things really are in the thirty-mile length of Greater Calcutta alongside the Hooghly River. Calcutta is merely said to be the place where thousands (or is it millions?) sleep on the streets at night. Where the poverty is so dreadful that everyone who knows it throws up his hands in horror and turns his back on it. Where there is violence and anarchy and raging Maoist Communism. All this is true. It is also true that Calcutta is not only the largest city in India but commercially, industrially and intellectually the most important. It is the richest city in India. And, paradoxically, set in one of the most ancient cultures known to man, it is one of the youngest cities in the world. Henry Hudson had dropped anchor off Manhattan and begun the history of New York eighty-one years before Job Charnock pitched his tents on the East bank of the Hooghly and made a start on Calcutta; Maisonneuve founded Montreal half a century earlier. What the traveller finds there today is therefore the creation and the legacy of the British.

Very few people have ever said anything nice about Calcutta, unless they were Bengali. Writing in 1863, Sir George Trevelyan was asking us to 'find, if you can, a more uninviting spot than Calcutta...it unites every condition of a perfectly unhealthy situation... The place is so bad by nature that human efforts could do little to make it worse; but that little has been done faithfully and assiduously.' Rudyard Kipling, who was there only for a short visit as a newspaper correspondent down from the Punjab, loathed the place and composed a rambling series of essays about it which he called *The City of Dreadful Night* (a title he also bestowed upon a verse epic about Lahore, for he was a repetitive man). A century and more before that, Robert Clive decided that it was 'the most wicked place in the Universe' though, admittedly, he had only England and Madras to compare it with. All these were stock responses of a kind Calcutta has generated from the start. There have been exceptions, though. A junior contemporary of Trevelyan was bowled over by the city when he came to it as a new recruit to the Indian Civil Service. 'Imagine,' William Hunter wrote home to his fiancée, 'Imagine everything that is glorious in nature combined with all that is beautiful in architecture, and you can faintly picture to yourself what Calcutta is.' He was, of course, in love and he'd just arrived from Peckham. But William Bentinck, who was much more sophisticated, and who was to rule India from Government House there, had decided in 1805 as soon as he discovered it that Calcutta was the richest city he had seen after London and 'the spectacle is altogether the most curious and magnificent I have met with'. At the other end of the nineteenth century Winston Churchill told his mother that 'I shall always be glad to have seen it — for the same reason Papa gave for being glad to have seen Lisbon — namely, that it will be unnecessary for me ever to see it again.' But he granted that it was a very great city and then made an unexpected comparison for 'at night, with a grey fog and cold wind, it almost allows one to imagine that it is London'. It put Reginald Heber, the second Bishop of Calcutta, in mind of Moscow. It put Mark Twain, who lectured there in 1896, in mind of very little but a vivid metaphor; he thought the weather of Calcutta 'enough to make a brass doorknob mushy', stayed only a day or two, and recalled the city years later merely as the place where he met an old girl friend, with whom he had a conversation which centred on the peculiarity of dried herring. But the most memorable observation of all was made by some anonymous fellow in a sentence which is usually, but incorrectly, attributed to Lenin. 'The road to world revolution,' wrote this unknown epigrammist one day, 'lies through Peking, Shanghai and Calcutta.'

The truth is that almost everything popularly associated with Calcutta is highly unpleasant and sometimes very nasty indeed. It is bracketed in the Western mind with distant rumours of appalling disaster, riot and degradation. The one incident in its history with which every schoolchild has always been familiar has been called the Black Hole of Calcutta, and nobody who knows it can ever have been surprised to learn that one of the most vicious weapons ever devised by man, the Dum Dum bullet, was invented and first produced in a small arms factory within a rifle shot of that splendid new airport.

The very name of Calcutta is derived from a symbol of fear and evil. There is no religion in the world richer than Hinduism in the number and variety of its gods. It enshrines a bewildering pantheon of figures who together are venerated for every conceivable reflex and incident in the human condition and philosophy. There are gods as jolly-looking as Ganesh, sitting comfortably with his elephant's head, who is invoked by writers to bring them success. There are goddesses as elegant as Sarasvati, riding upon her gorgeous peacock, patron of music and inventor of Sanskrit. And there are scores of godlings with more unfortunate connotations like Manasa, who is worshipped in Bengal as an antidote to snake bites, and Sitala, who is particularly idolised by people along the Hooghly during outbreaks of smallpox. There is no one at all more respected and feared than the goddess Kali who, like every other Hindu divine, has other names and forms as well; in Bengal she is more commonly known as Durga, in South India they sometimes call her Bhawani. All the representations of Kali are designed to frighten an illiterate and superstitious mind more thoroughly than anything else in creation. She appears with devilish eyes, or with a tongue dripping blood, with snakes entwined round her neck, or with a garland of skulls. She is Kali the Terrible and she is propitiated with daily sacrifice, as well as with flowers. When the Thugs strangled a traveller, they knotted in one corner of the handkerchief a silver coin consecrated to Kali, to give them a better grip.

Kali, says the mythology, was the wife of Siva the Destroyer; and Siva, together with Brahma the Creator and Vishnu the

Preserver, stands in a divine triumvirate at the head of the Hindu religion. When Kali died, Siva was both grief-stricken and angry. He placed her corpse on his shoulders and went stamping round the world in a dervish dance of mourning which became more furious the longer it lasted. The other gods realised that unless Siva was stopped the whole world would be destroyed by his rage, which was unlikely to end as long as he had his wife's body on his shoulders. So Vishnu took up a knife and flung it at the corpse, dismembering it into fifty-two pieces which were scattered across the face of the earth. By the side of a great river in Bengal the little toe of the right foot landed, and a temple was built there, with an attendant village, and the people called this place Kalikata.

Calcutta, indeed, is a mighty terrible and frightening place today. But there is another side to it, almost unheard of, rarely figuring in its reputation, sorely neglected by travellers from other parts of India as well as from farther afield, who dash in and transact their business, observe the miseries, then turn tail and run for it before they are totally overcome by violent claustrophobia. They go home and cry woe unto the city, take its taste out of their mouths with a gin and tonic or a Pepsi, and recall it thereafter only as an emblem of experience, to show that they now know the worst that Life has to offer. Yet to balance (just a little) this conventional rumour of Calcutta, the traveller can do no better than to spare himself a couple of hours from the commercial and social horrors of the city and take himself down to the Marble Palace. This, indisputably, is the richest, the quaintest, the eeriest, the most haphazard and the most ridiculous, the most astonishing and the most lovable and almost the saddest relic in what, by about the start of the nineteenth century, was beginning to be called the City of Palaces. You trace it – with some difficulty, no doubt, for the taxi-drivers of Calcutta are not very strong on navigation – down a side street among the pullulating alleys off Chittaranjan Avenue. The air reeks down here, like so many of the central thoroughfares, of worn-out engine fumes mixed up with half a dozen varieties of decay. The pushing and shoving and sidestepping past rickshaws and cows and people is almost as concentrated as anywhere. The noise is Calcutta's usual symphony of honks and clatters and clangs and rumbles and shouts, with transistored obligatos on the sitar. It feels and looks and is just about as unsavoury as its past; for this area was once called Chor Bagan, or the thieves' garden. But in the middle of this towering mess you find, unbelievably, a real garden of maybe an acre with a Palladian mansion set square in the centre. This could easily be a luxurious pocket in Rome, not Calcutta, and there is a fountain in the garden that would not be out of place in the Piazza Navona or at the bottom of the Spanish Steps; it has Neptune figures brandishing conch shells, with indeterminate water beasts gaping at them from the surrounding pool and four nubile naiads upholding a classical urn on top of the central column. The adjacent paths are bordered with a galaxy of busts that never quite add up to a rhythmic theme – a Caesar here, a Chinaman there, a Redskin over by the shrubbery – as though someone with a bent for sculpture couldn't make up his mind whether he was also a student of history or phrenology.

There are greater surprises inside the house. You enter a courtyard first, which is topped by a high gallery. The floor is patterned with diamond-shapes and lozenges of multi-coloured marble, the white walls are embellished with swagging in Wedgwood blue, there are wonderfully cool-looking maidens and men cut in stone, wrapped in togas and standing high on plinths. There are a couple of urns with a variety of aspidistra growing from the bowls. And there is a menagerie. Out in the garden, pelicans and peacocks, mallard and teal have been poking and prodding at the lawns or ducking and dozing in the pool. In this courtyard there are starlet macaws from Burma tethered to perches, albino mynahs from the back of Bihar whistling in cages, and pinioned parakeets from Northern Australia making a mess on the statues.

Beyond lie apartments and galleries, and in these the Marble Palace becomes a fantasy brought to earth. They are full, as no building was ever filled before, with art and objects from Bangkok to Bristol and back, though almost everything seems to have been picked up from the auctions and markets and dispossessed households of Europe. There is a very old Queen Victoria in plaster standing large as life by the main stairway and a very young Queen Victoria in oak, somewhat larger, dominating a red marble room where another squadron of busts glare at her from the shadows. There is marble everywhere, in ninety different varieties it is said, transported across the seas by the ton to provide floors and wall panels and table tops. There are great swathes of satin hanging round windows and enormous follies of crystal glass hanging in chandeliers from ceilings. There are mirrors from Venice and vases from Sèvres and goblets from Bohemia and stags' heads from the Trossachs and figures from Dresden and swords from Toledo and ormolu clocks from Paris and carvings from Bavaria and vast quantities of Victorian bric-à-brac that look as if they were scavenged in job lots from the Portobello Road on a series of damp Saturday afternoons in October; bronze boys on chargers all blackened with age, plaster fruit and stuffed kingfishers presented under glass domes, gewgaws in papier maché and firedogs in cast-iron. A long gallery is so cluttered with these things upon, between, under and around its marble table-tops, that there is scarcely room to lay a finger between the bits and pieces; all collecting a patina of dust and cobwebs in a creepy half light.

And then there are the pictures. They stagger up the stairways unevenly and they hang lopsided round all the rooms; the gilt of their frames is tarnished and flaked; they are desperate for restoration and some of the oil paint is beginning to slide from the canvases in the terrible humidity of Calcutta. This is catastrophe, for many of them are masterpieces; Reynolds is here and so is Murillo, and Titian is said to be lurking somewhere.

The guide books reckon there are four paintings by Rubens in this house: *The Marriage of St Catherine, The Martyrdom of St Sebastian, Minerva giving the loving cup to Apollo* and *The Return of Ulysses*. But when you stop before an aged and indistinct possibility and ask the old gentleman in the dhoti, who is taking you round, whether that is one, he just says 'Oh, yers. That's a priceless painting. Came from Europe. Oh yers. A priceless painting.' Then he cocks his head on one side and looks at you keenly; and you simply can't tell whether he is pulling your leg or wondering whether you are pulling his.

This is not a museum. It is a home, though you are very welcome to wander around it freely between the hours of ten and five for nothing more than your signature in the visitor's book. It belongs to the Mullick family, who had long service and good conduct under the Mogul Emperors of India and were eventually granted the zamindar title to farm taxes, which made them as rich and landed as any British grandee was to become. It was built in 1835 by Raja Rajendra Mullick Bahadur, who had been orphaned at three and given an English guardian, Sir James Hogg, by the Supreme Court. Sir James presented his ward with a few birds to go with the Marble Palace (which wealthy young Rajendra started making at the age of sixteen) and that was the beginning of the menagerie. The Mullicks have been there ever since, collecting their treasures and their trifles when abroad, establishing a legend of charity when at home. For at noon every day their durwans at the gate begin to hand food and paise, a little gruffly, to a long column of destitutes who have been waiting with clamour and patience since the dawn; and the donation, it is said, continues until the limit of four thousand people has been reached. Meanwhile, the Mullicks themselves count their investments and cultivate their thoughts and are occasionally discovered playing Chopin on a grand piano in a corner of the marble ballroom; while the heat bears down and causes a little more stucco to peel from the buff front of the Marble Palace, and the great wooden blinds are drawn deep between the classical pilasters, and even the figures on the pedimented roof seem to droop in the sun. And if it were not for that burning sun, that queue of beggars, that noise and that smell, that air of being trapped, it could very easily be 7,000 miles away to the West. It is a Chatsworth of a place, muddled up with scenes from an Indian *Great Expectations;* and it would be no surprise at all to encounter Miss Havisham reclining in a corner among the bric-à-brac, the shadows and the cobwebs.

This is Calcutta, too.

It was, all the same, lunacy for anyone not born and bred in Bengal (or, at least, in India) to settle down here and make an Empire from it. Everything in Nature was against it, the climate most of all. Calcutta is tolerable in winter, when the temperature is often in the 70s and when it can become even cooler in the evening; there was a freakish day in January 1899 when it dropped to 44.2 degrees, though it is hard to imagine the cold winds and foggy nights that made Winston Churchill think of London. But by the middle of March the heat is beginning to sear the city to the bone. Between then and the start of the monsoon it can rise to 120 degrees in this part of the world, the thermometer can stick over 100 for days on end, and it rarely falls below 80 even in the middle of the night. It becomes so hot that the tar liquifies on the roads and goes oozing down the drains, and the colossal steel mesh of the Howrah Bridge is habitually four feet longer by day than by night. People go out with black umbrellas for shade, including the policemen trying to sort out the chaos of traffic at the top of Chowringhee, who have umbrellas with special handles that slot into holsters at their belts so that their arms can remain free; and people without umbrellas are apt to hold briefcases and newspapers, books and letters and folds of saris between their heads and the sun; and men walk holding the hems of their dhotis out like sails, to catch any trace of breeze.

When Calcutta has a heat wave — which means something well over 100 degrees — the cinemas are packed, like the libraries and reading rooms, because they are almost the only public places in the city which run to air-conditioning. On top of the blistering heat comes the humidity, and it is commonplace for that to register 100 per cent.

There is occasional relief from this awful combination. There are odd evenings in April that bring a shower with blue electric flashes in the sky. You can get a storm that has the thermometer down and up again through 30 degrees in half an hour while the city is bombarded with hailstones an inch and a half across; and the crows caught in mid-flight twist and dodge like fighters in anti-aircraft fire to avoid them, while small boys alternately squeal with pain and yelp with delight as they try to catch the pieces of ice before they land. But, generally, Calcutta before the monsoon means being soaked with sweat after walking a slow fifty yards; it means not having an inch of dry skin except in air-conditioning; it means shivering with the shock as you walk off the street into a highly-equipped restaurant that feels like a refrigerator for the first few minutes.

And then, about the middle of May, the occasional puffs of cloud that have been in the sky for a week or two begin to roll up more thickly. This is the worst time of all unless the monsoon fails and anyone in his senses who could possibly get away would do so then. The monsoon breaks in the first week in June, unless there is to be calamity. It comes down in a torrent to a smashing of thunder. It rains for several hours in solid straight shafts of water. Then it stops and the city steams like a laundry in the sun. Then it rains again as before. It goes on like this for four months, while Calcutta collects almost all its annual quota of 64 inches rainfall. It comes down so fiercely and in such quantity, and Calcutta is so ill-equipped to bear this sudden blessing, that the streets are awash, the motor traffic is stalled, the trams can no longer move and only the rickshaw-pullers keep going through the floods, up to their knees and axles in water. This, too, is an awful time and the air is stickier than ever when the rain is not actually pouring. But without it Calcutta would be utterly lost. If the monsoon is delayed the city becomes insane with the tension of waiting in that smothering atmosphere; for it knows that if the monsoon failed, terrible things would happen to its people.

This is probably the filthiest climate on earth, then. But apart from the balmy uplands to the North around Darjeeling, it is much the same wherever you go in Bengal, which sits sodden astride the Tropic of Cancer. The thing that makes this the most impossible place of all in this part of India for metropolitan and imperial ambitions, is the structure of the landscape here. Calcutta lies within the wide flat wedge of delta country containing the outflows of both the Ganga and the Brahmaputra. The Hooghly is a diversion from the Ganga (which only the English-speaking have known as the Ganges) as it plunges towards the Bay of Bengal, eighty-odd miles to the South; and the Mother of the World finds her way to the sea through a hundred smaller channels besides. The whole area, thousands of square miles, is simply untamed tropical fen; 'new mud, old mud and marsh', as a geographer has called it. The only firm ground is by the river banks, so that villages straggle along the watercourses, surrounded by mangoes, palms, bamboos and endless expanses of swamp. When the rains come and the rivers flood, this delta becomes a gigantic inland sea. At any time, it is a perfect breeding ground for malaria and any other disease that thrives on moisture; some of Charnock's sailors found it so unhealthy that they christened their landing place Golgotha. Yet on this bog the British created their capital in India. Nothing but commercial greed could possibly have led to such an idiotic decision.

from

Places

JAMES MORRIS

Calcutta

SILENTLY, SILENTLY TRAIL THE PICKPOCKETS, AND SOMETIMES a sleeper stirs in the arcades of Wellesley Place, raises an arm and returns to the catacomb. Everyone knows about Calcutta. Beneath the fairy lights of Howrah Bridge the rickshaws, the ravaged double-deckers, the bullock-carts and the Indians move world without end towards the railway station. Policemen with Lee-Enfields clamber from lorries, beggars without faces huddle against walls. The terrible attendants of the Hogg Market, brandishing their baskets, fall demoniac upon the tourist taxis – Everything open madam!' 'Here madam here!' 'Come this way! Come this way!' – their ingratiating frontal smiles curdling into loathing through the back window. Everyone knows about Calcutta. Everyone has seen its tall tenements stuffed with disease, its rioting millions in the battened streets, its children sprawled dead or alive on the midnight pavement. If there is one name that stands for misery, it is the name of this fearful and astonishing city – 'Calcutta', as Mr. Eugene Fodor's guide expresses it, 'Vigorous, Vibrant, Versatile.'

I was looking for other images. I woke early and walked across Chowringhi into the green of the Maidan, before the sun rose and the heat-haze fell like a web upon us. It was lovely then in the park. Rooks cawed, kites hung, sparrows pecked, smiling pi-dogs padded by. Here and there across the grass white figures moved or loitered, and whenever I paused I was sympathetically accosted. 'What you are seeing is the Theatre, built in honour of our great poet Rabindranath Tagore.' 'If I may say so you would be more comfortable where there are not so many ants.' 'Wouldn't you like a game of golf. I am teaching golf, you see: here are my golf clubs.'

I persevered, and finding myself unattended at last, sat on the grass and concentrated on the distant silhouette of the city to the north. Presently my prospect cleared, for I am psychic that way. The office blocks dissolved; the high rise buildings fell; the muddle resolved itself; and there I perceived in visionary outline the City of Palaces – that first eager Calcutta, that landfall of modernity, which the British built long ago upon the banks of the Hooghly. There were the colonnades of Reason, there the elegant villas of Enlightened Profit, garden by garden along Chowringhi. Storks dozed upon the urns of Government House, and even as I sat there, out swept the Governor-General in his equipage, with Her Excellency muslined beneath her parasol – out through the great gate in billowing dust, the lancers fluttering and clattering behind, while the passing coolies dropped their loads to gape and salaam, and the redcoats presented muskets.

It did not last, of course. Soon the heat arrived, and the noises of the stirring city invaded the Maidan, and the pi-dogs pulled themselves together and started the day's long snarl. The professor of golf had gone off to his office. I rose myself to leave; and there behind me, high on her throne upon an ornamental bridge, Queen Victoria herself sat slumped and accusatory in bronze. 'It is the Queen of England. She is the Queen Victoria. You want to change money? You want anything?'

Where are the box-wallahs? Silent the thickened voices in
Spence's bar, absent the swaying Crimplene from the dance
floor of the Grand. Gone is all that hierarchy of commerce,
managing director to apprentice assistant, immortalized by the
Calcutta memoirists — *Life and Ledger Beside the Hooghly*, or Montague
Massey's classic *Recollections*, with a frontispiece of the Author
in a high starched collar and a buttonhole, and many amusing
anecdotes of life in the chummeries.

In the 1950s and 60s, that British business society still
thrived, and one often saw its wives out shopping, or argued
one's way laboriously into its presence when the front office
clerk declined to honour one's travellers' cheque. It was a direct
and living relic of the City of Palaces — itself a community of
box-wallahs, in the days when the Honourable Company humbly
received concessions from the Nawab of Bengal. The British
businessman made Calcutta. It sprang from the loins of five-
per-cent. There was nothing here before the Company came,
but out of the dividendal urge arose the first and most terrifying of all monuments to the westernization of the East.

Go-downs, factories, counting-houses were the core of the
city, and all around them the Bengalis swarmed in fascination —
a few hundred in 1690, a few thousand in 1750, 800,000 by
the 1890s, 3m. today. I love to wander around the city now
and see, submerged but still visible, the structures of that old
impetus; ramshackle warehouses, venerable banks; the long
line of wharves, Garden Reach to Howrah, along which in all
the old pictures lay the massed masts and smokestacks of the
merchantmen; faded announcements of Victorian enterprise,
saddlers and insurers and First Class Tailors, whose ornately-
lettered signs stand wistfully faded among the cinema posters;
even some stalwart survivors, ownership generally Indian but
pedigree boldly British — Hamilton the Jewellers, Spences Hotel
whose telegraphic address is *Homeliness, The Statesman* but not *The
Englishman,* or that noblest patron of imperial reminiscence,
Thacker, Spink the publishers.

The United Service Club is gone: but then it lost its point, did it not, when its committee overruled opposition to admit members of the Bengal Pilot Service. They have pulled down the Bengal Club, once Macaulay's residence. For twenty years after Indian independence the British liked to say that the Calcutta commercial community was larger than it had ever been. Now, like a tissue finally rejecting a graft, Calcutta has rejected the box-wallahs: the chemistry of nationalism, taxation, trade unionism has forced them out at last, and the transplant of three centuries has just this minute ended.

'Does he, do you think', tactfully inquired the Bishop of Barrackpore, 'expect a T∗I∗P?' But no, my guide was not ready for one yet, having high hopes of further services to be performed, so I joined the Bishop on his verandah, where during a lull before evensong he was eating peanut butter sandwiches with a kind Anglican lady in blue. I was surprised to find him there, for European bishops are rare in Calcutta; but the Anglican rite, I gather, thrives, messed about of course by ecumenical irrelevancies and unnecessary reforms, but still recognizably the faith of Bishop ('Icy Mountains') Heber, who was Bishop of Calcutta in the 1820s, and thought the nearest terrestrial equivalent to Paradise to be the Government Botanical Gardens. Certainly the Bishop of Barrackpore was all an aficionado of the tradition could ask: cassocked, distinguished, fatherly, concerned about that T∗I∗P. Soon, he told me, he would be retiring. Going home? I wondered, but he answered in grave italics: 'Staying in India — *for ever.*'

The metropolitan cathedral of Calcutta is St. Paul's, one of the two great imperial initiatives to which the Governor-General Lord Auckland gave his approval, the other being the catastrophic invasion of Afghanistan. I went to a festival service there, and found it packed. Forty-eight electric fans, by my surreptitious count during the first lesson, whirled above us like divine helicopters; the officiating canon, copiously bearded and gorgeously coped, spoke the kind of Oxford English I imagine Jowett or Arnold to have spoken. We sang the hymn that says the Lord's throne shall never like earth's proud empires pass away. I wiped away a self-indulgent tear, as usual (for they are *always* singing that hymn in ex-imperial cathedrals): and as I left the cathedral a Balliol voice called kindly across tine transept — 'I say! Excuse me! You do know where we are, don't you, if you're coming to the children's dance drama in the parish hall?'

'*Forever*', the Bishop said, while the lady replaced the tea-caddy with a significant air: and pressing his point with unnecessary force, I thought, he showed me the picture of an eminent predecessor's grave, high on a hill above Darjeeling — 'Milman', he said, 'son of the Durham Milman, you know'.

They invited me to play the gubernatorial baby grand in the ballroom of Raj Bhavan — once the palace of the Viceroys of India, and modelled upon the Curzon family home at Kedleston in Derbyshire. There is no denying that this house has come down in the world, since Wellesley extravagantly began its construction in 1799 — 'India should be governed', it was said then, 'from a palace, not a counting-house, with the ideas of a Prince, not with those of a retail dealer in muslin...' Reduced to the Governorate of Bengal when the capital was moved to Delhi in 1911, and to the Governorate of West Bengal after partition in 1947, its functions now rattle in it rather like a dehydrated pea in a juicy pod. The piano was badly out of tune, and seemed to want to play *Rustle of Spring*.

Still, the Indians have treated the building with respect, and showed it me most courteously. Calcutta is not, on the whole, vindictive about the Empire. Of course the lions, the unicorns and the imperial crowns have been prised away where priseable, but what remains is not abused. A king, three viceroys, a lieutenant-governor and an equestrian general still stand on their plinths in the Maidan: many more have been removed to retirement at Barrackpore, where they gaze sternly out of the garden shrubberies across the Hooghly river. They have not renamed Fort William, or Eden Gardens, or Hastings Square. They have not returned to the Burmese the pagoda which Lord Dalhousie looted from Prome in 1853. Nor have they toppled the weird column that commemorates good old David Octherlony, who was born in Massachusetts, whose thirteen Indian wives, they say, trundled about on thirteen elephants, and whose identity must be misty indeed to the passing Calcutta citizenry.

Among the most extraordinary sights in India is the stream of simple pilgrims that still flows awe-struck and amazed through the Victoria Memorial, that stately dome of white marble decreed by Lord Curzon to commemorate his monarch and himself. What are they thinking, these country families and groups of youths, as they pass from the Durbar Hall to Queen Mary's Room, and across to the Royal Gallery? Who can these bewhiskered magnates be, high and huge in their gilded frames? Why is the Female Aristocracy of Queen Victoria's Court perpetuated in massed lithography in the heart of Calcutta? Whose rheumy hand is this, thanking His Excellency for his condolences upon the death of the Prince Imperial? Reverentially they wander from hall to hall, gazing long at the ceiling mural portraying the prorogation of Parliament in July 1837, pondering deeply, as well they might, over the indescribable escritoire presented by King Edward in filial piety.

I would love to know what passes through their minds, and whose Raj they suppose this to have been. Sometimes they ask to see a picture in my guide book, as though it might elucidate a mystery, and they crowded around me in silent expectation when I sketched in my notebook the allegorical elevation across the east quadrangle: for there, looking past the central statue of the young Victoria, one sees perfectly aligned with her profile images of Lord Cornwallis and Sir Andrew Fraser, and Burne-Jones' great west window of St. Paul's — from the ear of the Queen, as it were, through the skulls of two satraps direct to the eye of God.

On a wall outside the Seth Sukhlall Karnani Hospital some verses are inscribed upon a plaque:

This day relenting God
Hath placed within my hand
A wondrous thing; and God
Be praised at his command.

Seeking His secret deeds
With tears and toiling breath,
I find thy cunning seeds
O million-murdering Death.

Here it was in 1898 that Surgeon-Major Ronald Ross, IMS, who was better at medicine than poetry, discovered the way mosquitoes spread malaria, one of the grand triumphs of the imperial experience.

I know this little thing,
A myriad men will save,
O death where is thy sting?
Thy victory, O grave?

Technique is what the British chiefly taught Calcutta. Profit brought them, faith blessed them, power kept them there and technique they left behind. System was their forte. School history books in India used to have a final chapter called Blessings of the English Raj. Exam papers always had questions about the Blessings, and seventy years ago every conscientious Calcutta schoolboy, looking around him at the electric tramways and the General Post Office, or the High Court built to the pattern of Ypres Town Hall, could enumerate them pat: law and order, public health, irrigation works, schools, roads, bridges, railways and telegraphs.

High above the city now, to be seen equally from the roof of the Hindustan International Hotel or the squalidest canyon of Chitpur, the ugly steel lattice-work of the Howrah

Bridge stands testimony to one kind of British technique: in a thousand grubby offices below the armies of bureaucracy, still consulting the precedents and cross-references of the Raj, bear inflexible witness to another. But the Blessings nowadays are harder to detect: they have not worn well in Calcutta, and are mostly corroded, or discredited, or buried in debris.

For this is like a city pursued by nightmares — chaos always at its heels, threats too hideous to contemplate and too shapeless to define. Technique itself has turned to anarchy, as though all the mechanism of modern urban life, grafted by the British in the days of the textbooks, no longer recognizes authority: the trams, the telephones, the dustbin trucks, the big bridge, the policemen jumping from their lorry, the massed faces of a hundred million officials, the stopped clock, the Hogg Market attendant — all are jumbled, fused and disintegrated, while around the wreck of the system those dream figures revolve, corrupting the examiners or stabbing Congress supporters or pissing against the bakery wall.

And silently trail the pickpockets — silently after the Blessings, for when I was crossing Howrah Bridge in a rickshaw one night, a thief crept behind me with a very sharp knife, and while leaving my person fortunately intact, slit a hole in my bag and stole my wallet.

from

India: A Million Mutinies Now

V. S. NAIPAUL

The Secretary's Tale:
Glimpses of the Indian Century

NIKHIL SAID ONE DAY, 'I KNOW A MAN HERE CALLED RAJAN. He is the private secretary of an influential politician and businessman. He says he met you in Calcutta in 1962.'

I couldn't remember, and I still didn't remember even when Nikhil took me one afternoon to Rajan's office. Rajan was a small, sturdy man of the South with a square, dark face. His office – or the suite of which it formed part – was one of the most spacious and stylish offices I had seen in Bombay. It was in the international style, in cool, neutral colours, and it was beautifully air-conditioned. Rajan was clearly a man of authority in that office. He wore a fawn-coloured, short-sleeved Mao outfit, which might also have passed as a version of Indian formal clothes, or might simply have been a 'safari' suit.

He said, 'You came to Calcutta in 1962, during or just after the China war. You were with some film people. In those days I myself took a great interest in films and the arts – it was the most hopeful period of my life. Someone from the Film Society at the end of one evening introduced me to you. My duty was to take you back to the drug-company guest house where you were staying.'

The painful war in the background, the mingled smoke and autumnal mist of Calcutta, the small, ceiling-lit rooms of the Film Society, full of old office furniture: one or two moments of the vanished evening began to come back, but they were the merest pictures, hard to hold on to. And nothing remained of the end of the evening.

'I was twenty-two,' Rajan said. 'I was working in an advertising agency. I was a kind of clerk. My salary was 315 rupees a month. I was tipped to be an assistant account executive, but that wasn't to be.' Three hundred and fifteen rupees, £24, a month.

'When did you leave Calcutta?'

'It's a long story,' Rajan said.

And later that afternoon — while we sat outside the club house in Brabourne Stadium, the old international cricket ground of Bombay, and had tea, and watched the young cricketers practising at the nets (at the other end of the ground: the high, scaffolded back of the big stage built for the Russian ice show, part of the visiting Festival of Russia) — and on another day, in a hotel room not far from his office, beginning after his office work, and talking on until late in the evening, Rajan told me his story.

'I was born in Calcutta in 1940. Our family came from the South, from what in British times was known as the province of Madras and today is the state of Tamil Nadu. My grandfather used to be some kind of petty official in one of the law courts near the town of Tanjore. He was respected by people for his honesty and courage. Courage in the sense that if something wrong happened, or if someone asked him to do something his heart wouldn't let him do, he would turn violent or resist it in any form he thought fit.

'A Britisher was above him. He wanted my grandfather to be a witness in a lawsuit and say what was not true. I know only that it ended up in a kind of fracas, and my grandfather took off his footwear and hit the Britisher. He realized that after that life would be difficult for him in Tanjore. He decided to migrate to the North with his only son, who was a student at that time. This would have been early in the century, between 1900 and 1905. He chose to move to Calcutta, which was the British headquarters. He could make a living there and have some kind of life.

'In Calcutta he stayed with some friend or distant relation till he found his feet. He got his son to learn stenography. South Indians, brahmins especially, had a better grasp of English because they were more exposed to it, and they would get jobs as secretary, stenographer, or even typist. These were probably the most widely followed professions for the South Indian or Tamil brahmins in British times — and this is something that has changed only in very recent years. Otherwise, as a class, South Indian brahmins worked as teachers or as priests or as petty clerks. Or, if they were lucky enough, they would take up a job in one of the government departments. These were the days when a 10-rupee-a-month government job was a most prized thing — it was the ultimate aspiration of the bulk of the Tamil brahmins who had done some schooling. And quite a few of them migrated to the North, to the big cities, Bombay, Calcutta, Delhi.

'After he settled, my grandfather lived in Howrah, on the other side of the river from Calcutta city. It was one of those typical Calcutta residential houses — a *pucca* house, a proper house, not *kaccha*, something unfinished or improvised, and it was in a respectable middle-class locality. These places could be rented. It was a locality where there were other people from the South who had similarly migrated, and it gave them some security to live among their own kind. There was no ill-feeling at that time towards South Indians in Calcutta — those times were different. In fact, South Indians were widely respected by the Bengalis. It's quite different today. Since the 1960s South Indians in Calcutta feel they don't belong, in spite of their having been there for many decades. Which is perhaps one reason why I left Calcutta and moved to Bombay – but that was many years later.

'My father became a stenographer when he was seventeen or eighteen. This would have been about 1909, and he would probably have worked in one of the British companies. He was a capable stenographer, and he told me he had twice won the 50-rupee government prize for speed in English shorthand and typing. He continued to live in Howrah, in my grandfather's dwelling, which was a portion of a residential house. In Calcutta there were no such things as flats or apartments or tenements. There were just parts of houses – with the landlord occupying a part of the house, and renting out the rest with little adjustments here and there.

'In a few years both my grandfather and grandmother passed away, not leaving much by way of money or property. But my father moved to better jobs over the years. A stage came, in the decade between 1915 and 1925, when he was quite well paid. He had enough money not only to look after his family more than comfortably, but also to acquire some status symbols, like horses and phaetons. He had a few Arab horses driven by Muslim coachmen. Why Muslim? In those days they were the most widely available for those jobs. In those days, for certain trusted jobs, Hindus wouldn't mind having Muslims around them.

'I myself don't have any memory of this period of my father's life. These are all versions narrated to me by my eldest sister, without me asking for it. And narrated also by people who used to know my father very closely. Some of them would come out with remarks like: "Rarely have South Indians lived in Calcutta in such status or style as your father did." When I was a kid, when I was thirteen, fourteen, fifteen, when I was at school, I heard this when I ran into them at some social gathering. There would be talk then of someone doing well in life, or of someone having failed, and there would be talk of my father's past glory. When I heard these stories I felt a mixture of both pride and sadness.

'My father, during this time of well-being, took to the typical British style of dressing – complete with top hat, the suit, the waistcoat, double-toned shoes, the tie. And he also spent his leisure hours playing tennis. He started a tennis club close to his house. As a South Indian, his living expenses were meagre. All South Indian or Tamil brahmins were vegetarians without exception in those days, of course. So 200 rupees a month was quite a sizeable salary. An average family could make do with 30 or 40 rupees.

'He was a deeply religious man, as most of the South Indian brahmins were. Apart from tennis, the only thing on which he would spend his time were his pujas and *bhajans,* devotional songs. He was quite recognized for his singing of bhajans. He became a leader of the community in the locality. With this result: he kept new migrants from the South, young men coming in search of a livelihood, in his house. He fed them and clothed them and trained them in shorthand and typing. There was almost a regular stenography class in our house. And he helped them into jobs with British firms.

'My father used to respect the British. His ability to get along with the British people, and his love for the English language itself, probably did not make him look at them only as some kind of people to be hated. He never had a bent for politics of any kind.

'My father got married three times. He lost his first wife, and then he married a second time, so that his second wife could look after his first two children. When his second wife died, leaving in turn two or three children, he was forced by his relations to marry a third time. In those days such marriages were not difficult. Despite their impecunious situation, the Tamil brahmins were invariably good breeders. They would be happy to give away their daughters to anyone who wanted to marry them, so long as they were sure of the basics – that the man belonged to the same community, and the man was capable of supporting his wife and family.

'In 1935, when my father married for the third time, he was forty-three. His third wife, my mother, was eighteen. There was a child in 1937, a boy, but he barely lived six months, largely because of my mother's poor health. I was born in 1940.

'By this time my father had married off his first two daughters, and he had one more daughter to marry off. He also had a son from his second marriage still going to school. These were the uncertain war years. My father at that time was a godown or warehouse keeper. It was a responsible job — most of the items in the godown were imported. The godown was owned by the Japanese firm of Mitsui. My father had taken this job with the Japanese in 1936, after he had married my mother. And he continued with it until, with the war, these Japanese operations in India were closed down. When this happened, my father moved to the newly created government department of the DGMP, the Directorate-General of Munitions and Production.

'When the war ended, my father gave up this job. About this time Mahatma Gandhi's independence movement was taking on more serious proportions, and the Muslims too were becoming agitated. In 1946 there were very bad Hindu–Muslim riots in Calcutta.

'But before this, my mother had fallen seriously ill. When my mother was close to death, she asked my elder stepsister — who had married a former army man — to bring me up. So when my stepsister and her husband left Calcutta, I went with them. I was six. My mother died a month later.

'Almost at the same time the big Hindu–Muslim riots took place in Calcutta. In the riots, the house in which we had been living was burned down. We had left Howrah long before and had moved to the city proper. When my father lost his job with the DGMP at the end of the war, we had moved to a single-room tenement in a large building. This was the building that was set on fire during the riots and burned down — with the room where my mother had died, and where we had stored almost everything that had belonged to us.

'My father was forced during the riot to get into a jeep and leave everything behind, paying all that he had, several thousand rupees, to save himself, paying that to the people who transported him. They dumped him and others like him, in, Howrah railway station, leaving them to take trains to their chosen destinations away from the city.

'I was with my sister and her husband far away, where my sister's husband was working as a food supply inspector for the state government. He had been discharged from the army, Auchinleck's army, in 1945. He had been one of the Viceroy's Commissioned Officers, as they were called, and when he left the army he had the rank of *jemadar*. These people, the VCOs, had been drafted into the army before the war, at a time when the British felt they would soon be facing a war situation. As a kid I used to admire him. I used to look forward to seeing him. In my eyes he was some kind of a hero. He was always well turned out. He had a lot of gifts for us — chocolates, canteen supplies. The only thing I didn't like about him was the smoking.

'I realized what was happening to my father in Calcutta. I used to see the photographs in the papers, and people talked about the horrors. This sequence — of my having seen my mother dying slowly over many months in one room, with my aged father nursing her; and then my being handed over to my sister's charge, and moving with her and her husband to an altogether new place, on the other side of India, where people spoke another language, Marathi, which I couldn't understand — this sequence put me into a spell of utter gloom and depression.

'I look at it as depression now. At the time what I did was just sit outside the house, on the steps, just crouching, leaning my head on my arms, sitting all by myself on the steps outside my stepsister's house. I spent hours like that, confused, not knowing what to think.

'Suddenly one morning my father landed, and I suppose he restored me to a certain amount of life. Then he left again, promising to take me away, back with him, after things settled down. This was just before independence.

'My brother-in-law started playing truant from his job. He would leave us, and go away for weeks on end, and not tell us where he was going. My sister wrote to my father for help. But my father was yet to settle down himself. He was almost fifty-five at this time. After various moves with my sister and her husband — who kept on changing jobs, and in every job kept going off, as he had been used to doing — my father came and took me and my sister away to Calcutta, where he had at last found a place to stay. He had also found a job, in an import company. This was in January 1948, the month when Mahatma Gandhi died.

'I spent some time with my father. Then my grandmother came and took me back to her village in the South, and put me in a school there. But this village life didn't suit me, and in 1950 I returned to Calcutta, to my father. He began to educate me at home. It was only in 1952, when I was eleven, that I actually entered a school. My father couldn't come with me. So I went to the school myself and got myself admitted after a test, in Class 8.

'My father was teaching me mainly English. He didn't attach much importance to the other subjects. Because of his love for the English language, and because he was now aged, he would get me to read out the editorials and leading articles from the *Statesman,* although often I didn't follow what I was reading. He would ask me to underline the difficult words and phrases, and leave me to write down the meanings as my home work for the afternoon.

'My father's income had gone down, and the place where we were living was in a locality where the rents were low. The locality had a sprinkling of leftover Britishers in the mansions around us, a sizable number of Muslims, and an equally large number of Anglo-Indians and Christians. The whole family — there were six of us now: my father, my stepbrother, my stepsister and her two children, and myself — had one very large room. About 20 feet by 16 feet or 18 feet. We had to share the common tap and toilet.

'There were few South Indians in that locality. The family didn't quite fit in. So my father decided to shift over to a place where mixing would be more easy, and my school would be closer. I had joined a South Indian school.

'I studied there for three years. I had problems every year at exam times with various minor ailments, and it was really only my general good performance that saw me through from one class to the other.

'We had moved to a three-room flat. My brother had started earning by then.

'I completed school in March 1955. My father passed away two months later, in a street accident very close to our house. My father was an early riser. He had gone to the market to buy flowers for the morning puja; and, as he was returning, a motorcycle on the wrong side of the road, with three people on it, dashed against him, and he fell unconscious. We found him in a pool of blood, with the vegetables and the flowers he had purchased strewn all over.

'We took him to the hospital by taxi, together with one of the men from the motorbike, the other two having vanished. This man wasn't injured. He was only pretending; and when he saw it was only my brother and me holding our father, he opened the taxi door at a street corner, and ran away. My father stayed in the hospital for three days. Three painful days. He never regained consciousness. He passed away.

'The whole family now had to live on my brother's 150-rupees income, £14 a month. He was working as a secretary to a British factory-manager, the factory being located in one of the suburbs. So we had to leave the three-roomed flat. We moved to a smaller place near to my brother's factory.

'I couldn't think in terms of going on to a college. I didn't want to be a burden on my brother. And I wanted to be on my own in any case. So I decided to learn the most obvious thing – typing, to begin with. There was a typing school not far off from our new place. The fees were four rupees a month. My brother paid in the beginning, but then I was able to earn some money to pay the fees myself. I did odd typing jobs at the institute. I was on the lookout then for any kind of employment, but things were not easy. Often I used to walk 10 or 12 miles to look up a friend, in the hope of finding a job through his help. I was about sixteen at this time.'

Rajan, though sturdy, was a short man. I wondered what his physical condition was like at the time he was talking about.

I asked him, 'Did you feel strong or weak?'

'I didn't feel physically energetic enough all the time. But what kept me going was the determination to be on my own. I'll tell you something I did one day. I even approached a Britisher in my brother's factory. He said, "You're too young. You should be at school." Another person I approached said, "But you haven't even grown a moush." A moustache.

'I suffered spells of gloom and melancholia. It was almost what I felt when I used to sit on the steps of my sister's house. I often even thought of ending my life. There were the suburban trains. And there was always the Hooghly River. But the counsel of a close friend of mine changed my mind.

'I had no adolescence. I stepped directly from childhood into adulthood. And I felt undernourished. Our food had gone down after my father's death, because my brother had to feed so many mouths on his meagre income. An added dimension to my none too happy life at this time was my relationship with my stepbrother, who was supporting us all. We could never get along. He was almost nine years senior to me, and he would always beat me up badly. It was on one of those occasions, when he had beaten me up badly, that I was driven to thinking in terms of ending my life.

'Things brightened up the next year, 1957, when I ran into a friend who said he could fix me up in a job in a Marwari concern. The Marwaris were taking over from the British in Calcutta, and were then the principal business people in the city — and they continue to be so. They were taking over the jute mills, the tea gardens, the coal mines, etc.

'I took a job with one of those family concerns as a typist. The salary was to be 90 rupees a month, seven pounds. I was just about able to get myself a second pair of trousers and a shirt. It was a long journey to the office and a long journey back. In that month I spent no more than 10 rupees on myself, and I handed over the rest of what I earned to my brother as my contribution to the family expenses. I travelled on the second-class train. I didn't go to a movie. I didn't spend more than two annas, one-eighth of a rupee, a penny, on my lunch.

'A month after I joined, I was summoned by one of the directors. I had put the carbon in the wrong way when I was typing out a statement. I was sacked. Luckily, within seven days, I ran into another friend — we were on the same tram — and he took me to another employer. This was also a Marwari. He interviewed me in his house. His company was a newspaper company, which is today India's largest.

'I was to work in their newly opened advertising department. I typed out advertising reports. I got 125 rupees. So I was doing slightly better. I contributed a full 200 rupees to the family, and spent 25 rupees on myself, including the tuition fees at an evening college I had just joined, doing Intermediate Commerce.

'We could now afford to shift back to the old locality in South Calcutta. We lived in a flat shared between two families. My relations with my brother continued as before. But he had stopped beating me, after I had one day returned a slap he had given me.

'I stayed for a year with the newspaper group. Then I left and went to Lipton's for a salary of 10 rupees a day. The manager there recommended me to his own advertising agency, and for six years, from 1958 to 1964, I worked with that advertising agency. That was when I met you. It was a good time for me. I was a member of the British Council. My love for the English language drew me to people proficient in the English language – journalists, film-makers, copywriters, and advertising people generally.

'I liked the advertising profession. It was different. It made me think. It was not drudgery. My other jobs had been drudgery. And I particularly liked the people in the profession – the artists, the account executives, the printers, the copywriters. I joined the advertising agency on 270 rupees. The senior director liked my English, and I worked for him. He liked the interest I showed in the work. He promoted me to assist him in various campaigns. Soon I was tipped to be an assistant account executive. I got on with other people in the firm as well, because I was the youngest of the lot, and could converse fluently in their language, Bengali. Bengalis appreciate that. I got an annual increment of 15 rupees. In 1964 I was getting 330 rupees. I was promised promotion, to be an assistant account executive. And finally, when it didn't come, I resigned in a huff.

'I became an assistant to an advertising and short-film producer who had taken a liking to me. I picked up the basics of film-making. He paid me 350 rupees. I even shot certain sequences on my own. But the Pakistani war of 1965 put an end to that kind of film-making company, and I had to find another job. During this time I met important people in the Calcutta creative world. That made me very happy. I always thought I had a creative urge in me, which hadn't found expression because I hadn't had a settled life and a proper foundation.

'Somebody told me I should go to England. It was because of that I took a job with Air India, for the free flight to England. At the end of my first year I went to England for a visit. But I had to return, because of that recurring problem in the family about my stepsister and her husband. At the end of my second year with Air India I made a trip to the United States.

'The Air India salary was 350 rupees. It was too low – the rupee had been devalued in 1967. I even had to do a part-time job in the evening. At last, I answered an advertisement from a manufacturing company. On the strength of my experience I was given a job in the management cadre, for thrice the Air India salary. The bosses soon promoted me and put me in charge of a purchasing department.

'So, after all these years, I found myself on the other side. But I couldn't identify myself completely with the management, because I knew too well what life was like for others. But then the political situation in Bengal was becoming turbulent. Labour was unruly. The leftists had more or less gained control of the unions and the state. And the physical conditions in the city also started deteriorating. More and more firms were coming under the control of the Marwari capitalists. And then there was the oil crisis of 1973. I was in charge of procurement of oil for the factory. I really faced a rough time. Plus the power shortages, the difficult transport, and the labour militancy I had to put up with as part of the management staff. You might say I had found the right kind of job, but at the wrong time. I hated going to work in the mornings.

'At the end of 1973 I quit – the problems in the job, the conditions of life in Calcutta. These things were compelling me to move out of Calcutta. I could only think of Bombay as the alternative, because my occasional trips to that city earlier – because of my job with Air India – had impressed me with its cosmopolitanism and its opportunities.

'So, without having a job in my hand, I moved to Bombay with my little savings. In Bombay I stayed with a relative almost my own age who was running a photographic studio in a distant suburb. He had no room. But I used to live in the studio, sharing the common toilet with other tenants in the building, and an open space for my bath. We used to store water for our photographic needs, and out of this I used to bathe.

'And I slept in a kind of loft that I specially made for myself. It was almost twice or thrice the size of an average coffin. It was just below the roof, and above the false ceiling of the front portion of the shop. I would climb into it by using the window bars as steps, and then I would slide myself into the small opening. I was comfortable. The air would come through the opening around the roller shutter. Often I would find this little loft to be the most convenient place for doing my reading and occasional writing – of letters, not articles.

'I was earning a meagre sum, having started working in the studio. I would send most of this back to my people, in Calcutta, because the four children of my sister were growing, and my stepbrother now had his own family to look after.

'Initially I thought I would be able to build up the photography business with my relative, as I knew a little bit of photography as an amateur. But after a while, my savings having dried up, my relation turned out to be none too helpful. When I needed money he wouldn't give it, and when I asked for the money I had already spent on the studio he wouldn't return it.

'So it was a strained relationship, although, helplessly, I continued to live there, sleeping and reading in my cubby hole, because accommodation of any kind was one real problem in Bombay. As the situation worsened, I decided to give up the idea of any photography business and having to depend on my relation.

'As a first step, I put an ad in the classified pages of the *Times of India.* That must have cost me about 14 or 15 rupees – the paper charged concessional rates for job-seekers. I got 40 replies.

'The advertisement I wrote read something like this: "South Indian secretary with over 10 years' experience, with impeccable English, seeks interesting position in advertising, public relations, travel, etc." I shortlisted the replies by choosing not to respond to companies located in the suburbs on the Central Railway, especially factories. The travelling conditions there were difficult and would involve a change of trains half-way from where I was living with my relation — that was an hour and a half away on the Western Railway line.

'I decided to attend only four interviews, all of which were to take place around the Victoria Terminal in Churchgate, and were in offices rather than factories or workshops. Nothing happened the first day. I didn't come to accept the jobs for varying reasons — salary, office atmosphere, and the interviewer himself. In fact, I told off one of the interviewers when he asked a very absurd question. "Why did you leave Calcutta after all these years? Those beautiful women there — you should have stayed at least for the *rasgolla*-like women there.' I thought that was too degrading to women. Probably he found I was more than he required. It was a trading company, and he was one of those uncouth characters who had suddenly come into money.

'The four interviews I had arranged were to last two days. Two a day. At the end of the first day I was somewhat despondent. I didn't want to return to Calcutta. On the other hand, I didn't want to make my life more miserable by being without much money and continuing to live with my relation. So I decided that if I didn't get a job the next day, I would have to return to Calcutta, from where my sister had been persistently writing to me.

'The following day I came all the way from the photographic studio to Churchgate. On arrival at Churchgate station I went to Satkar Restaurant opposite the station. The board said: "Tea and Snack Bar". I ordered myself an idli and a coffee — idli was about 60 paise and coffee was 40 paise — because I thought that was all I could afford, with my money touching the bottom.

'As I was finishing my coffee, I looked through the papers, the letters from the firms I had shortlisted, to see who were the people I still had to look up. And there I found this call from a man who described himself simply as "Municipal Councillor". His address was on "A" Road. I asked the waiter where "A" Road was. He said, "You are sitting on the very same road." I found that the address the municipal councillor had given was just a stone's throw away.

'I made for it, and discovered it was an office within a residence. After I had waited for a while, a gentleman came in. This was my first sight of the man with whom I was to work for the next 14 years. He was a tall man – no, average, five foot seven, five foot eight. Very fair, not heavily built. He looked well groomed, well dressed.

'He took me inside his office, and after a very brief conversation, 15 minutes, he straight away asked me to join him. Although I was readily impressed by the man, by his speed and quick decision, I did not accept his offer straight away, as I had to ponder over the salary offer he had made, which was 900 rupees. But he made no secret of his keenness to engage me. It looked almost as though he had guessed my situation, decided how much I should get, and made me an offer. To this day I don't know whether he knows much about me, my background, my life away from the office.

'He asked me to ring him back as soon as I had made up my mind, and he hoped he wouldn't have to wait too long, because he had made up *his* mind that I was the kind of man he was looking for. I went back to the restaurant – it was a different waiter – and, after weighing the situation, had very nearly come to the conclusion that a job in hand was better than none. I phoned him up the next day, and joined him the Monday following.

'When I got this job, there was an effort on the part of my relation in the photographic studio to patch up our relationship. But I didn't want it. I stayed for three months after that in the cubby hole in the studio. Then I continued to move from place to place as a paying guest with various families – with problems of their own, of all kinds. I had a suitcase of clothes and another suitcase of books and knick-knacks. Two suitcases of possessions – that was all I had.

'In my work for my employer I began to know people of importance. I enjoyed that. He was a civic leader and I could see that he was an ambitious man. I thought I would have opportunities of rising with him. And, indeed, he has risen in all directions. He is more famous and powerful and wealthy now than when I first went to work for him.

'People who deal with me in my office might say that I have risen with him. But I feel it hasn't been exactly in the manner I had hoped for. For a long time, while I worked here, my nomadic life as a paying guest continued, with my two suitcases, until I met a very kindly family — very hard to think of in a place like Bombay — who were generous enough to offer me a room all to myself, although in an old building. This was in 1980. I was forty years old. At that age, for the first time in my life, I had a room of my own. This was a dream in a place like Bombay, where people have to sleep on the pavement and in drainpipes — and it was perhaps the best thing to have happened to me.

'Until three years ago I lived on this charity, in a single room in that old house, with a common privy shared by 40 people. I couldn't think of marriage then. My salary, though very good by Bombay standards, couldn't have bought me a dwelling of any kind. But I've since been lucky, despite the odds, to acquire a flat or apartment of my own.

'And then a friend of mine felt I should settle down. This friend knew that I had seen my responsibilities to my sister's family through. He put an ad on my behalf in the matrimonial pages of the paper. It's the classified ad which has brought me things, and now again the ad came into my life and changed the course of events for me.

'Among the people who responded to the advertisement my friend had inserted for me was my prospective father-in-law. I had given my background and age in the ad. I had hidden nothing. I said I wanted a lady who would look forward to a simple life. I got about 90 replies, perhaps 100. They were from various parts of India. I think I got so many replies because I had said in the advertisement: "Caste, community, widows, divorcees, no bar." I wanted a lady, though, who was already in Bombay, because that would settle many problems. Bombay life is so hard – there are language problems for people not knowing Hindi – and transport is hard, and generally the style of life is hard here. It isn't an easy thing to get acclimatized to.

'In about half an hour with my prospective father-in-law he was able to understand my basic character. The meeting took place in the coffee shop of the Ritz Hotel. He had come over to my office, but I had to keep him there for a couple of hours, this seventy-year-old man, because I wasn't free when he came. He is a Keralite, but a brahmin. An average-sized man, bald, quiet-spoken, with the real stamp of patience on his face and in his demeanour. He was a retired electrical engineer in charge of purchase for a public-sector undertaking – part of industrializing India. He had been all over the country, and his children were broadminded.

'About a week after this meeting I went to their house at about 10.30 at night, after a full day's work. She was in bed. Her father woke her up. I spoke to her. She had been working for a nationalized bank for 10 years, took interest in yoga, and was not given to speaking much. She was average in her looks. She wasn't fat, but because of her height she didn't look lean. She was about four foot ten. She wore specs.

'And after conversing more or less through her father and her mother, I felt I should meet her again and let her speak her own mind in a private talk, without the parents. After three days I met her once again in her cousin's place. The cousin appreciated this attitude of mine, and made all appropriate arrangements, for privacy, etc. Over a cup of coffee we talked for a little over half an hour – she had just come back from her office in the bank. She wasn't a great dresser. I had the impression she didn't worry much about her attire.

'After three days I telephoned her at her office, and this time we met in a restaurant. And by and large we agreed that we

should get married. We got married in about 40 days. I wanted a
civil marriage — no dowry, no give, no take; no crowding around
with relations and friends; no party, no feasts, no gifts. But they
didn't want a civil marriage. So I called my cousin to perform
the rites. I was totally without religion myself; I had never made
a special effort to understand Hindu theology or principles.

'I am happy at last in having a purpose in life, now that
I have a family of my own. I've put an end to my otherwise
unsettled life. Marriage came to me when I was forty-five. My
wife was thirty-nine. We both had to wait a long time for this
mercy. And God has blessed us with this added happiness that —
at this late stage — we have had a child.

'I am still left with the feeling that I might have risen much
higher, given a little more understanding and sympathy. Or
perhaps in another country. What keeps haunting me all the
time is the feeling that I am doomed to rise no more than I
have risen. Even in this job I have been like a ship's ladder.
The sea rises, the ship rises, and the ladder rises with it. But
the ladder cannot rise on its own. I cannot be independent of
my employer and rise in life.

'And yet I have, positively, a sense of fulfilment. When
my father died, we were almost penniless, despite our earlier
well-being. My sister brought me up early. And when my brother-
in-law deserted her, it became my turn to take care of her and
rear her children. I was able to do it. Today they are all well
placed. I look upon them as symbols of my achievement.

'And yet, too, I thought I would be some kind of creative
person — like the persons I knew in Calcutta, when I first met
you in 1962. But that kind of life and companionship has always
eluded me. I started off as a secretary, and am still a secretary,
and shall probably end as a secretary. I haven't risen beyond what
my father and grandfather could rise to, at the beginning of
the century. The only consolation is that, even as a secretary, I
am not as badly off as most other secretaries are. And perhaps,
even, I no longer believe I am just a secretary.'

from

Begums, Thugs and White Mughals: The Journals of Fanny Parkes

FANNY PARKES

JANUARY 1824 — THE ADVANTAGES OF A RESIDENCE IN CALCUTTA are these: you are under the eye of the Government, not likely to be overlooked, and are ready for any appointment falling vacant; you get the latest news from England, and have the best medical attendance. On the other hand, you have to pay high house rent; the necessary expenses are great; and the temptations to squander away money in gratifying your fancies more numerous than in the *mofussil*.

A friend, now high in the Civil Service, contracted, on his arrival here about eighteen years ago, a debt of Rs 15,000, about £1500 or £1800. Interest was then at twelve per cent. To give security, he insured his life which, with his agent's commission of one per cent, made the sum total of interest sixteen per cent. After paying the original debt five times, he hoped his agents upon the last payment would not suffer the interest to continue accumulating. He received for answer, 'that interest never slept, it was awake night and day'; and he is now employed in saving enough to settle the balance.

I wish much that those who exclaim against our extravagances here knew how essential to a man's comfort, to his quiet, and to his health it is to have everything good about him — a good house, good furniture, good carriages, good horses, good wine for his friends, good humour; good servants and a good quantity of them, good credit, and a good appointment: they would then be less virulent in their philippics against oriental extravagance.

January 15th — The Governor-General has a country residence, with a fine park, at Barrackpore; during the races the Calcutta world assembles there; we went over for a week; it was delightful to be again in the country. Lady Amherst rendered the Government House gay with quadrilles and displays of fireworks but I most enjoyed a party we made to see the ruins of an ancient fort, near Cairipoor, belonging to the Rajah of Burdwan, about five miles from Barrackpore, and thought them beautiful.

The road was very bad, therefore I quitted the buggy and mounted an elephant for the first time, feeling half-frightened but very much pleased. I ascended by a ladder placed against the side of the kneeling elephant; when he rose up, it was like a house making unto itself legs and walking therewith.

We went straight across the country, over hedges and ditches, and through the cultivated fields, the elephant with his great feet crushing down the corn, which certainly did not 'rise elastic from his airy tread'. The fields are divided by ridges of earth like those in salterns at home; these ridges are narrow, and in general, to prevent injury to the crops, the *mahout* guides the elephant along the ridge: it is curious to observe how firmly he treads on the narrow raised path.

By the side of the road was a remarkable object: 'The appearance of a *fakir* is his petition in itself.' In a small hole in the earth lay a *fakir*, or religious mendicant; the fragment of a straw mat was over him, and a bit of cloth covered his loins. He was very ill and quite helpless, the most worn emaciated being I ever beheld; he had lain in that hole day and night for five years and refused to live in a village, his only comfort, a small fire of charcoal, was kindled near his head during the night. Having been forcibly deprived of the property he possessed in the upper provinces, he came to Calcutta to seek redress, but being unsuccessful he had, in despair, betaken himself to that hole in the earth. An old woman was kindling the fire; it is a marvel the jackals do not put an end to his misery. The natives say, 'It is his pleasure to be there, what can *we* do?' and they pass on with their usual indifference: the hole was just big enough for his body, in a cold swampy soil.

There is a menagerie in the park at Barrackpore, in which are some remarkably fine tigers and cheetahs. My *ayah* requested to be allowed to go with me, particularly wishing to see an hyena. While she was looking at the beast I said, 'Why did you wish to see an hyena?' Laughing and crying hysterically, she answered, 'My husband and I were asleep, our child was between us, an hyena stole the child, and ran off with it to the jungle; we roused the villagers, who pursued the beast; when they returned, they brought me half the mangled body of my infant daughter — that is why I wished to see an hyena.'

Before we quitted Calcutta, we placed the plate in a large iron treasure chest. A friend, during his absence from home, having left his plate in a large oaken chest clamped with iron found, on his return, that the bearers had set fire to the chest to get at the plate, being unable to open it, and had melted the greater part of the silver!

It appears as if the plan of communicating with India by steamboats will not end in smoke: a very large bonus has been voted to the first *regular company* who bring it about, and the sum is so considerable, that I have no doubt some will be bold enough to attempt it.

In Calcutta, as in every place, it is difficult to suit yourself with a residence. Our first house was very ill defended from the hot winds; the situation of the second we thought low and swampy, and the cause of fever in our household. My husband, having quitted college, was gazetted to an appointment in Calcutta, and we again changed our residence for one in Chowringhee Road.

Prince Jamh o Deen, hearing me express a wish to see what was considered a good *nach,* invited me to one. I could not, however, admire the dancing; some of the airs the women sang were very pretty.

Calcutta was gay in those days, parties numerous at the Government House, and dinners and fancy balls amongst the inhabitants.

A friend sent me a mouse deer, which I keep in a cage in the verandah; it is a curious and most delicate little animal, but not so pretty as the young pet fawns running about the compound with the spotted deer. The cows' milk generally sold in Calcutta is poor, that of goats is principally used: a good Bengali goat, when in full milk, will give a quart every morning; they are small-sized, short-legged, and well-bred. The servants milk the goats near the window of the morning room, and bring the bowl full and foaming to the breakfast table.

February 27th — My husband put into one of the smaller lotteries in Calcutta, and won thirteen and a half tickets, each worth Rs 100: he sent them to his agents, with the exception of one, which he presented to me. My ticket came up a prize of Rs 5000. The next day we bought a fine, high caste fiery Arab, whom we called Orelio, and a pair of grey Persian horses.

February 28th — Trial by Rice — The other day some friends dined with us: my husband left his watch on the drawing-room table when we went to dinner: the watch was stolen, the theft was immediately discovered, and we sent to the police. The *moonshee* assembled all who were present, took down their names, and appointed that day seven days hence for a trial by rice, unless, during the time, the watch should be restored, stolen property being often replaced from the dread the natives entertain of the ordeal by rice. On the appointed day the police *moonshee* returned, and the servants, whom he had ordered to appear fasting, were summoned before him, and by his desire were seated on the ground in a row.

The natives have great faith in the square *akbarabadee* rupee which they prefer to, and use on such occasions in lieu of, the circular rupee.

The *moonshee*, having soaked 2lb. weight of rice in cold water, carefully dried it in the sun: he then weighed rice equal to the weight of the square rupee in a pair of scales, and, calling one of the servants to him, made him take a solemn oath that he had not taken the watch, did not know who had taken it, where it was, or anything about it or the person who stole it. When the oath had been taken, the *moonshee* put the weighed rice into the man's hand to hold during the time every servant in the room was served in like manner. There were thirty-five present. When each had taken the oath, and received the rice in his hand, they all sat down on the ground, and a bit of plantain leaf was placed before each person. The *moonshee* then said 'Some person or persons amongst you have taken a false oath; God is in the midst of us; let every man put his portion of rice into his mouth, and having chewed it, let him spit it out upon the plantain leaf before him; he who is the thief, or knows aught concerning the theft, from his mouth it shall come forth as dry as it was put in; from the mouths of those who are innocent, it will come forth wet and well chewed.'

Every man chewed his rice, and spat it out like so much milk and water, with the exception of three persons, from whose mouths it came forth as dry and as fine as powder. Of these men, one had secreted two-thirds of the rice, hoping to chew the smaller quantity, but all to no purpose; it came *perfectly dry* from his mouth from the effect of fear, although it was ground to dust. The *moonshee* said, 'Those are the guilty men, one of them will probably inform against the others' and he carried them off to the police. It is a fact, that a person under great alarm will find it utterly impossible to chew and put forth rice in a moistened state, whilst one who fears not will find it as impossible to chew and to spit it out perfectly dry and ground to dust. An *harkara*, in the service of one of our guests, was one of the men whom the *moonshee* pronounced guilty; about a fortnight before, a silver saucepan had been stolen from his master's house, by one of his own servants.

Against another, one of our own men, we have gained some very suspicious intelligence, and although we never expect the watch to be restored, we shall get rid of the thieves. So much for the ordeal by rice, in which I have firm faith.

May 4th — The weather is tremendously hot. A gentleman came in yesterday, and said, 'this room is delightful, it is cold as a well.' We have discovered, however, that it is infested below with rats and muskrats, three or four of which my little Scotch terrier kills daily; the latter make him foam at the mouth with disgust. My little dog Crab, you are the most delightful Scotch terrier that ever came to seek his fortune in the East!

Some friends have sent to us for garden-seeds. But, oh! observe how nature is degenerated in this country — they have sent alone for vegetable-seeds — the feast of roses being here thought inferior to the feast of marrowfat peas!

[...]

July 17th — On this day, having discovered a young friend ill in the Writer's Buildings, we brought him to our house. Two days afterwards I was seized with the fever, from which I did not recover for thirteen days. My husband nursed me with great care, until he fell ill himself; and eleven of our servants were laid up with the same disorder.

The people in Calcutta have all had it; I suppose, out of the whole population, European and native, not two hundred persons have escaped; and what is singular, it has not occasioned one death amongst the adults. I was so well and strong — over night we were talking of the best means of escaping the epidemic — in the morning it came and remained thirty-six hours, then quitted me; a strong eruption came out, like the measles, and left me weak and thin. My husband's fever left him in thirty-six hours, but he was unable to quit the house for nine days: the rash was the same. Some faces were covered with spots like those on a leopard's skin. It was so prevalent that the Courts of Justice, the Custom House, the Lottery Office and almost every public department in Calcutta were closed in consequence of the sickness. In the course of three days, three different physicians attended me, one after the other having fallen ill. It is wonderful that a fever producing so much pain in the head and limbs, leaving the patient weak, reduced, and covered with a violent eruption, should have been so harmless; after three weeks, nobody appeared to have suffered, with the exception of two or three children whom it attacked more violently than it did grown-up people, and carried them off.

The politicians at home have anticipated us in reckoning upon the probability of a Burmese war. We have hitherto been altogether successful. I saw yesterday a gold and a silver sword, and a very murderous looking weapon resembling a butcher's knife, but on a larger scale. A necklace (so called from its circling the neck, for it was composed of plates of gold hammered on a silken string), and some little squab images, gods perhaps, taken from a chief, whom Major Sale of H. M. 13th dispatched in an attack upon a stockade, leaving the chief in exchange part of the blade of his own sword, which was broken in his skull by the force of the blow that felled him.

It is an unlucky business: the Company certainly do not require at present more territory on that side of India, and the expense to which Government is put by this elegant little mill, as Pierce Egan might call it, is more than the worthies in Leadenhall Street suppose.

I see Lord Hastings is made Civil Governor of Malta! 'To what base uses we may return!' I observe the motion to prevent the necessity of parents sending their sons to Haileybury has been lost. The grand object of the students should be the acquisition of the oriental languages; here nothing else tells.

If a young man gets out of college in three or four months after his arrival which, if he crams at college in England, he may easily effect, he is considered forthwith as a brilliant character and is sealed with the seal of genius. Likewise pockets medals and moneys and this he may do without knowing anything else.

To a person fresh from England, the number of servants attending at table is remarkable. We had only a small party of eight to dinner yesterday, including ourselves; three-and-twenty servants were in attendance! Each gentleman takes his own servant or servants, in number from one to six, and each lady her attendant or attendants, as it pleases her fancy. The *huqqa* was very commonly smoked at that time in Calcutta: before dinner was finished, every man's pipe was behind his chair. The tobacco was generally so well prepared that the odour was not unpleasant, unless by chance you sat next to a man from the *mofussil*, when the fume of the spices used by the up-country *huqqa bardars* preparing the tobacco, rendered it oppressive and disagreeable.

September 1st — The fever has quitted Calcutta, and travelled up the country stage by stage. It was amusing to see, upon your return to the Course, the whole of the company stamped, like yourself, with the marks of the leech upon the temples. Its origin has been attributed to many causes, and it has been called by many names. The gentlemen of the lancet are greatly divided in their opinions; some attribute it to the want of rain, others to the scarcity of thunder and lightning this season. There was an instance of the same general fever prevailing in the time of Warren Hastings. Not a single instance has been heard of its having proved mortal to adults.

Goodbye to Calcutta

ALAN ROSS

THE TEMPERATURE IS 105 DEGREES, HUMIDITY 100 PER CENT.
Between now and the monsoon in two months' time both
will get worse. Power cuts remain lengthy and unpredictable;
the Japanese-built telephone system rarely works, and that vast
trench running like a banked sewer through the centre of the
city and allegedly to become a metro has not only made travel
virtually impossible, but Calcutta hideous. As a child in the
1930s I thought Calcutta, that 'village of palaces', a heaven
on earth, and on each of four visits during the last 20 years
there appeared to be mitigating circumstances for evidence
of decline: the Bangladesh war, refugees, a Marxist government. The metro, unlikely ever to be finished, a permanent
disfigurement, seems the last straw.

It was the Russians a decade ago who foisted this folly, a
central government not a state project, on Mrs Gandhi, then
at her most susceptible. The advice of British, American,
Japanese and various European traffic experts to go for roads
or flyovers, easily constructed at a fraction of the cost, was

rejected: No one in Calcutta that I spoke to held out much hope for its successful completion or operation. Most believe that it would even now — despite the large waste of money and effort — be safer and more sensible simply to fill it in. Instead, because of political pride and bureaucratic intransigency, spasmodic digging will probably continue year after year until Calcutta grinds finally to a halt. No work can be done in the rains, and only a quarter of every rupee spent contributes to the construction. The idea of trains actually operating under ground in Calcutta — prone to subsidence, flooding, loss of power, extremes of heat, to say nothing of an inevitable invasion of pavement-dwellers — is even more appalling than the desecration of the city and its waste.

Meanwhile trams, buses, rickshaws, cows, cyclists, taxis, and old beat-up Ambassador cars jostle along what little remains of the streets. The public and private buses, carrying double their proper loads, frequently lose or squash their protruding passengers or overturn. In the suburbs or upcountry, pedestrians, who rarely look in either direction when crossing the road, are regularly knocked down, though in surprisingly few numbers, and when this occurs the offending bus, taxi or car is immediately surrounded and set on fire. The driver runs for his life and the passengers, too, if they are lucky.

Of course, Calcutta, that Brechtian city of the imagination — a metropolis beyond invention — has been, in the eyes of most people, in decline for over a century. Five generations of my family have lived there off and on, probably contributing to that, and a number of them have died there. The British cemeteries, in fact, are one of the few things that flourish. Though no longer a growth industry in the same way, their ghosts bloom under revived conservationist interest, pampered as few living things are in Calcutta.

One of my earliest memories of Calcutta is the racecourse, the most centrally situated of any major city in the world. That, at least, has not changed. A couple of minutes from the colliery-like inferno of Chowringhee and lying between the Victoria Memorial and the Hooghly, its track, paddocks and turreted stands form the same fine flourish to the southern end of the maidan. There may no longer be palatial residences at Garden Reach, the handsome colonial houses of Alipore are mostly company flats or taken over by Marwaris — those shrewd Rajastani entrepreneurs who have become the affluent scapegoats for all Bengal's economic injustices — and Kidderpore docks are only a shadow of their former glory, but the race-course, with its flags flying, its crisply-suited men and dazzling women, is as splendid as ever. From the boxes on the members' stand, with Chowringhee only discernible at roof level, it might still be as I used to dream of it through a decade of adolescent separation. Satyajit Ray, to whom I delivered a viewing-filter and who lives in the next street — huge shabby houses among palms and banana trees — where I used to visit my grandmother, says he could not imagine living anywhere else, so the dream must still be real for someone.

One thing the Bengal government learned from the Bangladesh war was that Calcutta can afford no more refugees. Accordingly, during the Assam atrocities, camps were set up in the frontier areas, and approaches to Calcutta sealed. Although criticism of Mrs Gandhi for persisting with the elections in Assam remains fairly general, tea-planters who have spent their whole lives there do not support it. According to them, there was little reason to predict butchery, certainly not on the scale that took place. Plainly, government advisers underestimated the real or contrived ferocity of local feeling, but if it was a misjudgment there was no precedent for acting otherwise.

In general it is impossible not to be amazed at the good humour and gentleness with which Indians, and the people of Calcutta especially, support the trials of their existence. Yet the violence when it erupts is horrifying. Large-scale demonstrations are no problem. Thousands mass on the maidan under local banners, the haranguing goes on all day, and then, when everyone is worn out, they disperse peacefully and return to their homes. It is the individual violence that shocks. Hardly a day passes without reports of an unwanted wife or daughter-in-law being set fire to and burned to death; last week, in a change of roles, a wife set fire to her husband.

There is no green quite like the green of Bengal. And once you are out of Calcutta the landscape assumes the timeless quality and serene beauty that haunt for ever those who fall prey to it: the raised, ruler-straight road lined with tamarind, peepul, bamboo, mango, gol mohur, ashoka; wheat and rice stretching away to the horizon; water buffaloes, only heads visible, motionless in hyacinth-filled lakes; the occasional cyclist under a black umbrella and, at the hour of the cowdust, creaking bullock carts. The villages are mere scatters of thatched huts and markets, rivers curve under coconut palms, women in turquoise, lemon or pink saris stride in their marvellous way under pitchers or copper bowls. Within half an hour Calcutta simply seems an aberration. The empty battlefield of Plassey, recorded by a single monument, or the Residency ruins at Lucknow have more immediacy than the broken sewage-pipe washing facilities and lightless suburbs of Calcutta.

No matter whom you ask, 'corruption' is always the answer when you try to assess responsibility for inefficiency and chaos; corruption among politicians, civil servants, petty officials, businessmen. Nothing proceeds without bribery, to such an extent that the inhabitants of Calcutta are disinclined to believe that this is not standard practice everywhere for everything. At the same time West Bengal, under its Marxist government, has one of the most honest and civilised administrations in India. Unfortunately, it is also a power-conscious one and investment in Bengal has as a consequence dried up. J.R.D. Tata, the 70-year-old head of the Tata empire and one of the shrewdest men in India, recently gave an interview to Calcutta's new newspaper the *Telegraph* (better written and printed than any of its older rivals) in which he laid much of the blame for India's present plight on Nehru's adherence to the Soviet pattern of industrial development and neglect of agriculture. According to Tata, the dismantling of bureaucracy, as recently achieved by Jayewardene in Sri Lanka, and a change from a parliamentary to an Indian-adapted presidential system offers the only hope of reversing the present slide into disorder and bankruptcy.

Affection for a city can blind one to almost anything. I don't think, all the same, that I shall ever want to return to Calcutta; not only because of its unsightliness and the relentless degradation of human life there, but because, for the first time, I felt it as a faintly hostile place. It was to be expected that all monuments to the Raj should be disposed of, but the painting out or removal of every single road sign in English and the replacement of familiarly named childhood streets by Lenin Sarani and Karl Marx Sarani etc. give one a strange feeling. It is as if the past had been rearranged to create not only confusion but a sense of alienation and dispossession.

Bengalis, for all their bureaucratic obstructiveness, can be marvellous people, and occasionally, at sunset or dawn, with the air sweet off the Hooghly, the old ties seemed to be re-establishing themselves. But if I ever had to live in India again it would certainly be Bombay or Bangalore, even Delhi, that I would choose, not Calcutta, and that is an admission I never expected I would have to make.

from

A Suitable Boy

VIKRAM SETH

7.30

WHEN THEY GOT TO THE PARK STREET CEMETERY, AMIT and Lata got out of the car. Dipankar decided he'd wait in the car with Tapan, since they were only going to be a few minutes and, besides, there were only two umbrellas.

They walked through a wrought-iron gate. The cemetery was laid out in a grid with narrow avenues between clusters of tombs. A few soggy palm trees stood here and there in clumps, and the cawing of crows interspersed with thunder and the noise of rain. It was a melancholy place. Founded in 1767, it had filled up quickly with European dead. Young and old alike – mostly victims of the feverish climate – lay buried here, compacted under great slabs and pyramids, mausolea and cenotaphs, urns and columns, all decayed and greyed now by ten generations of Calcutta heat and rain. So densely packed were the tombs that it was in places difficult to walk between them. Rich, rain-fed grass grew between the graves, and the rain poured down ceaselessly over it all. Compared to Brahmpur or Banaras, Allahabad or Agra, Lucknow or Delhi,

Calcutta could hardly be considered to have a history, but the climate had bestowed on its comparative recency a desolate and unromantic sense of slow ruin.

'Why have you brought me here?' asked Lata.

'Do you know Landor?'

'Landor? No.'

'You've never heard of Walter Savage Landor?' asked Amit, disappointed. 'Oh yes. Walter Savage Landor. Of course. "Rose Aylmer, whom these watchful eyes."'

'Wakeful. Well, she lies buried here. As does Thackeray's father and one of Dickens' sons, and the original for Byron's *Don Juan*,' said Amit, with a proper Calcuttan pride.

'Really?' said Lata. 'Here? Here in Calcutta?' It was as if she had suddenly heard that Hamlet was the Prince of Delhi. 'Ah, what avails the sceptred race!'

'Ah, what the form divine!' continued Amit.

'What every virtue, every grace!' cried Lata with sudden enthusiasm. 'Rose Aylmer, all were thine.'

A roll of thunder punctuated the two stanzas.

'Rose Aylmer, whom these watchful eyes –' continued Lata.

'Wakeful.'

'Sorry, wakeful. Rose Aylmer, whom these wakeful eyes –'

'May weep, but never see,' said Amit, brandishing his umbrella.

'A night of memories and sighs,'

'I consecrate to thee.'

Amit paused. 'Ah, lovely poem, lovely poem,' he said, looking delightedly at Lata. He paused again, then said: 'Actually, it's "A night of memories and of sighs".'

'Isn't that what I said?' asked Lata, thinking of nights – or parts of nights – that she herself had recently spent in a similar fashion.

'No. You left out the second "of".'

'A night of memories and sighs. Of memories and of sighs. I see what you mean. But does it make such a difference?'

'Yes, it makes a difference. Not all the difference in the world but, well, a difference. A mere "of"; conventionally permitted to rhyme with "love". But she is in her grave, and oh, the difference to him.'

They walked on. Walking two abreast was not possible, and their umbrellas complicated matters among the cluttered monuments. Not that her tomb was so far away — it was at the first intersection — but Amit had chosen a circuitous route. It was a small tomb capped by a conical pillar with swirling lines; Landor's poem was inscribed on a plaque on one side beneath her name and age and a few lines of pedestrian pentameter:

> *What was her fate? Long, long before her hour,*
> *Death called her tender soul by break of bliss*
> *From the first blossoms, from the buds of joy;*
> *Those few our noxious fate unblasted leaves*
> *In this inclement clime of human life.*

Lata looked at the tomb and then at Amit, who appeared to be deep in thought. She thought to herself: he has a comfortable sort of face.

'So she was twenty when she died?' said Lata.

'Yes. Just about your age. They met in the Swansea Circulating Library. And then her parents took her out to India. Poor Landor. Noble Savage. Go, lovely Rose.'

'What did she die of? The sorrow of parting?'

'A surfeit of pineapples.'

Lata looked shocked.

'I can see you don't believe me, but oh, 'tis true, 'tis true,' said Amit. 'We'd better go back,' he continued. 'They will not wait for us — and who can wonder? You're drenched.'

'And so are you.'

'Her tomb,' continued Amit, 'looks like an upside-down ice-cream cone.' Lata said nothing. She was rather annoyed with Amit.

After Dipankar had been dropped off at the Asiatic Society, Amit asked the driver to take them down Chowringhee to the Presidency Hospital. As they passed the Victoria Memorial he said:

'So the Victoria Memorial and Howrah Bridge is all you know and all you need to know of Calcutta?'

'Not all I need to know,' said Lata. 'All I happen to know. And Firpos and The Golden Slipper. And the New Market.'

Tapan greeted this news with a Kakoli-couplet:

'Cuddles, Cuddles, gentle dog,
Go and bite Sir Stuart Hogg.'

Lata looked mystified. Since neither Tapan nor Amit explained the reference, she went on: 'But Arun has said we'll go for a picnic to the Botanical Gardens.'

'Under the spreading banyan tree,' said Amit.

'It's the biggest in the world,' said Tapan, with a Calcutta chauvinism equal to his brother's.

'And will you go there in the rains?' said Amit.

'Well, if not now, then at Christmas.'

'So you'll be back at Christmas?' asked Amit, pleased.

'I think so,' said Lata.

'Good, good,' said Amit. 'There are lots of concerts of Indian classical music in winter. And Calcutta is very pleasant. I'll show you around. I'll dispel your ignorance. I'll expand your mind. I'll teach you Bangla!'

Lata laughed. 'I'll look forward to it,' she said.

Cuddles gave a blood-curdling growl.

'What's the matter with you now?' asked Tapan. 'Will you hold this for a second?' he asked Lata, handing her the leash.

Cuddles subsided into silence.

Tapan bent down and looked carefully at Cuddles' ear.

'He hasn't had his walk yet,' said Tapan. 'And I haven't had my milkshake.'

'You're right,' said Amit. 'Well, the rain's let up. Let's just look at the second great poetic relic and then we'll go out onto the Maidan and the two of you can get as muddy as you like. And on the way back we'll stop at Keventers.' He continued, turning to Lata: 'I was thinking of taking you to Rabindranath Tagore's house in North Calcutta, but it's quite far and a bit slushy and it can wait for another day. But you haven't told me if there's anything particular that you'd like to see.'

'I'd like to see the university area some day,' said Lata. 'College Street and all that. But nothing else really. Are you sure you can spare the time?'

'Yes,' said Amit. 'And here we are. It was in that small building there that Sir Ronald Ross discovered what caused malaria.' He pointed to a plaque affixed to the gate. 'And he wrote a poem to celebrate it.'

Everyone got down this time, though Tapan and Cuddles took no interest in the plaque. Lata read it through with a great deal of curiosity. She was not used to the comprehensible writings of scientists, and did not know what to expect.

This day relenting God
Hath placed within my hand
A wondrous thing; and God
Be praised, at his command.

Seeking his secret deeds
With tears and toiling breath,
I find thy cunning seeds
O million-murdering death.

I know this little thing
A myriad men will save.
O death where is thy sting
And victory, O grave?

Lata read it a second time. 'What do you think of it?' asked Amit.

'Not much,' said Lata.

'Really? Why?'

'I'm not sure,' said Lata. 'I just don't. "Tears and toiling", "million-murdering" — it's too alliterative. And why should "God" be allowed to rhyme with "God"? Do you like it?'

'Well, yes, in a way,' said Amit. 'I do like it. But equally I can't defend that feeling. Perhaps I find it moving that a Surgeon-Major should write so fervently and with such religious force about something he'd done. I like the quaint chiasmus at the end. Ah, I've just created a pentameter,' he said, pleased.

Lata was frowning slightly, still looking at the plaque, and Amit could see she was not convinced.

'You're quite severe in your judgment,' he said with a smile. 'I wonder what you'd say about my poems.'

'Maybe some day I'll read them,' said Lata. 'I can't imagine the kind of poetry you write. You seem so cheerful and cynical.'

'I'm certainly cynical,' said Amit.

'Do you ever recite your poetry?'

'Almost never,' said Amit.

'Don't people ask you to?'

'Yes, all the time,' said Amit. 'Have you listened to poets reading their work? It's usually awful.'

Lata thought back to the Brahmpur Poetry Society and smiled broadly. Then she thought again of Kabir. She felt confused and sad.

Amit saw the swift change of expression on her face. He hesitated for a few seconds, wanting to ask her what had brought it about, but before he could do so she asked, pointing to the plaque:

'How did he discover it?'

'Oh,' said Amit, 'he sent his servant to get some mosquitoes, then got the mosquitoes to bite him — his servant, that is — and when he got malaria soon afterwards, Ross realized that it was mosquitoes that caused it. O million-murdering death.'

'Almost a million and one,' said Lata.

'Yes, I see what you mean. But people have always treated their servants strangely. Landor of the memories and sighs once threw his cook out of a window.'

'I'm not sure I like Calcutta poets,' said Lata.

Flute–Music

RABINDRANATH TAGORE

Kinu the milkman's alley.
    A ground-floor room in a two-storeyed house,
Slap on the road, windows barred.
    Decaying walls, crumbling to dust in places
      Or stained with damp.
      Stuck on the door,
    A picture of Ganesa, Bringer of Success,
      From the end of a bale of cloth.
Another creature apart from me lives in my room
      For the same rent:
      A lizard.
    There's one difference between him and me:
      He doesn't go hungry.

      I get twenty-five rupees a month
      As junior clerk in a trading office.
I'm fed at the Dattas' house
      For coaching their boy.

At dusk I go to Sealdah station,
Spend the evening there
To save the cost of light.
Engines chuffing,
Whistles shrieking,
Passengers scurrying,
Coolies shouting.
I stay till half past ten,
Then back to my dark, silent, lonely room.

A village on the Dhaleśvarī river, that's where my aunt's people
live.
Her brother-in-law's daughter —
She was due to marry my unfortunate self, everything was fixed.
The moment was indeed auspicious for her, no doubt of
that —
For I ran away.
The girl was saved from me,
And I from her.
She did not come to this room, but she's in and out of my
mind all the time:
Dacca sari, vermilion on her forehead.

Pouring rain.
My tram costs go up,
But often as not my pay gets cut for lateness.
Along the alley,
Mango skins and stones, jack-fruit pulp,
Fish-gills, dead kittens
And God knows what other rubbish
Pile up and rot.
My umbrella is like my depleted pay —
Full of holes.
My sopping office clothes ooze
Like a pious Vaisnava.
Monsoon darkness

Sticks in my damp room
    Like an animal caught in a trap,
      Lifeless and numb.
Day and night I feel strapped bodily
    On to a half-dead world.

  At the corner of the alley lives Kāntabābu —
    Long hair carefully parted,
      Large eyes,
        Cultivated tastes.
    He fancies himself on the cornet:
  The sound of it comes in gusts
    On the foul breeze of the alley —
Sometimes in the middle of the night,
    Sometimes in the early morning twilight,
      Sometimes in the afternoon
    When sun and shadows glitter.
      Suddenly this evening
He starts to play runs in Sindhu-Bārōyā rāg,
    And the whole sky rings
With eternal pangs of separation.
  At once the alley is a lie,
False and vile as the ravings of a drunkard,
And I feel that nothing distinguishes Haripada the clerk
    From the Emperor Akbar.
  Torn umbrella and royal parasol merge,
    Rise on the sad music of a flute
      Towards one heaven.

    The music is true
  Where, in the everlasting twilight-hour of my
                wedding,
    The Dhaleśvarī river flows,
  Its banks deeply shaded by *tamal*-trees,
And she who waits in the courtyard
  Is dressed in a Dacca sari, vermilion on her forehead.

from

The Great Railway Bazaar

PAUL THEROUX

Through Berhampur and Khurda to Cuttack where children splashed, diving around buffaloes submerged to their nostrils in the wide Mahanadi River. This was the northeast corner of Orissa, smallpox capital of the world — Balasore, the very name suggesting some itching illness. The station signboards were captions to images I saw from the train: Tuleswar, a woman carrying a red clay water jar on her head, bringing contagion to a far-off village; Duntan, a defecating Bengali posed like Rodin's *Thinker*; Kharagpur, a man twisting the tail of his buffalo to make him go faster; Panskura, a crowd of children in school uniforms running along the tracks to their shantytown for lunch; and then the impacted precincts of Budge-Budge, where what I first took to be the poignant sight of an old man leading a small boy through the detritus of a train yard was a blind man with a devilish face squeezing the arm of the frightened child who was his guide.

The travelers on the Howrah Mail had a look of fatigued solemnity. They paid no attention to the hawkers and vendors who became more frequent as we neared Calcutta, getting on at suburban stations to make a circuit of the open carriages. A man gets on with a teapot, balancing a row of nesting clay cups on his arm. He squawks, urging tea on the passengers, waving the teapot in each person's face, and gets off: no sale. He is followed by a man with a jar of candy and a spoon. The candy man bangs his jar with the spoon and begins a monotonous spiel. Everyone is shown the jar, and the man continues to pound his spoon all the way to the door, where another enters with a tray of fountain pens. The pen man babbles and, as he does so, he demonstrates how the cap is unscrewed, how the nib is poised, how the clip works; he twirls the pen and holds it for everyone to see; he does everything but write with it, and when he has finished he leaves, having sold nothing. More get on with things to sell: buns, roasted chickpeas, plastic combs, lengths of ribbon, soiled pamphlets; nothing is sold.

At some stations Indians dived through the windows for seats, but when the seats were filled they squashed themselves at the door, maintaining only an emotional contact with the railway car. They were suspended from the ceiling on straps, stacked against the wall like cordwood, heaped on the benches holding their knees together, and outside the Howrah Mail they clung to the fittings with such agility, they seemed magnetized.

Near Howrah Station throngs of Biharis were throwing themselves into the greasy Hooghly River from sanctified *ghats.* Their festival, *Chhat,* was enlivening Calcutta, and it offered a chance for the Biharis to make a show of strength against the Bengalis, whose own Kali festival had sealed many streets with the chamber of horrors that is a Kali shrine: the goggle-eyed goddess twice life-size, with her necklace of human heads, sticking out a tongue as bright as a raspberry Popsicle and trampling the mortally wounded corpse of her husband. Behind Kali, plaster tableaux showed four doomed men, the first impaled on a bloody spear, the second having his neck wrung by a skeleton, the third flattened by a hag who is simultaneously severing the fourth's head. It was all a challenge to the Biharis, whose own processions involved tall mobile shrines draped in yellow cloth, carts loaded with women seated among heaps of banana offerings, looking deeply pious, and little troupes of transvestites dancing to bugle calls and drums.

'There go the Biharis, off to throw their bananas in the Hooghly,' said Mr. Chatterjee, from the chair car. A Bengali, Mr. Chatterjee wasn't sure of the purpose of the *Chhat* festival, but thought it might have something to do with the harvest. I said I didn't think the Calcutta harvest would be very large. He agreed, but said the Biharis enjoyed their annual chance to snarl Bengali traffic. At the head of every procession a black grinning boy, dressed as a girl, made the jerky movements of a dancer with his wrists and leaped in the air, his genitals whipping about in his crimson sari. From time to time, the young girls (who might have been boys) behind him dropped to the ground and prostrated themselves in the garbage-strewn streets.

The holy mob, the stink of sanctity, the legitimate noise: everything in Indian life seemed to sanction excess, and even politics had the *puja* flavor. While these religious festivals were going their bellowing way, the Socialist Unity Centre was organizing a *bundh* — a total work stoppage — and their preliminary rallies on the *maidan* with their flags and posters, processions and speeches, were practically indistinguishable from the displays of mass piety on Chowringhee's sidewalks and at the sloshing *ghats*. This aspect of Calcutta is the first that meets the traveler's eye, but the one that stays longest in the mind; it is an atmosphere of organized disturbance, everyone occupied in carrying out some program or other, so much so that those stricken thousands one sees uniformly — uniformly, because space is scarce — lying or sitting on the sidewalk have the look of nonviolent protesters having a long afternoon of dedicated *satyagraha* ('clinging to truth'). I imagined another group in an ambiguous posture when I read, in a Calcutta newspaper, 'The leftist leaders also decided to resort to mass squatting...'

From the outside, Howrah Station looks like a secretariat, with its not quite square towers and many clocks — each showing a different time — and its impenetrable brickwork. The British buildings in India look as if they have been designed to withstand a siege — there are hornworks and cannon emplacements and watchtowers on the unlikeliest structures. So Howrah Station looked like a fortified version of a mammoth circumlocution office, an impression that buying a ticket there only confirms. But inside it is high and smoky from the fires of the people who occupy it; the ceiling is black, the floor is wet and filthy, and it is dark — the long shafts of sun streaming from the topmost windows lose their light in dust on the way down.

'It's much better than it was,' said Mr. Chatterjee, seeing me craning my neck. 'You should have seen it *before* they cleaned it up.'

His remark was unanswerable. Yet at every pillar squatters huddled amid the rubbish they had created: broken glass, bits of wood and paper, straw, and tin cans. Some infants slept against their parents; others were curled up like changelings in dusty corners. Families sought refuge beside pillars, under counters and luggage carts: the hugeness of the station intimidated them with space and drove them to the walls. Their children prowled in the open spaces, combining their scavenging with play. They are the tiny children of tiny parents, and it's amazing how, in India, it is possible to see two kinds of people in the process of evolution, side by side, one fairly tall, quick, and responsive, the other, whose evolution is reduction, small, stricken, and cringing. They are two races whose common ground is the railway station, and though they come quite close (an urchin lies on his back near the ticket window watching the legs of the people in line) they do not meet.

I walked outside, into the midday chaos at the western end of the Howrah Bridge. In Simla, rickshaws were retained for their quaintness: people posed in them. In Calcutta, rickshaws, pulled by skinny running men in tattered clothes,

are a necessary form of transport, cheap, and easy to steer in
narrow back lanes. They are a crude symbol of Indian society,
but in India all symbols are crude: the homeless people sleeping in the doorway of the mansion, the commuter running
to his train accidentally trampling a station sleeper, the thin
rickshaw-*wallah* hauling his plump passengers. Ponies har-
nessed to stagecoaches labored over cobblestones; men pushed
bicycles loaded with hay bales and firewood. I had never seen
so many different forms of transport: wagons, scooters, old
cars, carts and sledges and odd, old-fashioned horse-drawn
vehicles that might have been barouches. In one cart, their
white flippers limp, dead sea turtles were stacked; on another
cart was a dead buffalo, and in a third an entire family with
their belongings — children, parrot cage, pots and pans. All
these vehicles, and people surging among them. Then there
was panic, and the people scattered as a tottering tram car
marked TOLLYGUNGE swayed down the bridge. Mr. Chatterjee
said, 'Too much of people!'

Mr. Chatterjee walked across the bridge with me. He was a
Bengali, and Bengalis were the most alert people I had met in
India. But they were also irritable, talkative, dogmatic, arrogant,
and humorless, holding forth with malicious skill on virtually every subject except the future of Calcutta. Any mention
of that brought them up short. But Mr. Chatterjee had views.
He had been reading an article about Calcutta's prospects.
Calcutta had been very unlucky: Chicago had had a great fire,
San Francisco an earthquake, and London a plague as well as a
fire. But nothing had happened to Calcutta to give planners a
chance to redesign it. You had to admit, he said, it had vitality. The problem of pavement dwellers (he put the figure at
a quarter of a million) had been 'somewhat overdramatized,'
and when you considered that these pavement dwellers were
almost exclusively engaged in ragpicking you could see how
Calcutta's garbage was 'most intensively recycled.' It seemed
an unusual choice of words, and it strayed close to claptrap:

vitality in a place where people lay dead in the gutter ('But everyone dies eventually,' said Mr C.), the overdramatized quarter of a million, the recycling ragpickers. We passed a man who leaned at us and put his hand out. He was a monster. Half his face was missing; it looked as if it had been clumsily guillotined — he had no nose, no lips, no chin, and clamped in his teeth, which were perpetually exposed, was the bruised plug of his tongue. Mr. Chatterjee saw my shock. 'Oh, *him!* He is always here!'

Before he left me at the Barabazar, Mr. Chatterjee said, 'I *love* this city.' We exchanged addresses and we parted, I to a hotel, Mr. Chatterjee to Strand Road, where the Hooghly was silting up so badly, soon all that would float on it would be the ashes of cremated Bengalis.

I stayed in Calcutta for four days, giving lectures, seeing the sights and losing my lecture fees at the Royal Calcutta Turf Club on the Saturday I decided to leave. On the first day the city seemed like a corpse on which the Indians were feeding like flies; then I saw its features more clearly, the obelisks and pyramids in Park Street Cemetery, the decayed mansions with friezes and columns, and the fountains in the courtyards of these places: nymphs and sprites blowing on dry conches, who, like the people living under them in gunny sacks, are missing legs and arms; the gong of trams at night; and the flaring lamps lighting the wild cows pushing their snouts into rubbish piles, vying with the scrabbling Indians for something edible. The high mock-Moghul tenements

> hustled it, and crushed it, and stuck brick-and-mortar elbows into it, and kept the air from it, and stood perpetually between it and the light...
>
> You groped your way for an hour through lanes and bye-ways, and court-yards and passages; and you never once emerged upon anything that might be reasonably called a street. A kind of resigned distraction came over the stranger as he trod those devious mazes, and, giving himself

up for lost, went in and out and round about and quietly turned back
again when he came to a dead wall or was stopped by an iron railing,
and felt that the means of escape might possibly present themselves in
their own good time, but to anticipate them was hopeless...

Among the narrow thoroughfares at hand, there lingered, here and
there, an ancient doorway of carved oak, from which, of old, the sounds
of revelry and feasting often came; but now these mansions, only used
for storehouses, were dark and dull, and, being filled with wool, and
cotton, and the like — such heavy merchandise as stifles sound and stops
the throat of echo — had an air of palpable deadness... In the throats and
maws of dark no-thoroughfares... wholesale dealers in grocery-ware
had perfect little towns of their own; and, deep among the foundations
of these buildings, the ground was undermined and burrowed out into
stables, where cart-horses, troubled by rats, might be heard on a quiet
Sunday rattling their halters, as disturbed spirits in tales of haunted
houses are said to clank their chains...

Then there were steeples, towers, belfries, shining vanes, and masts
of ships: a very forest. Gables, housetops, garret-windows, wilderness
upon wilderness. Smoke and noise enough for all the world at once.

There is more, and it is all good, but I think I have quoted enough
to show that the best description of Calcutta is Todger's corner
of London in Chapter IX of *Martin Chuzzlewit*. But having decided
that Calcutta was Dickensian (perhaps more Dickensian than
London ever was), and knowing that I could not share either the
excitement of the Bengalis, who agreed with the enormous bill-
board put up by the State Bank of India (CALCUTTA IS FOREVER),
or, what is more curious, the chummy regard of the Americans
I met there for this vast and yet incomplete city that I felt would
someday undo them, I decided to leave it and so leave India.

I was on my way when I saw the hopping man in the crowd
on Chowringhee. He was very strange: in a city of mutilated
people only the truly monstrous looked odd. This man had
one leg — the other was amputated at the thigh — but he did not
carry a crutch. He had a greasy bundle in one hand. He hopped

past me with his mouth open, pumping his shoulders. I went after him, and he turned into Middleton Street, hopping very fast on one muscular leg, like a man on a pogo stick, his head rising above the crowd, then descending into it. I couldn't run because of the other people, black darting clerks, swamis with umbrellas, armless beggars working their stumps at me, women proffering drugged babies, strolling families, men seeming to block the sidewalk with their wide flapping trousers and swinging arms. The hopping man was in the distance. I gained on him – I saw his head clearly – then lost him. On one leg he had outrun me, so I never found out how he did it. But afterwards, whenever I thought of India, I saw him – hop, hop, hop – moving nimbly through those millions.

from

Following the Equator

MARK TWAIN

Do not undervalue the headache. While it is at its sharpest it seems a bad investment; but when relief begins, the unexpired remainder is worth $4 a minute.

— PUDD'NHEAD WILSON'S NEW CALENDAR.

A COMFORTABLE RAILWAY JOURNEY OF SEVENTEEN AND A half hours brought us to the capital of India, which is likewise the capital of Bengal — Calcutta. Like Bombay, it has a population of nearly a million natives and a small gathering of white people. It is a huge city and fine, and is called the City of Palaces. It is rich in historical memories; rich in British achievement — military, political, commercial; rich in the results of the miracles done by that brace of mighty magicians, Clive and Hastings. And has a cloud-kissing monument to one Ochterlony.

It is a fluted candlestick 250 feet high. This lingam is the only large monument in Calcutta, I believe. It is a fine ornament, and will keep Ochterlony in mind.

Wherever you are, in Calcutta, and for miles around, you can see it; and always when you see it you think of Ochterlony. And so there is not an hour in the day that you do not think of Ochterlony and wonder who he was. It is good that Clive cannot come back, for he would think it was for Plassey; and then that great spirit would be wounded when the revelation came that it was not. Clive would find out that it was for Ochterlony; and he would think Ochterlony was a battle. And he would think it was a great one, too, and he would say, 'With three thousand I whipped sixty thousand and founded the Empire – and there is no monument; this other soldier must have whipped a billion with a dozen and saved the world.'

But he would be mistaken. Ochterlony was a man, not a battle. And he did good and honorable service, too; as good and honorable service as has been done in India by seventy-five or a hundred other Englishmen of courage, rectitude, and distinguished capacity. For India has been a fertile breeding ground of such men, and remains so; great men, both in war and in the civil service, and as modest as great. But they have no monuments, and were not expecting any. Ochterlony could not have been expecting one, and it is not at all likely that he desired one – certainly not until Clive and Hastings should be supplied. Every day Clive and Hastings lean on the battlements of heaven and look down and wonder which of the two the monument is for; and they fret and worry because they cannot find out, and so the peace of heaven is spoiled for them and lost. But not for Ochterlony. Ochterlony is not troubled. He doesn't suspect that it is his monument. Heaven is sweet and peaceful to him. There is a sort of unfairness about it all.

Indeed, if monuments were always given in India for high achievements, duty straitly performed, and smirchless records, the landscape would be monotonous with them. The handful of English in India govern the Indian myriads with apparent ease, and without noticeable friction, through tact, training, and distinguished administrative ability, reinforced by just and liberal laws – and by keeping their word to the native whenever they give it.

England is far from India and knows little about the eminent services performed by her servants there, for it is the newspaper correspondent who makes fame, and he is not sent to India but to the continent, to report the doings of the princelets and the dukelets, and where they are visiting and whom they are marrying. Often a British official spends thirty or forty years in India, climbing, from grade to grade by services which would make him celebrated anywhere else, and finishes as a vice-sovereign, governing a great realm and millions of subjects; then he goes home to England substantially unknown and unheard of, and settles down in some modest corner, and is as one extinguished. Ten years later there is a twenty-line obituary in the London papers, and the reader is paralyzed by the splendors of a career which he is not sure that he had ever heard of before. But meanwhile he has learned all about the continental princelets and dukelets.

The average man is profoundly ignorant of countries that lie remote from his own. When they are mentioned in his presence one or two facts and maybe a couple of names rise like torches in his mind, lighting up an inch or two of it and leaving the rest all dark. The mention of Egypt suggests some Biblical facts and the Pyramids – nothing more. The mention of South Africa suggests Kimberly and the diamonds and there an end. Formerly the mention, to a Hindoo, of America suggested a name – George Washington – with that his familiarity with our country was exhausted. Latterly his familiarity with it has doubled in bulk; so that when America is mentioned now, two torches flare up in the dark caverns of his mind and he says, 'Ah, the country of the great man – Washington; and of the Holy City – Chicago.' For he knows about the Congress of Religion, and this has enabled him to get an erroneous impression of Chicago.

When India is mentioned to the citizen of a far country it suggests Clive, Hastings, the Mutiny, Kipling, and a number of other great events; and the mention of Calcutta infallibly brings up the Black Hole. And so, when that citizen finds himself in the capital of India he goes first of all to see the Black Hole of Calcutta — and is disappointed.

The Black Hole was not preserved; it is gone, long, long ago. It is strange. Just as it stood, it was itself a monument; a ready-made one. It was finished, it was complete, its materials were strong and lasting, it needed no furbishing up, no repairs; it merely needed to be let alone. It was the first brick, the Foundation Stone, upon which was reared a mighty Empire — the Indian Empire of Great Britain. It was the ghastly episode of the Black Hole that maddened the British and brought Clive, that young military marvel, raging up from Madras; it was the seed from which sprung Plassey; and it was that extraordinary battle, whose like had not been seen in the earth since Agincourt, that laid deep and strong the foundations of England's colossal Indian sovereignty.

And yet within the time of men who still live, the Black Hole was torn down and thrown away as carelessly as if its bricks were common clay, not ingots of historic gold. There is no accounting for human beings.

The supposed site of the Black Hole is marked by an engraved plate. I saw that; and better that than nothing. The Black Hole was a prison — a *cell* is nearer the right word — eighteen feet square, the dimensions of an ordinary bedchamber; and into this place the victorious Nabob of Bengal packed 146 of his English prisoners. There was hardly standing room for them; scarcely a breath of air was to be got; the time was night, the weather sweltering hot. Before the dawn came, the captives were all dead but twenty-three. Mr. Holwell's long account of the awful episode was familiar to the world a hundred years ago, but one seldom sees in print even an extract from it in our day. Among the striking things in it is this. Mr. Holwell, perishing with thirst, kept himself alive by sucking the perspiration from his sleeves. It gives one a vivid idea of the situation. He presently found that while he was busy drawing life from one of his sleeves a young English gentleman was stealing supplies from the other one. Holwell was an unselfish man, a man of the most generous impulses; he lived and died famous for these fine and rare qualities; yet when he found out what was happening to that unwatched sleeve, he took the precaution to suck that one dry first. The miseries of the Black Hole were able to change even a nature like his. But that young gentleman was one of the twenty-three survivors, and he said it was the stolen perspiration that saved his life. From the middle of Mr. Holwell's narrative I will make a brief excerpt:

> *Then a general prayer to Heaven, to hasten the approach of the flames to the right and left of us, and put a period to our misery. But these failing, they whose strength and spirits were quite exhausted laid themselves down and expired quietly upon their fellows: others who had yet some strength and vigor left made a last effort at the windows, and several succeeded by leaning and scrambling over the backs and heads of those in the first rank, and got hold of the bars, from which there was no removing them. Many to the right and left sunk with the violent pressure, and were soon suffocated; for now a steam arose from the living and the dead. which affected us in all its circumstances as if we were forcibly held with our heads over a bowl full of strong volatile spirit of hartshorn, until suffocated; nor could the effluvia of the one be distinguished from the other, and frequently, when I was forced by the load upon my head and shoulders to hold my face down, I was obliged, near as I was to the window, instantly to raise it again to avoid suffocation. I need not, my dear friend, ask your commiseration, when I tell you, that in this plight, from half an hour past eleven till near two in the morning, I sustained the weight of a heavy man, with his knees in my back and the pressure of his whole body on my head. A Dutch surgeon who had taken his seat upon my left shoulder, and a Topaz (a black Christian soldier) bearing on my right; all which nothing could have enabled me to support but the props and pressure equally sustaining me all around. The two latter I frequently dislodged by shifting my hold*

*on the bars and driving my knuckles into their ribs; but my friend above
stuck fast, held immovable by two bars.*

*I exerted anew my strength and fortitude: but the repeated trials and
efforts I made to dislodge the insufferable incumbrances upon me at
last quite exhausted, me; and towards two o'clock, finding I must quit
the window or sink where I was. I resolved on the former, having bore,
truly for the sake of others, infinitely more for life than the best of it is
worth. In the rank close behind me was an officer of one of the ships,
whose name was Cary, and who had behaved with much bravery during
the siege (his wife, a fine woman, though country born, would not quit
him, but accompanied him into the prison, and was one who survived).
This poor wretch had been long raving for water and air; I told him I was
determined to give up life, and recommended his gaining my station. On
my quitting it he made a fruitless attempt to get my place; but the Dutch
surgeon, who sat on my shoulder, supplanted him. Poor Cary expressed
his thankfulness, and said he would give up life too; but it was with the
utmost labor we forced our way from the window (several in the inner
ranks appearing to me dead standing, unable to fall by the throng and
equal pressure around). He laid himself down to die; and his death, I
believe, was very sudden; for he was a short, full, sanguine man. His
strength was great; and, I imagine, had he not retired with me, I should
never have been able to force my way. I was at this time sensible of no
pain, and little uneasiness; I can give you no better idea of my situation
than by repeating my simile of the bowl of spirit of hartshorn. I found a
stupor coming on apace, and laid myself down by that gallant old man,
the Rev. Mr. Jervas Bellamy, who laid dead with his son, the lieutenant,
hand in hand, near the southernmost wall of the prison. When I had lain
there some little time, I still had reflection enough to suffer some uneasiness
in the thought that I should be trampled upon, when dead, as I myself
had done to others. With some difficulty I raised myself, and gained the
platform a second time, where I presently lost all sensation; the last trace
of sensibility that I have been able to recollect after my laying down, was
my sash being uneasy about my waist, which I untied, and threw from
me. Of what passed in this interval, to the time of my resurrection from
this hole of horrors, I can give you no account.*

There was plenty to see in Calcutta, but there was not plenty of time for it. I saw the fort that Clive built; and the place where Warren Hastings and the author of the Junius Letters fought their duel; and the great botanical gardens; and the fashionable afternoon turnout in the Maidan; and a grand review of the garrison in a great plain at sunrise; and a military tournament in which great bodies of native soldiery exhibited the perfection of their drill at all arms, a spectacular and beautiful show occupying several nights and closing with the mimic storming of a native fort which was as good as the reality for thrilling and accurate detail, and better than the reality for security and comfort; we had a pleasure excursion on the *Hoogly* by courtesy of friends, and devoted the rest of the time to social life and the Indian museum. One should spend a month in the museum, an enchanted palace of Indian antiquities. Indeed, a person might spend half a year among the beautiful and wonderful things without exhausting their interest.

It was winter. We were of Kipling's 'hosts of tourists who travel up and down India in, the cold weather showing how things ought to be managed.' It is a common expression there, 'the cold weather,' and the people think there is such a thing. It is because they have lived there half a lifetime, and their perceptions have become blunted. When a person is accustomed to 138 in the shade, his ideas about cold weather are not valuable. I had read, in the histories, that the June marches made between Lucknow and Cawnpore by the British forces in the time of the Mutiny were made in that kind of weather – 138 in the shade – and had taken it for historical embroidery. I had read it again in Serjeant Major Forbes-Mitchell's account of his military experiences in the Mutiny – at least I thought I had – and in Calcutta I asked him if it was true, and he said it was. An officer of high rank who had been in the thick of the Mutiny said the same. As long as those men were talking about what they knew, they were trustworthy, and I believed them; but when they said it was now 'cold weather,' I saw that they had traveled outside of their sphere of knowledge and were floundering. I believe that in India 'cold weather' is merely a conventional phrase and has come into use through the necessity of having some way to distinguish between weather which will melt a brass door-knob and weather which will only make it mushy. It was observable that brass ones were in use while I was in Calcutta, showing that it was not yet time to change to porcelain; I was told the change to porcelain was not usually made until May. But this cold weather was too warm for us; so we started to Darjeeling, in the Himalayas — a twenty-four hour journey.

Biographies

SIMON WINCHESTER (1944–)

A former foreign correspondent for the *Guardian*, Simon Winchester now writes books and divides his time between a farm in the Berkshire Hills of Massachusetts, a flat in Manhattan and a cottage in the Western Isles of Scotland. He is the author of the best-selling *The Surgeon of Crowthorne* (entitled *The Professor and the Madman* in the United States) and *The Map That Changed the World*, as well as numerous other books. His most recent books are *Krakatoa: The Day the World Exploded* and *The Meaning of Everything: The Story of the Oxford English Dictionary*.

RUPERT WINCHESTER (1966–)

Rupert Winchester is a writer, broadcaster and inveterate traveller. He currently lives in London with his American wife.

CLARK BLAISE (1940–) & BHARATI MUKHERJEE (1940–)

A novelist and short-story writer, Clark Blaise has taught at many universities across North America. Born in Calcutta, Bharati Mukherjee is a novelist, short-story writer and academic, whose writings often focus on migrants and their experiences. Blaise and Mukherjee married in 1963, and they are the co-authors of several books.

BUDDHADEV BOSE (1908–74)

Buddhadev Bose was a Bengali critic and educationalist, who wrote poetry, plays, novels, short stories and criticism, and translated European poets into Bengali. Seen by many as Rabindranath Tagore's true successor, he was a central figure in 20th-century Bengali literary life.

N. C. CHAUDHURI (1897–1999)

Nirad Chaudhuri was one of the more fascinating products of the meeting between Bengali and European culture, a writer touched by both Indian nationalism and European liberal thought. He worked as a radio journalist before moving to England and writing full time. His *Autobiography of an Unknown Indian* has been described as 'one of the great books of the century'. He wrote his last book at the age of 100.

WILLIAM DALRYMPLE (1965–)

Scottish travel writer and historian William Dalrymple wrote the highly acclaimed bestseller *In Xanadu* when he was twenty-two, and since then has gone on to write a number of highly acclaimed books on India, spirituality and history. He divides his time between London and Delhi.

ELIZA FAY (1756–1816)

Eliza Fay was a seamstress, teacher and unlucky merchant, who visited India four times between 1779 and 1816. Through her letters home to her family, we see India through the eyes of a woman blessed with a vivid sense of style, laced with great vitality and humanity.

GÜNTER GRASS (1927–)

The German novelist, poet, playwright and sculptor Günter Grass won the Nobel Prize for Literature in 1999. Politically active and committed to the peace and environmental movements, he is best known for his novel *The Tin Drum*.

PETER HOLT (1956–)

Author and journalist Peter Holt was educated at Eton. As a journalist he worked for various British national newspapers and spent ten years on Fleet Street with the London *Evening Standard*, before retracing his ancestor Robert Clive's journeys around south-eastern India. Peter Holt is married and lives in Shropshire, where he runs the family business.

RUDYARD KIPLING (1863–1936)

Rudyard Kipling was born in India but educated in England. He returned to India in the 1880s to work as a journalist but subsequently became chiefly known as a writer of short stories, and was celebrated as the successor to Charles Dickens. Kipling was the poet of the British Empire and the common soldier, whom he glorified in many of his works. Endlessly prolific, he achieved fame quickly, and was awarded the Nobel Prize for Literature in 1907.

DOMINIQUE LAPIERRE (1931–)

Dominique Lapierre is a French writer who made his name through both novels and non-fiction works with strong humanitarian overtones. In 1981, Lapierre founded an association rescuing leper children from the slums of Calcutta, which is supported by half the royalties from his literary successes. Lapierre's time in Calcutta gave him a huge international bestseller in *The City of Joy*.

ADRIAN LEVY (1965–) & CATHY SCOTT-CLARK (1965–)
Cathy Scott-Clark trained as a libel insurance underwriter, while Adrian Levy became a theatre director, but both separately moved into journalism. They met for the first time after being recruited by London's *Sunday Times*, where they became foreign correspondents. They covered regional conflicts and disasters from Kashmir to the Lebanon before leaving to become freelance writers, documentary film makers and broadcasters.

SUSANNA MOORE (1945–)
Susanna Moore is a prize-winning novelist, and author of *My Old Sweetheart, In The Cut, The Whiteness of Bones, Sleeping Beauties,* and a book of non-fiction, *I Myself Have Seen It.* She was born in Hawaii and now lives in New York.

GEOFFREY MOORHOUSE (1931–)
Geoffrey Moorhouse is one of Britain's best-loved travel writers, and his books on travel, history and cricket have been translated into many languages. He is a fellow of the Royal Society of Literature and of the Royal Geographical Society. He lives in a hill village in North Yorkshire.

JAMES MORRIS (1926–)
Morris was working for the *Times* when he was sent to the Himalayas in 1953 to cover the first successful ascent of Everest, and has been travelling and writing ever since. James Morris also wrote the highly acclaimed study of the British Empire, *Pax Britannica.* As Jan Morris, she continues to write and observe beautifully. She lives in Wales.

V. S. NAIPAUL (1932–)
Born in Trinidad, Vidiadhar Surajprasad Naipaul worked as a journalist before publishing his first novel in 1957. His work has grown steadily darker and more complex over the years, and he has written several travel books, including *An Area of*

Darkness: An Experience of India. Naipaul was knighted in 1990, and was awarded the Nobel Prize for Literature in 2001.

FANNY PARKES (1794–1875)
The daughter of a colonial officer, Fanny Parkes came to India as the wife of a minor civil servant. During the twenty-four years she lived in the country she travelled extensively, visiting Indian friends and assimilating herself into Indian culture and customs.

ALAN ROSS (1922–2001)
Calcutta-born Ross was a writer, poet and editor of great distinction. He wrote travel books, and a number of books on cricket. For many years he was editor of *London Magazine*, an ambitious literary and arts monthly, and he encouraged the careers of a large number of writers.

VIKRAM SETH (1952–)
The Indian novelist and poet Vikram Seth was born and raised in Calcutta. He studied at Oxford, did post-graduate study in economics at Stanford University and studied classical Chinese poetry at Nanjing University in China. He is best known for his novels: *The Golden Gate*, about San Francisco, written in verse as a very long sequence of sonnets; and *A Suitable Boy*, a huge and brilliant examination of Indian social mores.

RABINDRANATH TAGORE (1861–1941)
A Calcutta-born poet and philosopher, playwright, novelist, painter and educationalist, Tagore is far and away the most revered figure in the pantheon of Bengali intellectuals. In 1901 he founded a communal school to blend Eastern and Western philosophical and educational systems. He received the Nobel Prize for Literature in 1913, the first Asian to do so, and was knighted in 1915 – an honour which he resigned in 1919 as a protest against British policy.

PAUL THEROUX (1941–)

Massachusetts-born Theroux published his first novel, *Waldo*, in 1967. His highly acclaimed travel books include *Riding the Iron Rooster, The Great Railway Bazaar, The Old Patagonian Express* and *Fresh Air Fiend. The Mosquito Coast* and *Dr Slaughter* have both been made into successful films. He divides his time between Cape Cod and the Hawaiian Islands, where he is a professional beekeeper.

MARK TWAIN (1835–1910)

Born Samuel Langhorne Clemens in Missouri, Twain was apprenticed to a printer at age 13. In his 20s he was commissioned to write a series of comic travel letters, but he decided to become a steamboat captain instead. In the 1860s he moved to San Francisco to work as a reporter. He subsequently travelled the world writing accounts for papers in California and New York. His best-known novel, *The Adventures of Tom Sawyer,* was published in 1876.

Acknowledgments

CLARK BLAISE & BHARATI MUKHERJEE
From *Days and Nights in Calcutta* © Clark Blaise and Bharati Mukherjee 1977. Reprinted by permission of the authors.

BUDDHADEV BOSE
From *Tithidore*, translated by Ketaki Kushari Dyson © 2001.

N. C. CHAUDHURI
From *Autobiography of an Unknown Indian* © N. C. Chaudhuri 1951. Reprinted by permission of Macmillan, London, UK.

N. C. CHAUDHURI
From *Thy Hand Great Anarch!*, Chatto & Windus, London, 1987.

WILLIAM DALRYMPLE
From *White Mughals* © William Dalrymple 2002. Reprinted by permission of HarperCollins Publishers Ltd and Viking Penguin, a division of Penguin Group (USA) Inc.

SUSANNA MOORE
From *One Last Look* © Susanna Moore 2003. First published in the United States by Knopf in 2003, first published in Britain by Viking in 2003. Reprinted with the permission of Penguin Books Ltd and The Wylie Agency, Inc.

GEOFFREY MOORHOUSE
From *Calcutta* © Geoffrey Moorhouse 1971. Reprinted with the permission of Weidenfeld & Nicolson.

JAMES MORRIS
From *Places* © James Morris 1972. Reprinted with the permission of the author.

V. S. NAIPAUL
From *India: A Million Mutinies Now* © V. S. Naipaul 1990. Reprinted with the permission of Gillon Aitken.

FANNY PARKES
From *Begums, Thugs and White Mughals: The Journals of Fanny Parkes*, edited by William Dalrymple. (Sickle Moon, London 2002, pp28-33.)

ALAN ROSS
'Goodbye to Calcutta', first published in the *Spectator*, 30 April 1983.

VIKRAM SETH
From *A Suitable Boy* © Vikram Seth 1993. Reprinted with the permission of Weidenfeld & Nicolson and Curtis Brown Group Ltd.

RABINDRANATH TAGORE
'Flute-Music', from *Rabindranath Tagore: Selected Poems* (translated by William Radice), Penguin, 1985. Copyright © William Radice 1985. Reproduced by permission of Penguin Books Ltd.